The Trekker's Gu  ırs

By

Published by Dragon Wing Express

Cover photo courtesy of Jordan Davis

Copyright © 2021

ISBN: 9798732594089

First Edition: April 2021

DWE

Table of Contents

For my father, who only watched Voyager because of Seven of Nine

Introduction: About this Book

Call it the return of Plan A. Nearly twenty years after Paramount had promised fans a new *Star Trek* series that would serve as the anchor for a new television network—which subsequently morphed into Plan B: a motion picture project that would launch the *Star Trek* film series—the original idea was brought back in the 1990s. With *TNG* winding down its run on television and *DS9* a ratings success, Paramount Chairman Kerry McCluggage approached producer Rick Berman about the idea of continuing to run two *Star Trek* shows concurrently with the creation of a new series. By 1995, *Star Trek: Voyager*, featuring Captain Janeway and her crew, was off and running.

Unfortunately, with "franchise fatigue" setting in and a host of new science fiction shows, not to mention a new science fiction cable channel, providing increasing competition, a lot of people missed out on their weekly adventures. Happily, never before have the episodes been so accessible. Today's technology allows even non-*Star Trek* fans to instantly watch just about any episode of *Voyager*, thanks to the internet and streaming services. (And fans have definitely been doing so, with data showing the Voyager episodes among the most commonly streamed of the old *Star Trek* offerings.) And yet, even big fans can be forgiven if they have difficulty sorting out the hundreds of hours of *Star Trek* available—save for a quick check online which may also yield spoilers and misinformation.

That's where this series of books, with this being the fourth volume, comes into play. Throughout this edition, every episode of *Voyager* is graded, reviewed, and analyzed…and all without giving away plot points and surprises that make *Star Trek* worth watching. If knowledge of one episode is important to enjoy another, or if there's a prequel or sequel, the review includes that information as well.

These books are *not* a substitute for watching *Star Trek*. After all, what is? It's been said that a dozen people watching the same episode or movie will have twelve different experiences, and many *Star Trek* fans have strong personal bonds to specific episodes for their own special reasons. But what I will do with this book is share and explain my thoughts and opinions, not to supersede the reader's own thoughts and viewing experiences, but to enhance them with another perspective.

And just who am I, anyway?

I'm J.W. Braun, a guy from Wisconsin. I was born in 1975 and grew up with a family that loved science fiction and fantasy, becoming a *Star Trek* fan in the 1980s after discovering, in succession, *Star Trek: The Animated Series*, the *Star Trek* movies, and *Star Trek: The Next Generation*.

Me at Captain Janeway's statue in Bloomington, Indiana

Today, I'm an unabashed fanboy who spends too much time analyzing entertainment and seeking out the people who make things like *Star Trek* possible so I can share what I learn with others. As I review the work, I try to be honest and fair. I can ask no more of you as you read this book!

Grading the Episodes

At the top of the reviews, you'll see grades for the episodes. I use the standard American letter grade scale you may remember from school because it's easy to understand. But to spell it out (pardon the pun), here's a guide.

A: Excellent (nearly perfect)
B: Very good (exceeds expectations)
C: Average (par for the course)
D: Poor (below standard)
F: Failure (ugh)

Each review will also include vital information about the episode, including a plot description, the original air date, and the writing and director credits.

Terminology

As you read through the reviews, you'll probably notice that I casually throw out certain terms that not everyone is familiar with. As such, I've included this quick glossary for reference.

Bottle episode: a ship-based episode that only uses existing sets to free up money for effects or another episode. The term was coined by the cast and crew of *TOS*, who compared these episodes to a ship in a bottle.

CGI: an abbreviation for computer generated imagery, effects created by computer after shooting has completed.

Cinematography: the art of recording motion. This includes everything from lighting and framing to the choice of lenses and colors (or lack thereof). It's sort of the kinetic version of painting works of art.

EMH: Emergency Medical Hologram (*VOY's* Doctor).

MacGuffin: something that is only included in the story to serve as a motivator for the protagonists and antagonists.

Plot or storytelling device: something contrived to create a story.

Show/episode: words I do not use interchangeably. I use "show" to refer to a TV series as a whole (such as *Voyager*) and "episode" to refer to a single installment of a show (such as "Caretaker"). Thus, I use the term "bottle episode" rather than "bottle show," even if the latter is more fashionable.

Story credit, teleplay credit and written by credit: writing acknowledgements based on the genesis of the episode. Story credit goes to those who come up with the story idea, teleplay credit goes to those who actually write the scripts the director and actors use, and "written by" is used to acknowledge someone who does both.

Teaser: an opening sequence that attempts to hook the viewer before the theme song and opening credits play.

Technobabble: futuristic shop talk (made-up technical jargon).

TOS: *The Original Series*, the show with Captain Kirk (1966–1969)
TAS: *Star Trek: The Animated Series* (1973–1974)
TNG: *Star Trek: The Next Generation* (1987–1994)
DS9: *Star Trek: Deep Space Nine* (1993–1999)
VOY: *Star Trek: Voyager* (1995–2001)
ENT: *Star Trek: Enterprise* (2001–2005)
DSC: *Star Trek: Discovery* (2017–present)
PIC: *Star Trek: Picard* (2020–present)

Trope: a commonly recurring element or storytelling device. For example, *Gilligan's Island* (1964–1967) is famous for endings in which attempts to escape the island inevitably fail for the main characters, keeping the overall premise of the series intact. *Rashomon* (1950) popularized a technique where we see an event from multiple characters' viewpoints, with variations in each. And *Lost* (2004–2010) is known for weaving flashbacks and flash-forwards into its stories.

And with all that in mind, let's engage, warp factor four!

Planting Seeds

VOY, the fourth of the *Star Trek* spinoff shows, had an unprecedented advantage. When it began preproduction, there were two other *Star Trek* shows still on the air that could prepare the audience for the arrival of a new sister series. What follows are my reviews for the episodes of *TNG* and *DS9* that planted the seeds that would ultimately germinate in *VOY's* pilot. These episodes include:

1. *TNG's* "Journey's End"
2. *DS9's* "The Maquis, Parts I & II"
3. *TNG's* "Preemptive Strike"

TNG's Journey's End

TNG's "Journey's End": B

A colony of Native Americans refuses to evacuate per treaty agreement, pitting Wesley Crusher against Picard.

Air date: March 28, 1994
Written by Ronald D. Moore
Directed by Corey Allen
TV rating: 11.9

"What you're doing down there is wrong. These people are not some random group of colonists. They're a unique culture with a history that predates the Federation and Starfleet." —Wesley

TNG finishes up Wesley Crusher's story with this spiritual Native American relocation episode. With an outstanding guest performance from Tom Jackson (Lakanta) and a thoughtful, new age musical score by Jay Chattaway, this character-driven episode includes two plotlines, giving us a healthy dose of Wesley and Picard while developing deep enough dilemmas to ensure there is never a dull moment before a twist is thrown in that's delightfully unpredictable.

At the same time, "Journey's End" does move slowly, with the Wesley plot lacking direction for much of the episode, and the Picard portion—featuring a political allegory so close to its inspiration, even Picard comments on it—that is mostly comprised of diplomatic discussions that go nowhere.

The action picks up toward the end, with the Cardassians and the growing conflict between Wesley and Picard driving the drama before a decision, ultimately accepted by all sides, lays the groundwork for the creation of the Maquis.

Did you know? *VOY's* Chakotay was originally conceived as one of the elder Native Americans from this episode's colony, but as the new show was being developed, the producers began to consider that Chakotay, as first officer, might be in charge of many away missions and opted for a more youthful character inspired by *TNG's* Commander Riker. One of the actors from "Journey's End," however, did go on to play a relative of Chakotay's. In fact, Ned Romero can be seen in three different *Star Trek* shows, playing a Klingon in *TOS's* "A Private Little War, the leader of the tribal council in *TNG's* "Journey's End," and Chakotay's grandfather in *VOY's* "The Fight." Romero died in 2017 at age ninety.

DS9's "The Maquis, Parts I & II": B

When a Cardassian freighter explodes at Deep Space Nine, the Cardassians blame a rogue group of Federation colonists.

Air dates: April 24, May 1, 1994
Teleplays by James Crocker & Ira Steven Behr
Story by Rick Berman, Michael Piller, James Cocker,
Jeri Taylor & Ira Steven Behr
Directed by David Livingston & Corey Allen
TV rating: 8.6, 8.3

"Without any help from either one of us, they've managed to start their own little war out here." —Dukat

In this two-parter, the politics from *TNG's* "Journey's End" spill over into *DS9*, setting up *VOY* while still being pretty darn entertaining in its own right. In fact, both halves are Sisko episodes, with the whole thing beginning with a bang before turning into a tense political thriller.

"Part I" itself doesn't spend a lot of money on effects, but it does create a large scope on a small budget by using the dialogue and tactical displays to make it seem like more is going on than we actually see.Meanwhile, a number of guest stars give the plot its moving parts, with Tony Plana playing a human conspirator, Bernie Casey playing a Starfleet attaché, Richard Poe playing a Cardassian, and Marc Alaimo reprising Gul Dukat. The latter is the breakout character, with Alaimo and Avery Brooks finally given time together to develop the relationship between their characters, leading to many more scenes between the two in future episodes. As Dukat becomes more three dimensional, *DS9* gains a more interesting antagonist, and here it puts Sisko (and the audience) in the difficult position of hearing two different viewpoints of what's going on, making the situation more difficult to gauge. As this is happening, the other guest stars contribute to the story in small ways without overstaying their welcome, with Casey's performance being the most memorable of the bunch.

In "Part II," the story gets more talky, with Avery Brooks, as Commander Sisko, paired up with each of the major guest stars in a succession of scenes. These guests—including Natalija Nogulich as Admiral Nechayev—give Brooks some generous performances to play off of, and with each new scene, the plot becomes more personal and Brooks becomes more intense. As the episode approaches its conclusion, the big money is finally thrown onto the screen in the form of a space battle with some nifty special effects for 1990s television.

Did you know? Bernie Casey accepted the part of attaché Cal Hudson specifically so he could work with Avery Brooks, whom he had admired as an actor since seeing Brooks's work in *Spenser for Hire* (1985–1988) and *A Man Called Hawk* (1989).

TNG's "Preemptive Strike": B

Ro Laren infiltrates the Maquis only to sympathize with them, testing her loyalty.

Air date: May 16, 1994
Teleplay by René Echevarria
Story by Naren Shankar
Directed by Patrick Stewart
TV rating: 11.8

"When you sent me on this mission, I thought that I could do it. Now I'm not sure where I stand." —Ensign Ro

The penultimate *TNG* episode is full of heart and has much to like, but its success hinges completely on the guest performance of Macias, Ro's surrogate father figure. Without a cunning, powerful, and likeable character on the same level as Picard, it doesn't matter what Michelle Forbes (Ro) does for her final *Trek* appearance, there would be no believable drama of a woman torn between her two mentors. Fortunately, by its seventh season, *TNG* was such an established ratings hit, the producers were able to find actors like John Franklyn Robbins, an English actor who, with his charm and boyish grin, brings such warmth and innocence to Macias, the pieces to the drama fall right into place, making Patrick Stewart's final directorial outing a breeze.

To be fair, Forbes herself is outstanding as well, playing up the internal conflict writer Echevarria successfully develops throughout the course of the hour. With the Maquis plight presented here much more sympathetically than on *DS9* (which would later turn it into a literal version of *Les Misérables*), Forbes, much like Wil Wheaton in "Journey's End," brings out new layers to her character amidst a backdrop that eschews black and white for shades of grey, making Ensign Ro's ultimate choice all the more poignant.

Did you know? This episode includes Gul Evek, a Cardassian played by Richard Poe who threads his way through the *Star Trek* universe over the course of a year. He appears in:

DS9's "Playing God" (February 27, 1994)
TNG's "Journey's End" (March 28, 1994)
DS9's "The Maquis, Part I" (April 24, 1994)
TNG's "Preemptive Strike" (May 16, 1994)
DS9's "Tribunal" (June 5, 1994)
VOY's "Caretaker" (January 16, 1995)

Season One

Production Order
(with air date order in parentheses)

1. "Caretaker" (1st)
2. "Parallax" (2nd)
3. "Time and Again" (3rd)
4. "Phage" (4th)
5. "The Cloud" (5th)
6. "Eye of the Needle" (6th)
7. "Ex Post Facto" (7th)
8. "Emanations" (8th)
9. "Prime Factors" (9th)
10. "State of Flux" (10th)
11. "Heroes and Demons" (11th)
12. "Cathexis" (12th)
13. "Faces" (13th)
14. "Jetrel" (14th)
15. "Learning Curve" (15th)

The First Season Cast

Captain Janeway: Kate Mulgrew
Commander Chakotay: Robert Beltran
B'Elanna Torres: Roxann Biggs-Dawson
Kes: Jennifer Lien
Tom Paris: Robert Duncan McNeill
Neelix: Ethan Phillips
The Doctor: Robert Picardo
Tuvok: Tim Russ
Harry Kim: Garrett Wang

Notable Guest Stars

Basil Langton
Armin Shimerman
Josh Clark
Martha Hackett
Cully Fredricksen
Angela Dohrmann
Larry A. Hankin
Vaughn Armstrong
Francis Guinan
Ronald Guttman
Anthony De Longis
Marjorie Monaghan
Carolyn Seymour
Brian Markinson
James Sloyan

"Caretaker": A

(Pilot) The newly commissioned starship Voyager and a Maquis raider are flung into the remote Delta Quadrant by a powerful entity known as the Caretaker.

Air date: January 16, 1995
Teleplay by Michael Piller & Jeri Taylor
Story by Rick Berman, Michael Piller & Jeri Taylor
Directed by Winrich Kolbe
TV rating: 13.0

"Captain, if these sensors are working, we're over seventy-thousand light-years from where we were. We're on the other side of the galaxy." —Ensign Kim

Written primarily by the same man who stabilized *TNG's* writing staff and wrote *DS9's* pilot, "Caretaker" skillfully launches *Voyager* with a two-hour romp that simultaneously works well as a beginning and as a standalone story. Like *TNG's* pilot, the story is basically a mystery mixed with a powerful alien, though here the elements are better interwoven and no expense is spared. At $23 million, this is *Star Trek's* most expensive episode of the 1990s, giving the story ample location shooting and visual effects to jumpstart the series and launch a network.

Benefitting from exposition planted in *TNG* and *DS9*, *VOY's* pilot opens with a *Star Wars*-like crawl and then kicks into gear, cutting a quick pace as it moves along to introduce the characters. Surprisingly, the most important of these initially is not the captain, but Tom Paris, who serves as the gateway into the story at large. It's an interesting choice, with Paris being an outcast, but his character arc helps sum up what the show's all about: a new life. *TNG* fans, of course, will remember Robert Duncan McNeill as Nicholas Locarno from "The First Duty," a character with nearly the same backstory as Paris. Naturally, it's easy to wonder why *Star Trek* invents Paris rather than just reusing Locarno, but the truth is that McNeill's character in "The First Duty" is (appropriately) selfish

11

and arrogant, which is the cause of his trouble. Paris, on the other hand, though similar in demeanor, is more selfless and full of self-doubt. While *VOY* could (and almost did) reuse Lacarno and try to recharacterize him, there's no reason to go to so much trouble because of one *TNG* episode. Instead, giving the actor a blank slate allows the show to introduce Paris to us in a new way and develop him throughout the episode and series without being tethered to the past.

In the meantime, the pilot still offers Kate Mulgrew plenty of opportunities to put her stamp on Captain Janeway, and she uses them to create a character that's vulnerable in private but unquestionably in charge in public. Mulgrew gives a performance that's not just extraordinary but extraordinarily important for *Star Trek*. It might seem sexist today, but after a poor performance by Geneviève Bujold as Janeway before a casting change, there was some doubt from the Paramount executives as to whether a woman could actually front a show they were relying on to launch UPN. Mulgrew, however, owns the part, giving Janeway a Kathryn Hepburn-like quality while proving she's just as good as any leading man.

Meanwhile, with seven other regulars to introduce, some characters get shortchanged. The Doctor, who would go on to be one of the show's breakout stars, gets in a couple funny lines but little more. Seska. who is not a regular but does factor into the first two seasons, doesn't appear at all. But while some have more to do and some less, most of the major characters get a chance to at least outline the basics of their personalities and relationships. (And a visit to Deep Space Nine even gives us a Quark cameo.)

Always remaining a favorite for the cast, crew, and fans alike, the events in "Caretaker" come back into play in several episodes of the series, starting with Season Two's "Projections." Sadly, however, "Caretaker" is the last *Star Trek* pilot written by Piller. But his work here is superb. In fact it's so good, the show never has to employ an idea planted in the pilot specifically to set up a quick way to get back home if the show's concept were to prove unpopular: a second caretaker. (For the sake of completion, the show cleans up this loose thread in Season Two's "Cold Fire.")

"Caretaker" went on to be nominated for Emmys for hairstyling, costume design, and visual effects, winning for the latter.

Did you know? When the cast and crew began shooting "Caretaker," Mulgrew sported shoulder length hair, which nearly everyone agreed was best. But Paramount Chairman Kerry McCluggage was unhappy with the choice, and Mulgrew was asked to return to reshoot many of her scenes with a new style. Writer/producer Michael Piller once joked, "'Caretaker' is probably the only *Star Trek* pilot in which the hairdressing cost more than the special effects." Janeway's hair would continue to be a hot topic amongst the producers and executives throughout the series, driving Mulgrew crazy. "She would do a really hard day's work," Berman recalls, "and the next day she'd be told to do it again because someone didn't like her hairdo." Mulgrew herself commented, "There were days I envied Patrick Stewart."

"Parallax": C+

Investigating a distress call, Voyager becomes trapped inside the event horizon of a quantum singularity.

Air date: January 23, 1995
Teleplay by Brannon Braga
Story by Jim Trombetta
Directed by Kim Friedman
TV rating: 9.2

"Wait a minute, let me get this straight. We were cruising along at warp seven, then we pick up a distress call and moved in to investigate. But now you're saying that the other ship is actually just a reflection of us and that the distress call is actually just the captain's opening hail?" —Paris

Taking the baton from *TNG*, *VOY* uses a sci-fi conundrum to bring B'Elanna Torres and Captain Janeway closer together in the first bottle episode of the series. Beneath the technobabble, it's purely a paint-by-numbers plot as old as the hills: people have doubts about Torres, but the plot provides her a test and gives her a chance to prove herself to everyone.

Fortunately, the story includes quite a bit of Janeway, who proves herself no dummy. A trap for plots of this kind is to suddenly have the leader appear more incompetent than usual to set the stage for the lesser character to save everyone. But here, Janeway hangs with Torres each step of the way as they work through the crisis, keeping Janeway a strong character and turning a story about "earning respect" into a two way street. (Janeway also has some great moments with Chakotay, with the early part of the plot drawing him into the mix to weave some drama out of their new working relationship.)

For her part, Torres goes through all the motions of the typical TV redemption plot. It's somewhat uninspired, and the crisis itself is similar to dozens of *TNG* episodes, but that's not really the point of it all. It's about establishing a character, and Biggs-Dawson does so just fine.

Did you know? Martha Hackett debuts as Seska in this episode. Hackett had previously appeared as a Romulan in *DS9's* "The Search," directed by Kim Friedman. While that part didn't work out as the recurring role it was originally intended to be, Friedman, a fan of the actress, personally cast Hackett as Seska in "Parallax."

"Time and Again": B

While investigating a massive explosion that destroyed all life on a planet, Janeway and Paris are swept back a day in time to just before it happened.

Air date: January 30, 1995
Teleplay by David Kemper & Michael Piller
Story by David Kemper
Directed by Les Landau
TV rating: 8.8

"Alright, here's the truth. We're from the future." —Janeway

This Chernobyl episode has quite a concept! Like the previous episode, this one has fun playing around with cause and effect. But whereas "Parallax" uses a time distortion/reflection, "Time and Again" uses good old-fashioned time travel. With Janeway and Paris one day behind the rest of the crew, each on opposite sides of an apocalyptic disaster, the episode cleverly weaves its A and B story together by intercutting between the past and the present at the same locations.

Unfortunately, the premise, which requires Janeway and Paris to fit in with the aliens, dictates that the planet's culture be just like Earth. It's something other *Trek* incarnations do once in a while, but with Voyager being on the other side of the galaxy, it seems out of place and certainly fails to highlight how far the crew is from home. Perhaps worse, the script attempts to turn Kes into Guinan, giving her the same "beyond time and space" intuitive sense. Whoopi Goldberg knows how to pull it off, but Jennifer Lien isn't a good enough actress to make it work. To make matters worse for Lien, her character's visit to The Doctor gives Robert Picardo a chance to upstage her, and he takes full advantage of the opportunity.

Still, the premise itself is strong, and "Time and Again" has enough interesting bits to make it one of *VOY's* better first season episodes.

Did you know? When *VOY* commenced principal photography on September 6, 1994, the ages of the actors were:

Kate Mulgrew: 39
Robert Beltran: 40
Roxann Biggs-Dawson: 35
Jennifer Lien: 21
Robert Duncan McNeill: 29
Ethan Phillips: 39
Robert Picardo: 40
Tim Russ: 38
Garrett Wang: 25

"Phage": B

Aliens steal Neelix's lungs.

Air date: February 6, 1995
Teleplay by Skye Dent & Brannon Braga
Story by Timothy DeHaas
Directed by Winrich Kolbe
TV rating: 8.5

"The Doctor says whoever did this used some kind of transporter to beam the lungs directly out of his body." —Chakotay

Boy, when you're creating a *Star Trek* episode, it takes guts to remake "Spock's Brain," but that's basically what this one is, with Neelix's lungs serving as the MacGuffin. This time, the writers get it largely right, turning it into a medical drama that gives Robert Picardo an opportunity to show off his stuff. Stepping into his first "Doctor" episode, Picardo has plenty of sardonic wit, but he hasn't developed too much more for the character, leaving plenty of room for improvement in future episodes. Fortunately, starting simple before growing throughout the series works for a hologram who was just "born," giving him a meaningful character arc in the long run. As for the here and now, Picardo needs help carrying "Phage" and gets it. Ethan Phillips and Jennifer Lien step into the roles of a paraplegic and his loved one respectively and turn this into arguably their best episode together. Lien has already established Kes as polite but assertive by this point, and it works especially well within the context of the plot. Phillips meanwhile, gets plenty of opportunities to develop Neelix, with the Talaxian experiencing a broad range of activities: setting up a makeshift kitchen, exploring a planet, and waking up on a medical table unable to move.

In the B story, Janeway hunts down Neelix's lungs, thankfully not running into any miniskirted girls in the process. It's pretty standard fare for the most part, but it does lead to an unexpected conclusion and gives us the first real display of how protective the captain is of her crew.

The organ-harvesting Vidiians return in several more episodes, beginning with "Faces" later in the season

Did you know? Before joining the cast of *VOY*, Robert Picardo played doctors on *China Beach* and *The Golden Girls*.

"The Cloud": D

The crew of Voyager unknowingly puts itself in danger while looking for resources inside a cloud-like anomaly.

Air date: February 13, 1995
Teleplay by Tom Szollosi & Michael Piller
Story by Brannon Braga
Directed by David Livingston
TV rating: 7.9

"Find yourself a seat with a good view because just like Jonah and the whale, you're going in." —Captain Janeway

This episode dances all over the place, with an A story that takes forever to get going and B and C stories that wander around aimlessly.

The main plot features the titular cloud, a nebula-like thing, which Voyager investigates. After beginning as a mystery, this story develops into a medical drama of sorts, but with more technobabble than substance. Meanwhile, to help fill out the hour, Paris creates a pool hall and Chakotay teaches Janeway how to find her spirit animal. All together, the stories are about as memorable as one of the redshirts from *TOS*, though it is funny to see The Doctor give a description of Dr. Zimmerman and jokingly throwing out the idea of programming a family, both the subject of future episodes.

Unfortunately, in the meantime, none of the ideas here blossom into anything meaningful. It's as if the writers want to do *Pulp Fiction* in an effort to develop the characters but can't find the right stories to weave together to make it worthwhile. Unfortunately, there are worse episodes to come, but thankfully most are better.

Did you know? From bar patrons to an accordion player, "The Cloud" features a wider variety of extras than most other episodes. How did the supervising producer, the guy in charge of limiting extras to keep the show within its budget, let the director get away with this? Well, in this case, the supervising producer *was* the director.

"Eye of the Needle": B+

Voyager uses a wormhole to make contact with a ship in the Alpha Quadrant.

Air date: February 20, 1995
Teleplay by Bill Dial & Jeri Taylor
Story by Hilary J. Bader
Directed by Winrich Kolbe
TV rating: 7.7

"I am Captain of the cargo vessel Talvath, location Alpha Quadrant, sector one three eight five. What is your location?" —Telek

With its exquisitely laid out plot, "Eye of the Needle" is a fascinating bottle episode with a tease of home that has enough story dynamics to overcome its *Gilligan's Island*-like conclusion.

The A story begins with the simple discovery of a wormhole and lays out its cards one at a time, giving the viewer quite a journey as the acts progress. Teleplay writer Jeri Taylor doesn't rush a single step, letting each moment breathe and allowing the characters to interact to provide depth and build anticipation.

There's also a B story with Kes serving as a counselor for The Doctor as well as his advocate. In fact, Lien deserves some credit for helping develop Picardo's character, using Kes to push Picardo into adding layers to the hologram, with the two clearly having some chemistry together when there's give and take. And what's great about this substory is how easily it folds into the A story toward the end. Just as Kes is helping The Doctor become a more respected being and a true member of the crew, he's faced with the possibility of having it all come to an end as the crew discovers a way they might use to get home.

It all makes for a heck of an episode and all the better for being something only *VOY* could do, though *DS9* does a variation of sorts in its Season Six episode, "The Sound of Her Voice". (*VOY* itself takes the idea and runs with it further in Season Four's "Message in a Bottle.")

Did you know? A throwaway line by Torres in this episode would later become the focus of Season Seven's "Lineage."

"Ex Post Facto": C–

While visiting an alien world, Lieutenant Paris is convicted of murder.

Air date: February 27, 1995
Teleplay by Evan Carlos Somers & Michael Piller
Story by Carlos Somers
Directed by LeVar Burton
TV rating: 8.0

"Let the record show that the sentence of the court has been carried out. For the rest of his natural life, once every fourteen hours, Thomas Eugene Paris will relive the last moments of his victim's life." —Alien doctor

This is basically a redo of *TNG's* third season murder-mystery, "A Matter of Perspective," but whereas that one is essentially *Rashomon*, using the different characters to give different accounts of the same acts, this one is *Citizen Kane*, using the different characters to color in different parts of the story.

Paris serves as the focal point, but "Facto" really becomes a Tuvok episode once it gets going, with the Vulcan at the center of the film noir-like narrative, using his logic to get to the bottom of things. Unfortunately, a story with a smoking housewife and her dog again does little to take advantage of *VOY's* far-out premise, and with all the film noir elements, the unusual punishment for Paris, despite being the catalyst for the episode, gets lost in the shuffle.

There is a funny bit where The Doctor considers taking the name of a famous doctor as an homage and mentions several possibilities, such as Galen, Salk, and Spock. (Benjamin Spock was a pediatrician who wrote the bestselling book, *The Common Sense Book of Baby and Child Care*, in 1946.) And it's interesting to see *Star Trek*, within the sci-fi device, shoot in black and white for the first time. But while director LeVar Burton does an admirable job of somehow turning the limited story into a watchable episode, there's no getting around the lack of originality in the teleplay.

Did you know? Ex post facto is Latin for "from a thing done afterward" and is often cited in a legal setting when someone attempts to retroactively make a legal but morally questionable action illegal after it's been committed in an attempt to bring a charge against the perpetrator. This is not allowed in most nations, including the United States where the Constitution specifically forbids it.

"Emanations": B

While investigating an asteroid, Harry Kim is transported to another dimension where people believe he's come from the afterlife.

Air date: March 13, 1995
Written by Brannon Braga
Directed by David Livingston
TV rating: 7.1

"I have to admit, there is a little voice inside me that's terrified of dying. And since I've been talking to you, that little voice has started to get louder."
—Garan

Religious beliefs are, of course, considered sacred ground by most people, and yet they're an area full of possibilities to explore in fiction. Ironically, it's more common for the popular culture to use it for comic fodder than drama because perhaps, as Data might say, humans often use humor as a shield when they discuss deeply personal topics. Yet there are many interesting facets of these beliefs that can be explored in a dramatic setting, and science fiction offers an opportunity to do so in a way that, while still uncomfortable for some, offers a forum that's more acceptable to the masses.

"Emanations" meets the challenge head on, presenting a kind, loving society and forcing some of them to question their religious beliefs, as well as euthanasia, for the first time.

Harry Kim gets the A story, stepping into the Riker/O'Brien everyman role and finding himself accidentally sent from a culture's "Heaven" (an asteroid full of dead bodies) to their homeworld in another dimension. This makes for a rather uncomfortable conversation when one of the aliens, Garan, who is scheduled to die, starts asking Kim what he can look forward to in the afterlife. (Garan's culture believes that when they die, their corporeal bodies are sent to another place so they can live again and associate with lost loved ones.) Kim tries to avoid the question, but coming from "the other side," there are lots of people who are curious about what he knows, not to mention some who feel threatened by what he might say. The late Jeffrey Alan Chandler plays Garan with a sweetness that serves the part well, while Jerry Hardin uses his gravitas to nearly steal the show, playing the planet's chief thanatologist.

Meanwhile, dead people from the planet keep getting sent to Voyager instead of the asteroid, which helps Janeway and her crew to start putting the pieces together and figure out what's going on. This turns into the obligatory "trying to recover a lost crewmember" B story, but it's certainly one of the more creative variations.

When "Emanations" first aired, it generated some controversy, with some deeply religious people mistaking it as an allegory for atheism. In fact, what the episode is really about is exploring how people handle the challenge of considering that their most important and cherished beliefs might be wrong. The problem for some people, however, is that doubt is such a foreign concept to their way of thinking, they can't help but view the writers and the episode (and life) in black and white terms: the story is either validating their beliefs or attacking them. It's a frame of mind that's not exclusive to religion, often showing up in politics and nationalism.

Sadly, the episode is only able to scratch the surface of the issue in the time allotted. There's much more that could be mined, including Kim's effect on the society as a whole and the danger to him as a result. In fact,"Emanations" would make for an interesting two-parter; but then that's something the show would be more likely to do later in its run.

VOY does, however, return to this story concept in Season Four's "Mortal Coil."

Did you know? Garrett Wang once said, "I really enjoyed a lot of the work in 'Emanations,' and some of the moments we discovered were quite fantastic, but in terms of the timing of that episode, it would have been nice to have it later in the season so Kim comes into the second season a wiser soul."

Wang in 2007 (photo courtesy of Nihonjoe)

"Prime Factors": C+

Voyager discovers a planet that has the technology to send people across the galaxy. However, the planet's leader is more interested in hosting the crew than helping them leave.

Air date: March 20, 1995
Teleplay by Michael Perricone & Greg Elliot
Story by David R. George III & Eric A. Stillwell
Directed by Les Landau
TV rating: 7.3

"We cannot share our technology. Once it's out of our control, it might fall into the hands of those who would abuse it, and our canon of laws strictly forbids that." —Labin

Voyager suffers from the flip side of the Prime Directive, opening up several possibilities for the episode to explore. Does the crew attempt to barter? Do they secretly study the technology? Do they try to steal it? The answer is all of the above, which gives just about everyone something to do, save for The Doctor, Kes, and Chakotay. The latter is rather conspicuous by his absence, with Janeway struggling with her conflicting emotions and the Maquis running amok. (Maybe he's off with his spirit animal.)

Unfortunately, the aliens, with a leader that comes across as the poor man's Mr. Roark, are a swing and a miss. The Sikarians, possessing a technology that allows them to appear almost anywhere in the quadrant, were conceived as one of the show's recurring species; but their poor performance (thanks mostly to Ricardo Montalbán-wannabe Ronald Guttman) sinks their ship, forcing them to join the Vians, the Mintakans, and Tosk in the one and done club.

The true focal point of the episode, however, is Tuvok, By using him as Janeway's moral compass, the writers skillfully set up a twist ending that's somehow both surprising and logical, giving them a way to pay the whole premise off without resorting to another *Gilligan's Island* gimmick.

It's a fine example of a show early in the go developing its characters and finding its way. *VOY* would go on to tell better stories, but for a first season offering, "Prime Factors" isn't a bad episode.

Did you know? The Sikarians' method of long distance travel, where they fold space to bring origin destination points closer together, is a fictional idea that previously appeared in *A Wrinkle in Time*, a 1962 book, and *Super Dimension Fortress Macross*, a 1982 anime series.

"State of Flux": B

When evidence indicates that Voyager has a traitor aboard, Chakotay narrows it down to two suspects.

Air date: April 10, 1995
Teleplay by Chris Abbott
Story by Paul Robert Coyle
Directed by Robert Scheerer
TV rating: 6.5

"Why would anyone on this ship betray us? We're all in this together."
—Janeway

This good old mystery traitor story has some surprising and some not so surprising twists and turns en route to its resolution. It's a Chakotay episode that gets a lot of mileage out of his Maquis past, even building in a backstory about a relationship between him and Seska to enrich the plot. (Coming out of nowhere, this is the sort of thing that risks feeling contrived, but the writing and acting are good enough to make it seem like an organic part of the series.)

Robert Beltran himself is an underrated actor. He's not as flamboyant or memorable as some of *Star Trek's* more famous performers, but there's a sincerity and sensitivity to his Chakotay that makes his stories work. Truth be told, the idea of Chakotay being the first officer of Voyager is itself a bit of an artistic liberty. On a real ship, no captain would ever give a renegade faction leader a rank higher than qualified, loyal officers, no matter what the circumstances were. (Tuvok would seem the obvious choice for the position.) But the show isn't meant to be a model for realistic command structures; it's a forum for storytelling, and it's episodes like these where Beltran proves his worth. As a bonus, the irony of Tuvok serving legitimately under Chakotay here after having done so as a spy gives their relationship an added layer that makes conversations like the one they have at the end of this episode all the more meaningful.

The episode holds back just enough information throughout to keep its mystery alive, and of the two characters suspected of treachery, the show chooses the better actor to be the guilty party. It's a wise choice that lets the show do several follow-up episodes built around the same character, beginning with Season Two's "Maneuvers."

Did you know? Kate Mulgrew was ill for much of this episode's shoot and doesn't appear in some scenes she was scheduled for as a result.

"Heroes and Demons": B

When several crewmembers disappear inside Harry Kim's holodeck program, The Doctor is the only one who can rescue them.

Air date: April 24, 1995
Written by Naren Shankar
Directed by Les Landau
TV rating: 6.4

"Think of this as your first away mission, Doctor. I can understand your hesitation. But there are three lives at stake, and you have the best chance of anyone on this ship to save them." —Janeway

VOY does its first malfunctioning holodeck story with a *Beowulf* fantasy that winds its way into a breakthrough episode for The Doctor...who doesn't even appear until about one quarter into the episode!

Written by *TNG* vet Naren Shankar, who conceived the story over a dinner with Brannon Braga, "Heroes" has many humorous touches, and gives Robert Picardo a chance to show off his comedic talents. (It's sort of *VOY's* equivalent of *TNG's* "Qpid.") The use of The Doctor in the holodeck works particularly well, because we not only get to see him outside of sickbay for the first time, we get to see him step out of his programmed occupation. Both of these serve as the template for his future development, and as a holographic character himself, it makes his interactions with the characters in the "holonovel" especially interesting because these, after all, are his own people.

With these elements and the unique medieval look and style that *Beowulf* brings to *Star Trek*, the result is one of the most popular *VOY* episodes from Season One and one that earned an Emmy nomination for its cinematography. (Incredibly, everything was shot on indoors on stages, including a forest which could easily pass for the real thing.) Even composer Dennis McCarthy cuts loose, conjuring up a memorable score that's more melodic than the norm, earning an Emmy nomination as well.

Did you know? Naren Shankar, who previously worked as a science consultant and writer for *TNG*, wrote this episode as a freelancer, never having any regular involvement with *VOY*.

"Cathexis": C–

When Voyager's crew attempts to investigate a mysterious force, an unknown entity keeps turning them back.

Air date: May 1, 1995
Teleplay by Brannon Braga
Story by Brannon Braga & Joe Menosky
Directed by Kim Friedman
TV rating: 6.4

"It seems to have the ability to jump from person to person. If that's true, it could be in any one of us, controlling our actions without us realizing it."
—Janeway

Taking its title from an ancient Greek word meaning "occupation," this paranoia bottle episode is another one of those old "non-corporeal creatures taking over the crewmembers" stories. For the most part, it's nothing new, meandering along for a while before finally kicking into gear in the last act. By then, it's too little, too late to save it from being *VOY's* least memorable episode of the season. What's sad is the teaser, showing Captain Janeway participating in a Gothic holodeck program set in 19th century England, seems like a much more interesting premise, though the show would probably not want to do two holonovel stories in a row.

Whatever the case, as writer Brannon Braga later lamented, the main problem with "Cathexis" is that it's not actually about anything.

Did you know? Wanting Janeway to have a recurring holonovel program, the writers first conceived of a simulation set in the Wild West, with Janeway playing the part of a pioneer woman on the move in a covered wagon. Producer Jeri Taylor thought the situation—being far from home, meeting new people, and not knowing what was around the corner—was an appropriate metaphor for Voyager's predicament in the Delta Quadrant and an unusual way of both enhancing and developing the persona of the captain. Unfortunately, the idea of repeated location shooting with horses and horse wranglers sunk the idea due to budget limitations, and so the writers came up with an indoor story with shades of *Jane Eyre*, *Rebecca*, and *The Turn of the Screw* to replace it. The Gothic holonovel continues in the Season One finale, "Learning Curve."

"Faces": C–

Lieutenant Torres is captured and separated into two entities, one Klingon and one human.

Air date: May 8, 1995
Teleplay by Kenneth Biller
Story by Jonathan Glassner & Kenneth Biller
Directed by Winrich Kolbe
TV rating: 6.1

"So, you're what's left over when all the Klingon DNA is taken out." —Torres

B'Elanna Torres finds herself in a variation of the *Dark Crystal* story, separated into two contrasting characters by the Vidiians, the creepy aliens first introduced in "Phage." But while this gives Roxann Biggs-Dawson a double role and lets her explore diverse character traits much like William Shatner in "The Enemy Within," the plot itself is a clunker.

Taking place largely on the cave set, the premise basically evolves into a "great escape" story with the two halves of Torres ultimately having to team up to find their way out. Dawson is so good at playing and differentiating the two parts, it's easy to forget the two roles are played by the same person, but as with most *Star Trek* "escape" stories, the episode relies too heavily on the characters sitting around talking rather than having them exploring, discovering, and doing.

Still, the episode has its moments, including Brian Markinson in a double role that allows the Vidiians to do some creepy face grafting, and it ends with an ambitious conclusion.

"Faces" would go on to be nominated for an Emmy for make-up. Meanwhile, *VOY* would return to the "Phage"-well in Season Two's "Lifesigns."

Did you know? While this episode was being shot, actress Nana Visitor of *DS9* wandered onto the *VOY* sets by mistake. "Oh my God," she said, before excusing herself to search for the *DS9* set she was scheduled to be on.

"Jetrel": B

Neelix comes face to face with Jetrel, an alien who designed a weapon that decimated Neelix's homeworld and killed his family.

Air date: May 15, 1995
Teleplay by Jack Klein, Karen Klein & Kenneth Biller
Story by James Thomton & Scott Nimerfro
Directed by Kim Friedman
TV rating: 5.8

"Something as enormous as science will not stop for something as small as a man." —Jetril

VOY presents a Hiroshima-like fallout story with Neelix having to confront the man whose weapon did his people great harm. It's a stroke of science fiction brilliance, taking an idea similar to that which real victims and great physicists have had to cope with and turning it into a deeply personal story by forcing a Weapons of Mass Destruction creator and someone suffering the consequences of his weapon to look each other in the eye and come to terms with one another as people, like a *Reader's Digest* story come to life.

Truth be told, while the weapon is obviously a stand-in for the atomic bomb, the title character, Jetril, is quite different than J. Robert Oppenheimer, the scientist who led the Manhattan Project. Oppenheimer was never broadly criticized for his research and had no regrets about his country using the bomb on Hiroshima, though he thought the attack on Nagasaki was unnecessary. (It's U.S. President Harry Truman who has taken the brunt of the criticism for those decisions, with a good argument to be made that he didn't try hard enough to resolve World War II diplomatically during the summer of 1945, though Japan's government was probably more so to blame.)

Jetril, however, can be thought of as a composite of Oppenheimer and Wernher von Braun, the German scientist whose early rockets Hitler used to destroy much of England and whose later rockets the Americans used to win the Space Race. (Von Braun used to say "I aim at the stars." Others would add, "Sometimes I hit London.")

Needing a mixture of guilt and pride for the part, *VOY* gives the role to James Sloyan. It's a good choice. Having already proved he could handle such emotions as the titular character in *TNG's* "Defector" and the scientist who discovered Odo on *DS9*, the role is right in his wheelhouse, and while there can be fears about casting a familiar actor in a new role, why risk someone else striking out when you know Sloyan's going to hit a homerun?

The real star of the episode, however, is Ethan Phillips. With several long speeches intended to tug on the heartstrings, the script asks a lot from him, and he delivers. *VOY* often uses Neelix for comedy more than drama, and it's easy to

Ethan Phillips and James Sloyan
(photos courtesy of Beth Madison)

stereotype the character as *Star Trek's* version of Jar Jar Binks. But Phillips is capable of much more, and it's exciting to see what he does here with some serious material. Helping enhance Phillips's talents, Dennis McCarthy provides a more sensitive score than *VOY* is usually known for.

Unfortunately, an episode that stands out as one of the finest of the series proved to be a ratings dud, garnering the worst numbers of Season One. But it has found a second life, thanks to on demand viewing in the 21st century.

Did you know? While Hiroshima was chosen by the U.S. as the first target of an atomic bombing attack, Nagasaki was not initially chosen to be the second. In fact, it only replaced Kyoto on the list of possible targets after Kyoto was removed when Truman's Secretary of War, who had fond memories of his honeymoon there, argued against its inclusion. Even so, Kokura was ultimately chosen to be the primary target for the second bomb, and a B-29 bomber was dispatched to drop it there. Fortunately for the people of Kokura, as the bomber circled the city three times, clouds and drifting smoke obscured the aiming point, forcing the bomber to divert to the secondary site, Nagasaki, which had only been added to the list of possible targets two weeks before.

"Learning Curve": D

Tuvok attempts to teach some former Maquis members how to be Starfleet officers. (Season finale)

Air date: May 22, 1995
Written by Ronald Wilkerson & Jean Louise Matthias
Directed by David Livingston
TV rating: 6.1

"Good morning. We have assembled here because Captain Janeway feels you would all benefit from additional Starfleet training." —Tuvok

It's basic training with Tuvok for four former Maquis crewmembers in a tedious episode that pulls out all the old military training clichés along with a variation of the old Kobayashi Maru scenario to go with a B story about the physical ship itself becoming ill. Neither bit is very compelling, with Tuvok's attempt to earn the respect of the Maquis coming across like a B story itself. (And wasn't Tuvok with the Maquis before being rescued by Voyager? You wouldn't know it by this episode.)

The ship's sickness, which takes advantage of the idea of biological gel packs introduced in the pilot, is a more creative concept, but it's just there to add tension, and it never really develops.

Built around Tuvok, this bottle episode is really just a water-downed, boring reincarnation of "The Galileo Seven."

Did you know? As originally written, this episode was supposed to end with an interaction between Neelix and Tuvok that demonstrates Tuvok made a bigger impact on his Maquis students than he realized. "There was a trick that Tuvok had been trying to teach the students which involved holding a rod a certain way," writer Ron Wilkerson explains. "None of the students could do it properly, but ultimately Neelix showed Tuvok he could do it, implying that he had learned it from Maquis. It was a cute moment, but it didn't make the final cut."

Season One Roundup

In 1993, when producer Rick Berman was asked to create a new *Star Trek* show, he was hesitant. He had just launched *DS9*, with the plan that it would air concurrently with *TNG* while working out the kinks and establishing itself before it became the sole *Trek* on television. Meanwhile, *TNG* would not disappear but would continue on in feature films, creating an ideal scenario for him as a producer. Kirk and company would be put out to pasture, and Berman would oversee the two remaining *Star Treks* in two separate environments, giving Picard and Sisko their own space while giving the fans, pardon the pun, the best of both worlds. With all this going on, he wondered, was it really a good time to start up another show?

But even as Berman was having his doubts about starting a new project in the midst of all this, Paramount began planning a new network. After it had aborted plans to launch one in 1978, the Fox Broadcasting Company had successfully filled the void in 1986, and by early 1993, with Warner Bros. laying the groundwork for a network of its own, Paramount executives were worried that if they didn't act fast, they'd miss the boat once again. They didn't need a full slate of programming, they reasoned. They just needed some cornerstone programming they could use to entice stations to join, and they could gradually grow the network from there. And what better cornerstone could anyone ask for than a new *Star Trek* show? By summer, Paramount Chairman Kerry McCluggage told Berman the new show was going forward—with or without him.

So Berman reached out to *DS9* co-creator Michael Piller and said, "Okay, they want us to do another one," and the two began brainstorming. With *DS9* set on a station, the new show would take place on a ship. With *DS9* featuring a male lead, the new show would feature a female in charge. And with Piller uncertain how long he would remain on staff, not to mention the advantage of having a female point of view while developing *Star Trek's* first permanent female captain, they recruited *TNG* writer and executive producer Jeri Taylor to help them fine-tune the details from there.

Their chief concern? How to create conflict aboard a ship to drive the drama. While running *TNG*, Gene Roddenberry developed a strict rule Berman and Piller wanted to adhere to: no conflict among Starfleet officers. They had gotten around this on *DS9* by populating the station with non-Starfleet characters, but how could the creative team recreate this on a Starfleet ship? The answer was to create a new faction of officers called the Maquis: a group that had broken away because its members didn't hold with Starfleet ideals. And then they would strand Starfleet and the Maquis aboard one ship in a far off region of space, forcing them to work to survive together out of contact with everyone back home. And with that, *VOY* was born.

Like any show, of course, it would need a team of artisans to take shape and make it into viewers' living rooms. Fortunately, with *TNG* coming to a close, there were many qualified people with *Star Trek* experience willing to continue working for the franchise. Brannon Braga, Merri Howard, and Peter

Lauritson, who had each worked their way up the *TNG* ladder, took positions on the new show as producers. Robert Blackman and Michael Westmore, who were pulling double duty respectively as the costume designer and make-up man for *TNG* and *DS9*, agreed to do the same for *DS9* and *VOY*. Ditto for Michael Okuda and Rick Sternbach, who brought their experience in graphics and design to the new frontier, with Sternbach, who had previously designed the Deep Space Nine space station, designing the Voyager starship itself. Other experienced personnel included Dan Curry, who would continue his work as visual effects producer, and composers Jay Chattaway, Dennis McCarthy, and David Bell, who would take turns scoring the episodes. The producers, hoping for a look that was halfway between *TNG* and *DS9*, were even able to poach Marvin Rush from *DS9* to serve as cinematographer. There was, however, one notable name that wasn't very familiar to *Star Trek* fans. Kenneth Biller, who had begun his career writing a handful of episodes for *Beverly Hills, 90210* and *The X-Files*, was chosen to be the show's first executive story editor.

"I was friends with René Echevarria, originally a writer for *TNG* but later a writer/producer for *DS9*," Biller recalls. "And he offered me a chance to write for *DS9*, but I didn't really feel it was a good fit, so I turned it down. Then a few months later I needed some extra money so I called Rene and asked, 'Hey, can I still do that episode?' He said, 'Actually, they're starting this new series called *Voyager*.' So he gave some of my writing samples to Jeri Taylor and one thing led to another, and I was invited to join the staff."

In 1994, *TNG* wrapped up its television shoot and went straight into shooting its first feature film, with a story featuring the end of the Enterprise D. (Counselor Troi finally gets a chance to fly the ship and totals it, leaving the bridge in ruins.) After that, *TNG's* sets were turned over to *VOY* to repurpose for itself, with a new bridge built right over the old. (The stage sets for engineering, the transporter room, the corridors, and the holodeck, meanwhile, were modified to be reused.) Eventually, everything was polished up and ready for a new crew, with the producers searching high and low for the right actors to play the new parts. Some choices were easy. Everyone liked Robert Duncan McNeill as Lieutenant Paris, a character inspired by McNeill's Nick Locarno from *TNG's* "The First Duty," and Tim Russ, who had guest starred on several *Star Trek* productions, was an obvious choice for Tuvok. Other roles were more difficult to fill, with Robert Beltran not in place until after shooting on the pilot had already commenced, and the producers still disagreeing on who should play Janeway even as the cameras began rolling.

"Geneviève Bujold came to us," Rick Berman recalls, "and she's a remarkably talented woman. So Michael and Jeri were just so emphatic about how much they loved her, and I couldn't talk them out of it. But she was used to film. So I took her out to lunch, and I tried to talk *her* out of it. 'You're going to be shooting until two or three in the morning. You're going to be doing it ten months a year. You're going to be working with directors you don't know.' And I went on, basically to see how she'd respond. And a couple days later, she called and said, 'Rick, I have talked to my children, and my answer is oui.' So we hired her. But I told Michael and Jeri this was going to be a nightmare. And after a day and a half of shooting, the whole deck of cards fell apart. She said to me, 'There are people touching my hair who I don't know. I have all these pages. I can't discuss every line with the director, and they're asking me to do things at a certain speed. I just can't do it!' It was every single thing I tried to tell her. I went to Kerry McCluggage's office and I said, 'This isn't going to work. This woman is a great actress, but she was not designed to be the star of a science-fiction television show that shoots in seven or eight days.' So we stopped production and went back to our second, third and fourth choices. One was Susan Gibney [familiar to *Star Trek* fans as Dr. Leah Brahms in *TNG's* "Booby Trap" and "Galaxy's Child"] and another was Kate Mulgrew. And we ultimately went with Mulgrew, who was thankfully still available."

"Kate was a great actress," Robert Picardo says, "but what really set her apart was her voice. For our series, that was so important because the captain does all the narration. 'Captain's log, blah blah blah.' That's what made William Shatner and Patrick Stewart so important to their shows, and that's what we needed. We couldn't have just anyone in that position. Imagine Edith Bunker saying those lines."

In the months that followed, *VOY* finished shooting its pilot and shot an additional eighteen episodes as well: enough for the United Paramount Network to air fifteen in an abbreviated first season (which, similar to *DS9's* first season, ran from January to May), with another four episodes donated to Season Two.

The producers' hope was to avoid the problems that had plagued the first seasons of *TNG* and *DS9*, with both shows having budget issues that undermined the quality of the episodes as the season progressed. "With *DS9* in particular," Michael Piller once said, "the overages on the pilot were astonishing. A result of that was a lack of scope in the early shows. And the audience seemed to be telling us very early on that they felt claustrophobic on the space station." *VOY* would therefore employ plenty of location work early in an attempt to rope in viewers with stories told on a grander scale. "With this show," Piller said, "I was hoping that rather than getting intimate with these characters so quickly, the audience would have more of a stake in who they are after they had gone through a number of adventures together as a family."

And yet in those early days, the structure of the show itself was still in flux. Following a two-hour pilot comprised of a teaser and eight acts, the next four episodes were shot like *TNG* and *DS9*, intended to feature a teaser and five acts. But before those episodes aired, UPN executives requested a change in the formatting so *VOY* would seem less like a syndicated show and more like a network show: they wanted a teaser and just four acts, like the hour-long dramas that were playing on ABC, CBS, and NBC. Through some shrewd editing, the four episodes in the can were modified to feature one less commercial break, and the scripts for the following episodes were reformatted as well, with shooting commencing on "Eye of the Needle" with four acts in mind. But a short time later, UPN, worried about the loss of revenue the new structure was costing it, asked *VOY* to change back to a teaser and five acts. The net result is that six episodes feature four acts and eight episodes feature five.

So amidst all the chaos, how did Season One turn out? Not surprisingly, it's a mixed bag. The Kazon, based on the Los Angeles street gangs and meant to be the show's bad guys, flop right out of the gate, coming across as simply another set of actors wearing rubber masks, hardly different from the background aliens on *TNG* and *DS9*. Meanwhile, the hoped for Maquis/Starfleet conflict begins to fizzle, with the premise of the show itself making the Federation irrelevant and everyone on the ship realizing quite quickly they have to cooperate to get back home. On the other hand, the main characters themselves are well played, and the cast quickly develops a chemistry of its own, with the writers playing up their unique bond.

But as the heir to *TNG*, the real question is how good the episodes are, with *VOY*, like the previous show, focusing on individual stories rather than serial arcs. Happily, there are several that stand out, with "Caretaker," "Eye of the Needle," and "Jetrel" considered instant classics while none are outright duds, though "The Cloud" and "Learning Curve" come close. Meanwhile, the season as a whole netted nine Emmy nominations, with wins for visual effects (from "Caretaker") and the theme song (composed by Jerry Goldsmith).

The ratings themselves began higher than *DS9's*, with 21.3 million viewers watching "Caretaker," before the viewership eroded throughout the season, due primarily to two problems. First, the decision to postpone four episodes until Season Two led to more reruns than usual. Second, UPN was, in general, aiming for a different audience than the usual *Star Trek* fans, with *VOY* out of place in a Monday night lineup that also featured *Pig Sty* and *Platypus Man*. (Perhaps Lieutenant Torres needed a pet targ.)

But UPN was satisfied with what it ultimately got from *Star Trek*. In fact, of the five shows that debuted with the network, only *VOY* was given a second season, making Season One a success where it mattered most.

Season Two

Production Order
(with air date order in parentheses)

1. "Projections" (3rd)
2. "Elogium" (4th)
3. "Twisted" (6th)
4. "The 37's" (1st)
5. "Initiations" (2nd)
6. "Non Sequitur" (5th)
7. "Parturition" (7th)
8. "Persistence of Vision" (8th)
9. "Tattoo" (9th)
10. "Cold Fire" (10th)
11. "Maneuvers" (11th)
12. "Resistance" (12th)
13. "Prototype" (13th)
14. "Death Wish" (18th)
15. "Alliances" (14th)
16. "Threshold" (15th)
17. "Meld" (16th)
18. "Dreadnought" (17th)
19. "Investigations" (20th)
20. "Lifesigns" (19th)
21. "Deadlock" (21st)
22. "Innocence" (22nd)
23. "The Thaw" (23rd)
24. "Tuvix" (24th)
25. "Resolutions" (25th)
26. "Basics, Part I" (26th)

The Second Season Cast

Captain Janeway: Kate Mulgrew
Commander Chakotay: Robert Beltran
B'Elanna Torres: Roxann Biggs-Dawson
Kes: Jennifer Lien
Tom Paris: Robert Duncan McNeill
Neelix: Ethan Phillips
The Doctor: Robert Picardo
Tuvok: Tim Russ
Harry Kim: Garrett Wang

Notable Guest Stars

Sharon Lawrence
David Graf
Aron Eisenberg
Patrick Kilpatrick
Dwight Schultz
Nancy Hower
Jennifer Gatti
Warren Munson
Henry Darrow
Martha Hackett
Anthony De Longis
Alan Scarfe
Raphael Sbarge
Brad Dourif
Gerrit Graham
John de Lancie
Jonathan Frakes
Susan Diol
Michael McKean
Carel Struycken
Tom Wright

"The 37's": B

The crew traces an SOS call to a planet and discovers the fate of Amelia Earhart.

Air date: August 28, 1995
Written by Jeri Taylor & Brannon Braga
Directed by James L. Conway
TV rating: 7.5

"From what we can tell, all eight of the people in that stasis chamber were taken from Earth in the 1930s and brought here." —Chakotay

Much like Kirk meeting Abraham Lincoln in "The Savage Curtain," Janeway meets her idol in a captain-based episode that is ultimately about decision making. Shot as the Season One finale but held back to kick off the second season instead, "The 37's" is a unique episode that lacks focus but somehow works in spite of it.

The showpiece of the episode is the Voyager crew eschewing the transporters for technical reasons and physically landing the ship on a planet. With live action shot on location at Bronson Canyon (and a matte painting covering the Hollywood Sign), this visual is quite a sight, and it pairs perfectly with the unique look inside the ship itself, with the blue sky spilling in through Voyager's windows. Amidst this backdrop, Janeway contemplates what it would be like for the crew to settle down and start a new life as opposed to continuing what might be a hopeless journey. (In this way, the episode *would* work better as a season finale than a season premier, but with Amelia Earhart, a 1936 Ford, and an assortment of ideas scattered throughout the episode, there are enough interesting bits to hold an audience's attention either way.)

Unfortunately, the story leaves quite a bit on the table, seeming more like a "Part I" to a nonexistent "Part II." Earhart herself doesn't really contribute much, budget issues prevent us from seeing the amazing cities that make everyone homesick, and the true plot doesn't kick in until the last act. Worse yet, while Sharon Lawrence is fabulous as Earhart herself, John Rubinstein is terrible as her navigator, Fred Noonan, with a penchant for overacting.

But seeing Janeway and Earhart meet is an iconic *Star Trek* moment, and though the episode takes the scenic route to get to where it's going, it's actually a lot of fun to try to figure out what it's all about as the adventure twists and turns along its path.

Did you know? Originally, Harry Manning, a radio operator, was supposed to be Amelia Earhart's navigator for an attempt to fly around the world. Then Fred Noonan, a skilled navigator in his own right, joined their team. But after the threesome's first attempt to circle the globe failed, Manning pulled out, leaving Earhart and Noonan to make another attempt on their own. Unfortunately, neither Earhart nor Noonan had any radio experience, which complicated their search for Howland Island in the Pacific Ocean, where they were supposed to land before returning to the United States. Earhart and Noonan never made it, but Manning lived for another 37 years, dying at age 77 in 1974.

"Initiations": C

Chakotay becomes caught up in a young alien's rite of passage.

Air date: September 4, 1995
Written by Kenneth Biller
Directed by Winrich Kolbe
TV rating: 5.9

"I'm stranded here with you because for some reason that escapes me at the moment, I keep saving your life." —Chakotay

It's that episode where Nog plays a Kazon with *DS9's* Aron Eisenberg guest starring as a Kazon adolescent on *VOY*. As a Chakotay/Kazon episode, it's a perfectly acceptable hour of television but nothing more.

Chakotay, apparently needing a whole solar system to himself to perform a ritual, borrows a shuttlecraft and drifts into Kazon space in a "just go with this" beginning written by Ken Biller. This decision by the first officer is dangerous, because the Kazon are territorial and gang-like, modeled after the clans in *TNG's* "The Vengeance Factor," which is a curious choice because that episode isn't particularly good. Eisenberg, for his part, plays a pint-sized Kazon named Kar who reluctantly bonds with Chakotay while the two go on the run from the other gang members as a B story plays out about Voyager's hunt for the crew's lost man.

With location shooting at the same Vasquez Rocks where Kirk fights the Gorn (though the show is careful not to show the iconic jagged peaks), the episode is nothing we haven't seen before, though the script is well written and attempts to find something for each character to do. Unfortunately, the Kazon continue to have no great actors to establish the race. (Even the Borg know how important this is. When they can't have a Mark Lenard or Robert O'Reilly, they recruit Patrick Stewart as their spokesperson!) Eisenberg is a bright spot, playing his part well, but the producers, deciding his voice is too recognizable to *Star Trek* fans, don't bring him back. That turns "Initiations" into a one and done filler episode, but as such, it's entertaining enough for a viewing or two.

Did you know? Aron Eisenberg died in 2019. He was fifty.

"Projections": B

The Doctor considers the possibility that he's a real person and that the ship and the rest of the crew are part of a malfunctioning holographic program.

Air date: September 11, 1995
Written by Brannon Braga
Directed by Jonathan Frakes
TV rating: 6.1

"This is just a simulation, Lewis! None of this is real, and unless you destroy this ship that you think you're on, you're going to die." —Lieutenant Barclay

Brannon Braga and Jonathan Frakes team up for a mind-bending bottle episode similar their *TNG* hit, "Frame of Mind" (and reminiscent of *TOS's* "The Mark of Gideon"), this time with Frakes in the director's chair and The Doctor put through the wringer. Like "The 37's," it's another holdover from the first season and proves that good things come to those who wait. Dwight Schultz reprises *TNG's* Lieutenant Barclay, a holographic character who, in the spirit of *Quantum Leap*, serves as "Al" to The Doctor's "Sam," with the two revisiting the events of the pilot as Barclay tries to get The Doctor to leap home (in a manner of speaking). It's a high concept that simultaneously allows us to return to the show's roots while logically allowing The Doctor to go anywhere on the ship. Adding Dwight Schultz is the cherry on top, as he has mad chemistry with Robert Picardo. Both actors bring something quirky to their characters, and with Braga's writing, they make a great comedy duo. (I particularly like the inside joke about the Caretaker, with Barclay tossing out the name "Banjo-man," the Caretaker's name in the script.)

From the opening teaser, the episode is really a character-based mystery story, with The Doctor trying to figure out what's real and the audience wondering where Braga is going with the whole thing. No viewer buys the premise that the show is just a holographic illusion, of course, but that doesn't really matter; the fun is in the journey. Like "Frame of Mind," the explanations in the end aren't as intriguing as the mystery in the beginning, but they do lay the groundwork for the real Jupiter Station, along with Dr. Zimmerman and Lieutenant Barclay, to appear in the future.

Barclay, who ends up appearing in more episodes of *VOY* than *TNG*, returns in Season Six's "Pathfinder."

Did you know? When creating the *VOY* characters, the producers initially thought about having Dwight Schultz play a holographic Doctor created in Barclay's image.

"Elogium": D

Space-borne life-forms affect Kes's reproductive cycle.

Air date: September 18, 1995
Teleplay by Kenneth Biller & Jeri Taylor
Story by Jimmy Diggs & Steve J. Kay
Directed by Winrich Kolbe
TV rating: 5.7

"But you, you don't understand. The elogium occurs only once. If I am ever going to have a child, it has to be now!" —Kes

Elogium
(noun)
1. The praise bestowed on a person or thing
2. Puberty for Kes's people
3. A poor VOY episode

With a swarm of alien sperm creatures attracted to Voyager and Neelix and Kes considering having a child, this bottle episode (another holdover from the first season) places a heavy emphasis on instinct and hormones. The idea of a child growing up on Voyager is an interesting notion considering the crew's unique situation, and the episode even strays close to the issue of teenage pregnancy. Unfortunately, most of the plot sees Neelix and Kes struggling (separately) to decide whether they want to be parents or not, an interesting subject in the abstract sense but one that can and has been done on just about every kind of TV show.

The swarm of sperm is notable for being an early CGI success for televised *Star Trek*, but it amounts to nothing more than a vanilla "ship-in-peril" B story, being similar to the B story of *TNG's* "Galaxy's Child," where an alien space baby mistakes the Enterprise for its mother.

The interlacing of the two stories does neither any favors, though with Neelix and Kes being the dullest couple in *Star Trek* history, it's an uphill battle either way. The most memorable bit is at the end, where we're teased with the foreshadowing of a character who does, in fact, appear later in the season.

Did you know? The writers felt this episode would have been a more fitting Season One finale than "Learning Curve," but the episode was held back for Season Two because some felt it was too much like Season One's "The Cloud" and wanted to give each episode its own space.

"Non Sequitur": B

Harry Kim finds himself in an alternate timeline where he was never assigned to Voyager.

Air date: September 25, 1995
Written by Brannon Braga
Directed by David Livingston
TV rating: 6.0

"Your shuttle intersected one of our time streams and boom! A few things were altered as the result of the accident. History and events were scrambled a bit, and you ended up here." —Cosimo

Finally, Nomad's catch phrase, Latin for "does not follow," serves as the title for a *Star Trek* episode, and boy does this one take it literally.

This Earth-based story steps outside the usual *VOY* formula for a memorable Harry Kim story that makes good use of Paramount's New York street back lot.

Waking up in an alternate reality, Kim gets a good look at a "What if?" scenario, playing out as if he was never able to join Voyager for her first mission. Inside this idea, the writers try to do the *It's a Wonderful Life* thing where Paris and the guy taking Kim's place on the ship are worse off due to the new timeline (because the writers need a reason for Kim to try to change things back). Really, they could have just made the whole thing a Paris episode, with Paris discovering a new reality where he's turned down the Voyager assignment and is confined to a penal colony, forcing him to escape and go on the run to set things right. He could even still meet up with Kim, who in this alternate reality missed his opportunity to join the Voyager crew when Paris wasn't there to help him on Deep Space Nine just before Voyager was set to embark. But, the writers, wanting more Kim-based episodes, give the ball to Garrett Wang instead, and he does just fine, giving us one of the more interesting Season Two stories.

In fact, in a way, it's a small-scale version of *TNG's* finale, "All Good Things," with the aliens, like Q, explaining the nature of what's going on in the middle rather than the end, and Kim, with no proof of what's going on, having to rely on his closest friends to help him set things right. That includes his girlfriend, Libby, played by Jennifer Gatti. Last seen in *TNG's* "Birthright" as Worf's romantic interest, Gatti plays it much the same here, giving Libby a sweetness and innocence while the writers find creative ways to show her half naked throughout the episode. Libby even gets in on the story's action, blocking an exit to stop Starfleet Security from chasing Kim, which you might think wouldn't work considering she weighs about a hundred pounds. (Fortunately for her, the security personnel seem to be *Star Trek's* equivalent of the Keystone Cops, bumbling their way through the whole episode.)

40

Like Season One's "Emanations," it's a bit surprising that this ambitious episode isn't a two-parter to allow it to dig deeper into the plot and spread out the cost of the unique environment. As a standalone episode, however, it's lots of fun, with the editor shrewdly using stock shots from *Star Trek* movies and past episodes to help sell the idea that the episode was made on a bigger budget than it really was.

Did you know? Are you a Starfleet officer on the run? Here's the Federation's how-to guide for evading your enemies.

• The Klingons: Use an English to Klingon translation book to impersonate and confuse them (as demonstrated by the crew of the Enterprise in *Star Trek VI: The Undiscovered Country*).
• The Romulans: Ask a Vulcan to flirt with their captain to distract her so you can steal her cloaking device (as Kirk has Spock do in *TOS's* "The Enterprise Incident").
• The Borg: Pull out one of their hoses, causing them to break down like an old Chevy truck (as demonstrated by Picard in *TNG's* "Descent").
• Starfleet Security: Have your girlfriend run interference while you make your getaway (as Kim has Libby do in *VOY's* "Non Sequitur").

"Reistance is somewhat possible."
(photo courtesy of Patric Butler)

"Twisted": C–

Voyager encounters an anomaly that reconfigures the ship.

Air date: October 2, 1995
Teleplay by Kenneth Biller
Story by Arnold Rudnick & Rich Hosek
Directed by Kim Friedman
TV rating: 5.6

"I can't find the cargo bay, and I can't find my security team." —Lieutenant Baxter

This one's premise (which J.K. Rowling would whimsically use later in the 1990s in her first *Harry Potter* book) is the perfect idea for a bottle episode: when the characters try to get to someplace on the ship, they find themselves randomly somewhere else. (So, for example, they may think they're walking from the ready room to the bridge, but instead they find themselves walking into a crewman's quarters.) The concept, however, needs something more to sustain interest for the duration of the episode, such as some action, a mystery, or…something. Unfortunately, "Twisted," another holdover from Season One, lacks such an X factor, with the crew figuring out what's going on early in the go, and the story meandering on from there without coming up with anything new.

Considering the characters all pair off to wander around like an episode of Scooby Doo, having the cause be more of a mystery would probably be better, with the crew not figuring out what was going on until the last act. In fact, while the old "malfunctioning holodeck" story was something the writers were trying to avoid by the time this episode was being written, if any episode cries out for such a device, it's this one. Having Janeway and company discover at the end that they been walking around in a malfunctioning holographic replica of the ship (and interacting with holographic crewmembers), would explain everything in a much more believable way.

Whatever the case, as is, the episode comes off as largely forgettable, with some meaningless scenes even tossed in after it was discovered the episode was running some eight minutes short. However, with the premise making it so unpredictable as to what's going to be behind the doors or around the corner as the crew moves from place to place, it's fun to watch anyway. (Will it be the bridge? Engineering? Some half-naked crewman's quarters?) And if the episode doesn't get the mileage it should out of the premise, at least it can take comfort in the fact that the first *Harry Potter* movie doesn't either.

Did you know? Prior to "Twisted" being slotted for a spot in Season Two, there was a rumor that it was so bad that UPN had decided not to air it.

"Parturition": D

When Neelix and Paris discover a new life-form on a planet, they become its caretakers.

Air date: October 9, 1995
Written by Tom Szollosi
Directed by Jonathan Frakes
TV rating: 5.9

"And you expect to take care of this thing until what? It graduates from high school, college? And what if Mom doesn't come back? Are you planning to bring this with us back on the ship?" —Paris

With Neelix's jealousy and possessive issues the most grating part of the character in the first two seasons, this episode brings good and bad news. The good is that the issues are finally put to bed. The bad is that it takes an episode all about them to do so.

Neelix and Paris, sharing the A story, work out their issues together while stranded on a planet as the rest of the crew get the standard B story about the search for their missing people. Along the way, the writer tosses in some inside jokes, having the characters mention longtime backstage terms "planet hell" and "technobabble" and finds a way to work in the plot of *Three Men and a Baby*. (Sadly, we don't get to hear Neelix and Paris sing "Goodnite, Sweetheart, Goodnite")

In a way, the episode stays true to the roots of *Star Trek*, demonstrating respect for all life-forms, and at least Neelix and Paris simply look after an alien baby as opposed to giving birth to one as the title suggests. (Besides, the director of *Three Men and a Baby* was supposedly a *Star Trek* fan, so he probably enjoyed contributing to the franchise, if only in a small, indirect way.) But all the same, the alien portion seems more like something from the *Dinosaurs* sitcom (1991–1994) than *VOY*.

Did you know? *Three Men and a Baby* (1987) was directed by Leonard Nimoy.

"Persistence of Vision": C

Something causes the crew to suffer hallucinations.

Air date: October 30, 1995
Written by Jeri Taylor
Directed by James L. Conway
TV rating: 6.1

"Captain, until I am able to determine the cause of these hallucinations, I'd prefer that you return to your quarters." —The Doctor

Janeway's Gothic holonovel is back one last time, continuing from where it left off in "Learning Curve," but this time it works its way into a surreal plot. A ship-based bottle-show, "Persistence" makes up for its lack of new visuals with a plethora of characters, including Janeway's husband, Tuvok's wife, and Paris's father.

While the episode uses the ensemble well, it's Janeway who's the center of attention in the first few acts, simultaneously allowing Kate Mulgrew to show them youngins' how it's done while allowing the plot to take on more importance than if it was about a lesser character. Unfortunately, the uneven script abandons Janeway near the end in favor of using Kes for a vague, underwritten conclusion. It's well played by Jennifer Lien, but with Kes in the background for most of the episode, it doesn't feel right to have her in control of the climax.

Sadly, Janeway's gothic adventure, a brilliantly textured idea, never returns for a resolution. (When the series first aired, there were many fans that objected to the notion, misunderstanding it to be Janeway's secret fantasy and finding it puzzling.) Happily, the series doesn't discard the holonovel concept altogether, however, including several more in the future.

"Persistence" was nominated for an Emmy for hairstyling.

Did you notice? For this episode, the show tweaks the color of the warp core, with the previous pinkish-blue replaced by a more whitish-blue, a change that would stick for the remainder of the series.

"Tattoo": C

Chakotay investigates a group of aliens who seem to be connected to his own people.

Air date: November 6, 1995
Teleplay by Michael Piller
Story by Larry Brody
Directed by Alexander Singer
TV rating: 5.8

"It's an ancient myth. Sky Spirits from above created the first Rubber People in their own image and led the way to a sacred land where the Rubber People would live for eternity." —Chakotay

The past and present unite for Chakotay in a story that, like an episode of ABC's *Lost*, weaves a childhood memory into current events. With ample location shooting and a mystical score, "Tattoo" creates quite a different feel for *Star Trek* while giving Robert Beltran an opportunity to explore the spiritual side of his character. And yet neither the past nor present offers much of an adventure, with both amounting to little more than a walkabout with an all too predictable conclusion.

To lighten the mood, the episode also includes a comedy runner where The Doctor suffers from a holographic flu. Picardo (who suggested the idea to begin with) nails it, making the symptoms believable and hilarious at the same time.

Overall, however, "Tattoo" comes across as a soft, forgettable offering, though it does what it does quite well, and Henry Darrow, who died in 2021, deserves special praise for his performance as Chakotay's father.

Did you know? By 1995, Michael Piller and some of the other *Star Trek* writers were becoming concerned that *Star Trek* wasn't keeping up with the faster pacing other television shows were moving toward, with sitcoms like *Seinfeld* (1989–1998) driving the medium toward shorter and more plentiful scenes, making *VOY* feel lethargic in comparison. With "Tattoo," Piller intentionally tried to inject some urgency into his script, transitioning in and out of scenes quicker.

"Cold Fire": C+

The Voyager crew discovers a second Caretaker and a colony of Kes's people.

Air date: November 13, 1995
Teleplay by Brannon Braga
Story by Anthony Williams
Directed by Cliff Bole
TV rating: 6.0

"I'm sure you care for them very much. I'm sure they're wonderful people. They certainly seem that way to me, but it's time that you began to accept how different you are from them." —Tanis

With a story thought up by an assistant manager of advertising for Paramount, "Cold Fire" invokes the pilot's idea of a second Caretaker and combines it with Kes's developing mental abilities to create a decent episode.

Gary Graham, who Berman & Piller considered for the part of Sisko on *DS9*, is the main guest star, playing a hybrid of Yoda and the Emperor and teaching Kes the ways of the force. It's a part that requires movie star gravitas, and Graham, unfortunately, doesn't have it, sabotaging what the writers are going for. (Graham is actually a fine actor who would return to play a recurring Vulcan on *Enterprise*. This just isn't his sort of role.) What the part really needs is an actor with more stage experience and more charisma, such as Jerry Hardin or Ian McKellen. Jennifer Lien on the other hand, hits all the right notes as Kes to help make up for Graham's shortcomings.

As it winds its way to its conclusion, the episode turns into a mini horror movie (which is not surprising if you've seen the preview, since it gives away most of the story) before maddeningly hitting the reset button at the end.

Still, for an uneven episode with casting issues, "Cold Fire" is a rather entertaining hour.

Did you know? This was the first of ten *VOY* episodes directed by Cliff Bole, who previously directed twenty-five *TNG* episodes and seven *DS9* episodes.

"Maneuvers": C+

After Seska steals vital transporter technology from Voyager, Chakotay sets off on his own to recover it.

Air date: November 20, 1995
Written by Kenneth Biller
Directed by David Livingston
TV rating: 5.4

"Conventional tactics aren't going to work with Seska. We'll need to come at her with a few surprises of our own." —Chakotay

Martha Hackett returns as Seska in this Chakotay episode that's a sequel to Season One's "State of Flux." Starting out as a cat and mouse game, it quickly turns into a POW story that's as much about Seska and the Kazon as Voyager.

Most of it is uninspired, with Voyager conveniently having some major security lapses when necessary for the plot. Meanwhile, tough guy Chakotay laughs off his hostile interrogators, and Janeway blows a clear opportunity to force the Kazon to return Seska to the ship. Along the way, we learn a little more about the Kazon, but the casting department ages them up too greatly to continue the original idea of a gang culture.

Seska's a fun character however, and it's interesting to see how transporter technology can shift the power within the Kazon culture. It's sort of like watching a small gang from a city that's never seen firearms and seeing what they can do with a gun.

Seska returns in "Alliances."

Did you know? Shortly before this episode began shooting, Martha Hackett learned she was pregnant.

The Seven Essential Seska Episodes:

"State of Flux"
"Maneuvers"
"Alliances"
"Investigations"
"Basics, Part I"
"Basics, Part II"
"Worst Case Scenario"

"Resistance": B

After an away mission goes awry, Janeway accepts the help of a delusional resistance fighter to help free Tuvok and Torres.

Air date: November 27, 1995
Teleplay by Lisa Klink
Story by Michael Jan Friedman & Kevin J. Ryan
Directed by Winrich Kolbe
TV rating: 5.9

"You did save me. Now I'm returning the favor." —Janeway

Opening mid-crisis to toss the viewer right into the fray, "Resistance" is a planet-based Janeway episode that's sort of a cross between Season One's "Time and Again" and Miguel de Cervantes's *Don Quixote*.

Newcomer Lisa Klink proves her mettle by crafting an ambitious teleplay that balances quite a few elements, having A, B, and C stories, while not losing sight of the episode's heart. We have Chakotay on the bridge of Voyager being stonewalled by a figurehead from the planet of the week, Torres and Tuvok bonding in prison, and guest star Joel Grey (who won a Tony and an Academy Award for *Cabaret*) nearly stealing the show as Caylem, a lovable nut. Yet through it all, the focus remains on Janeway, with Kate Mulgrew taking full advantage of the opportunity to show the captain in a different environment than usual. (UPN, unfortunately, used this to create a misleading preview, showing a moment where she dresses up as a prostitute to distract the guards and making it seem like she has to sell herself to save her crew. "Just how far will she go? Tune in next week!")

More than anything however, Mulgrew and Grey work well together and give each scene some poignant moments, the last being the most powerful of all. The two flesh out a plot that could be done in any *Star Trek* incarnation and turn it into a unique and special episode for *VOY*.

Did you know? In 2007, writer Lisa Klink appeared on Jeopardy and won five games, amassing $71,150. She returned in 2009 for a Tournament of Champions, winning an additional $5,000.

"Prototype": C+

Torres attempts to save a mechanical man and his race.

Air date: January 15, 1996
Written by Nicholas Corea
Directed by Jonathan Frakes
TV rating: 5.9

"They've learnt to make repairs to themselves, some pretty complex, but the construction of a power module, the device that sustains them, is beyond their grasp. It's an incredible challenge, Captain, but with enough time to study their systems, I might be able to do it." —Torres

Automatons make a *Star Trek* comeback in this throwback episode that's sort of a sophisticated combination of *TOS's* "I, Mudd" and "The Doomsday Machine" that features B'Elanna Torres.

Beginning unusually from the robot's point of view (including a rare, first person transporter effect), director Jonathan Frakes gives the episode a feature film quality before settling into more standard television shots as the episode develops its plot.

Corea's script, polished by Ken Biller, includes a few Data references and establishes enough dots for the episode to connect as it moves along, though both the story and backstory it develops lack the complexity needed to really stand out. (I'm not in the business of spoilers, but I could probably tell you all you need to know about the episode in a few sentences.)

Despite its simplicity, however, "Prototype" entertains because it has an interesting premise and everyone works hard to pay it off. Rick Worthy, in particular, deserves credit for his work as the robot itself.

Curiously, a similar premise, with more complexity, would appear again just a few episodes later in "Dreadnought."

Did you know? In 1770, just as the first Industrial Revolution was gaining steam, Hungarian inventor Wolfgang von Kempelen revealed his latest creation: a mechanical man who could play chess. Known as The Turk, the supposed automaton chess player was attached to a desk with cabinet doors that allowed its creator to show off an interior filled with gears, cogs, and levers. Over the course of the next several decades, audiences gasped the mechanical player matched wits with some of the most famous chess players of the time, including Benjamin Franklin and Napoleon Bonaparte. But it was all a hoax. The desk itself was designed like a prop for a magic show, allowing a human chess master to hide inside, view the game from below, and operate the Turk's arm. It was, nonetheless, an ingenious bit of engineering for the time and inspired others to create their own machines, including Charles Babbage, an English engineer who played The Turk twice and went on to invent the first mechanical computer.

49

"Alliances": B–

Janeway seeks an alliance to secure Voyager's passage through Kazon space.

Air date: January 22, 1996
Written by Jeri Taylor
Directed by Les Landau
TV rating: 5.4

"You've made an interesting proposal. I've discussed it with Seska and she assures me that you would not make this gesture unless you were sincere. I will talk with you." —Culluh, leader of the Kazon-Nistrim

With Voyager getting bullied by the Kazon, Janeway agrees to bend on the whole Prime Directive issue, and if you know anything about the *Star Trek* writers, you know how that's going to turn out.

Featuring Seska, the Kazon, and the Trabe, the latter making their first appearance after being mentioned in "Initiations" and "Maneuvers," this episode moves through the motions of diplomacy and backstabbing to flesh out the politics of the area before building a story on top of it. The situation itself is really an allegory for the America's relationship with Middle Eastern nations, with the U.S. intolerant of immoral acts when it comes to nations like Iraq or Iran while ignoring the same acts when it comes to Saudi Arabia or other nations which have chosen to be friendly to the Western world. This sort of idea, unfortunately, continues to weaken the Kazon as characters, turning them into more of a messy bureaucracy than a threatening group of gangs.

As it moves along, "Alliances" eventually winds its way to a "surprise" ending that can be seen a mile away, but as an episode about the internal struggles of Janeway and the Voyager crew in a topsy-turvy universe, it works alright...if you can get past the after school special moral at the end.

Raphael Sbarge, impressing the show's powers-that-be as Crewman Jonas, returns for the next several episodes to continue a mini-plotline begun here.

Did you know? Raphael Sbarge and Ed Begley Jr (who appears in "Future's End") went on to found Green Wish in 2009, a non-profit organization that helps fund environmentally friendly community projects.

"Threshold": F

After Paris successfully breaks the warp 10 speed barrier, he begins to change into an amphibious creature.

Air date: January 29, 1996
Teleplay by Brannon Braga
Story by Michael De Luca
Directed by Alexander Singer
TV rating: 6.2

"I don't know how this is possible, but it appears that his entire biochemistry is changing." —The Doctor

Star Trek fan Michael De Luca contributes to *Star Trek* with disastrous results, though it's not all his fault. With the regular *VOY* writers adding some ideas of their own to the plot, "Threshold" ends up as a jumble of concepts. There's *Star Trek's* version of the breaking of the sound barrier, the plot of "The Fly," and bits from *TOS's* "Where No Man Has Gone Before" and *TNG's* "Identity Crisis" all in one. The end result makes "Spock's Brain" look like intelligent science fiction.

At the core, it's all a Tom Paris episode, and teleplay writer Braga tries to develop it around the notion of Paris searching for redemption, though the point is largely lost in the shuffle (or the mess). The real thrust of the plot is an effort to illustrate the idea that evolution isn't really about the development of more intelligent or socially savvy species but is instead about survival of the fittest (with the fittest being those who are able to have the most offspring live to reproduce). Unfortunately, as *Star Trek* is prone to do, the episode attempts to distill the idea down to an individual, taking all the sense out of it. Some other episodes, such as *TNG's* "Genesis," get away with it because they use the junk science as a conceit to tell an interesting story; but here, the junk science *is* the story, and it results in some very confusing explanations and an ending that's too implausible for even science fiction.

"Threshold" won an Emmy for make-up (beating out *DS9's* "The Visitor").

Did you know? In the 1990s, Michael De Luca was a pop culture visionary. As president of production at New Line Cinema, his films included *The Mask*, *Rush Hour*, and *Austin Powers*, turning Jim Carrey and Mike Myers into box office commodities. New Line producer Mark Ordesky once told me, "At New Line, we couldn't make traditional star-driven films. We were not a company that was going to get access to Tom Cruise. The star-driven vehicles were going to go to Paramount, or Warner Bros., or one of the more traditional studios before us. So Mike De Luca used to say, 'Because we can't afford stars, we need to create stars.'"

51

"Meld": B

Tuvok is disturbed by a senselessness murder.

Air date: February 5, 1996
Teleplay by Michael Piller
Story by Michael Sussman
Directed by Cliff Bole
TV rating: 5.1

"Vulcan mind-melds: utter foolishness. Anybody with an ounce of sense wouldn't share his brain with someone else." —The Doctor

With a story by intern Mike Sussman and the first guest appearance by Brad Dourif, this Tuvok bottle episode examines the effects of a creepy ensign on the normally unemotional Vulcan.

Using a script that benefits from input from the California Institute for the Mentally Insane, Brad Dourif, the voice of Chucky from *Child's Play* and the actor who plays Wormtongue in *The Lord of the Rings* movies, is the perfect choice for Ensign Suder and works well with Tim Russ in this character piece that uses a mind-meld to overlap their personalities. The story, avoiding a cliché murder-mystery, focuses on the nature of random violence and how to deal with the perpetrators, with Russ finally allowed to cut loose and Tuvok having some interesting conversations with Janeway about the treatment of prisoners. Still, while it's a breakout episode for Russ and a memorable episode for the series, "Meld" is a dark installment that's hard to enjoy, and it doesn't dig as deep into the issue of capital punishment as it could. (More on this topic would come in Season Seven's "Repentance.")

To lighten the mood, Piller tosses in a Paris B story about gambling. Originally meant to superficially tie into the A story, its final scene is cut, leaving it a dangling thread that's instead paid off in "Investigations."

Ensign Suder returns for the season finale, "Basics Part I." Later on, *VOY* redoes the plot of "Meld" with the Season Four episode "Random Thoughts."

Did you know? Mike Sussman later became a writer and co-producer for *ENT*.

"Dreadnought": B

A missile B'Elanna Torres programmed during her time with the Maquis is threatening a planet in the Delta Quadrant.

Air date: February 12, 1996
Written by Gary Holland
Directed by LeVar Burton
TV rating: 6.0

"Who would have thought two years ago, after all those weeks we spent together perfecting your program, that we'd end up out here trying to kill each other?"
—Torres

Based on a story by an executive at Paramount's advertising division and featuring a teleplay written by the uncredited Lisa Klink, this Torres episode gives Biggs-Dawson a double role as both Torres and the voice of the titular missile, Dreadnaught.

It's basically the Hal story from *2001: A Space Odyssey*, with Dreadnought as the stubborn computer and Torres, in Kirk-like manner, attempting to argue against the cold logic of a machine hell bent on carrying out a mission.

Klink lays out the episode nicely, putting Voyager and Dreadnought in a cat and mouse game, with Dreadnought always a step ahead before a one-on-one showdown with Torres and the weapon. That puts the episode on Dawson's shoulders, and she comes through, playing Dreadnought with an almost Vulcan-like personality and Torres with a mixture of guilt and desperation as she essentially butts heads with herself. Meanwhile, Kate Mulgrew and guest star Dan Kern lend an assist in a B story about Janeway attempting to warn an alien leader of Dreadnought's planetary target.

Director Burton, using a Steadicam for Dreadnought's interior stage set to give it life and unpredictability, builds the momentum with a quickening pace as the episode approaches its climax and pays it off with an ending that wisely doesn't overstay its welcome.

Did you know? Referencing Season Two episodes "Faces," "Prototype," and "Dreadnought," Dawson noted, "I had an episode where I played opposite myself, then opposite a machine, then opposite a machine with my voice. Hopefully, next year I get to talk to a real person."

"Death Wish": A–

A member of the Q Continuum seeks asylum aboard Voyager so he can commit suicide.

Air date: February 19, 1996
Teleplay by Michael Piller
Story by Shawn Piller
Directed by James L. Conway
TV rating: 6.8

"Will you send him to prison for eternity or will you assist in his suicide plan?"
—Q

TNG vets John de Lancie (Q) and Jonathan Frakes (Commander Riker) guest star in this high profile *VOY* episode thought up by Michael Piller's son, Shawn, with *VOY* using the Q Continuum for a rare story where the protagonist fights for death and the antagonist fights for life.

Frakes himself has only a glorified cameo (originally meant for LeVar Burton, though the latter's shaved head made him unusable as La Forge), with Mulgrew, de Lancie, and guest star Gerrit Graham doing the heavy lifting in a story about Graham's character and the philosophical question of whether a person has the right to choose to die or not.

After beginning with some superfluous Q whimsy, including an inside joke where Voyager becomes a Christmas tree ornament, the episode settles into the weighty subject matter in a courtroom-like setting with the characters carefully positioned into their roles. Graham's character is the defendant, Tuvok serves as the defense attorney, de Lancie's Q is the prosecutor, and Janeway is the judge.

The case, of course, is shamelessly set up in the protagonist's favor, with no family or friends around to illustrate the selfish side of suicide. The trial, nonetheless, opens the door for some interesting questions about the matter, such as why a society feels it's okay to have a death penalty but wrong for someone to kill him or herself. And being tucked inside a Q Continuum story, it allows the writers to be creative, with the prosecution and the defense both presenting some unusual evidence. (This is where Riker comes in, with de Lancie's Q summoning several historically important Earth people to show how their lives have been touched by the defendant. It comes across like a *Forrest Gump* spoof and adds little to the episode, though thankfully Michael Jordan and Bill Gates declined invitations to appear.) Most notably, the defense creates an abstract facsimile of the Q Continuum, thanks to location shooting in Lancaster, California, giving the race some depth that would inspire future Q episodes.

Within this framework, Graham, serving as a counterpoint to de Lancie, gives a poignant performance that cuts through the Q silliness to give the episode its drama and meaning. The other actors, probably recognizing a rich script, work hard as well. (Paramount was smart to hold this episode back to air during sweeps, even if it gets plopped into the middle of some episodes with an ongoing story arc involving Paris and Jonas.)

John de Lancie's Q, who uses "Death Wish" to build a rapport with Janeway, returns in a loose sequel of sorts in Season Three's "The Q and the Grey".

Did you know? For this episode, Andrew English was cast as a background security officer. He would go on to appear in twenty-nine other episodes, including "Future's End, Part II," "Equinox," "One Small Step," "Fury," "Flesh and Blood," "Author, Author," and "Endgame."

"Lifesigns": B

The Doctor falls in love with a Vidiian patient.

Air date: February 16, 1996
Written by Kenneth Biller
Directed by Cliff Bole
TV rating: 5.6

"By the way, Danara, I've been meaning to tell you: I'm romantically attracted to you and wanted to know if you felt the same way." —The Doctor

This Doctor episode sees *VOY's* holographic physician begin dating. Credited to Biller but polished by Piller and Taylor, the script allows Robert Picardo to get out of the sickbay set and explore some teenage angst in The Doctor's own way.

Guest star Susan Diol plays Danara, giving her character both an inner strength and a vulnerability for Picardo to play off of. The sci-fi idea of transferring her consciousness temporarily from her diseased body to a temporary holographic healthy body opens up a lot of new story ideas. There's a bizarre situation where she, in the new body, helps The Doctor work on her old body, her true self. Then there's her concern about what The Doctor will think of her diseased self and her reluctance to return to her old body even if it means a shorter life as a beautiful hologram. It also sets up a unique situation where The Doctor is dealing with a hologram who happens to be real, which makes the romance all the more complex.

While Picardo and Diol carry the episode, Robert Duncan McNeill also gets quite a few things to do, with Paris and Kes helping out the lovebirds and Paris and Chakotay having a falling out. Meanwhile, Crewman Jonas, when not recording songs with his brothers, continues his own plotline with the Kazon.

Almost a cost saving bottle episode, "Lifesigns" does include some nice location shooting on Mars for a holographic date. *VOY* does more great Doctor episodes in later seasons, but this one remains a standout for the character and one of *Star Trek's* more successful romantic offerings.

Danara returns later in the season in "Resolutions."

Did you know? When *VOY* began shooting, the show's crew enjoyed having a bit of extra space by the main sets where they could store equipment. For Season Two, however, a new set was built right in this location: The Doctor's medlab. This proved inconvenient and led to a lot of complaining, as the equipment had to be moved to and from locations farther away. But as Rick Berman told his people, "Sets are what get filmed, make the show, and pay the bills, so you'll just have to make do."

"Investigations": B–

Neelix searches for a traitor aboard Voyager using his morning news program.

Air date: March 13, 1996
Teleplay by Jeri Taylor
Story by Jeff Schnaufer & Ed Bond
Directed by Les Landau
TV rating: 4.9

"I believe someone on this ship has been making covert transmissions and erasing the evidence." —Neelix

Using Neelix's investigative journalism as a frame, this episode picks up the threads of Crewman Jonas and Lieutenant Paris left by previous episodes and turns them into a *Columbo*-style crime puzzle with a twist.

Essentially broken into a Neelix A story and a Paris B story, it's not really a "whodunnit" so much as a "howcatchem," ultimately ending with a fight reminiscent of *TOS*. Featuring plenty of heart, action, and suspense, not to mention a resolution, "Investigations" is one of the more notable offerings of the season. Curiously, however, the A and B story eventually become concurrent attempts to solve the mystery, minimizing the scope of the episode and the stakes for Paris and Neelix. (After all, only one has to truly succeed.) Does it all add up to a good episode? Yes. But it leaves a lot of potential on the table. Having Neelix unknowingly stumble across a secret plot and a secret attempt to thwart it is a good start, but if this were used as the sole plot of the episode, it would allow time for more roadblocks to overcome, more mystery, and a more powerful conclusion, all revealed through the lens of Neelix's TV show. Meanwhile, future episodes could establish Paris as a double agent on board the Kazon vessel, which seems like where this episode is going. What we get instead is a half-baked version of both ideas sandwiched together to give Neelix some action and quickly clean up character issues with Paris the writers wish they hadn't introduced.

Did you know? Abdullah bin al-Hussein, who would go on to be the King of Jordan, plays a character talking to Harry Kim in the teaser before Neelix approaches.

"Deadlock": A–

Voyager is duplicated by a spatial phenomenon.

Air date: March 18, 1996
Written by Brannon Braga
Directed by David Livingston
TV rating: 5.8

"As strange as it sounds, Captain, according to these readings, another Voyager is right here, right now, occupying the same point in space-time that we are."
—Harry Kim

This fast-paced, action-packed ensemble piece is an ambitious story that borrows *TOS's* "Mirror, Mirror" idea and takes it to the next level by linking the twin Voyagers, forcing the two crews to work together to escape.

The true brilliance of the story lies in the execution of the narrative structure, which begins with *VOY's* longest teaser, continues with all hell breaking loose (leading to what's probably the longest damage report in *Star Trek* history) before the episode works its way to seemingly hitting the reset button...only to subsequently pull the rug out with a mind-bending conclusion. It's a roller coaster ride with twists and turns only Brannon Braga could come up with, and yet the wild, implausible story is so intelligently laid out, it's easy for the casual fan to follow without getting confused. (David Livingston deserves credit as well, giving the opening and close a frantic pace while slowing things down for the explanations in the middle.)

As "Deadlock" approaches its climax, it becomes a Janeway episode, with Mulgrew even getting a one-on-one scene one with herself. (Perhaps Biggs-Dawson should file a grievance.) Of course, *Trek* has done the twin thing in the past many times, but here it comes across as less of a gimmick and more as an organic part of the plot than twin Datas or twin Kirks. Just as another episode might need a curmudgeon old man to tell its story and the part is appropriately cast, this one needs another Janeway, and Mulgrew generously guest stars on her own series. The result is awesome-squared.

Like *DS9* and the future *Trek* shows, *VOY* never gets a chance at a feature film, but this one comes pretty close. With big battles and little character moments that utilize the entire cast, it's easy to imagine how a few more scenes could have turned "Deadlock" into a satisfying *Star Trek* movie experience. Instead, it serves as a delightful hour of sci-fi television that makes Schrödinger's cat paradox accessible to the masses.

Did you know? Thanks to a number of sci-fi twists, Captain Janeway dies seventeen times throughout *VOY's* seven seasons.

"Innocence": C–

Tuvok is trapped on a moon with a group of children who are disappearing one by one.

Air date: April 8, 1996
Teleplay by Lisa Klink
Story by Anthony Williams
Directed by James L. Conway
TV rating: 5.1

"Near the end of life, we reach the age of complete innocence." —Alcia

Tuvok babysits some alien kiddos in this planet-based episode that also features a first contact B story on the ship.

Teleplay writer Lisa Klink plays up the mystery of the children, and the child actors are rather good. But this "Tuvok as a parent" story just runs in place until its conclusion. Tuvok promises to look after the kids, the kids hug him. Tuvok tells a bedtime story, the kids hug him. Tuvok sings a lullaby, the kids hug him. Meanwhile, Janeway deals with a xenophobic race that's short on communication skills until it's time for the big reveal.

Both plots come together for a satisfying last act that almost makes up for the pedestrian journey to get there, but looking back at successful episodes with similar themes, they either have more to them (such as *TNG's* "Disaster") or spread out their sci-fi twist instead of saving it for the end (such as *TAS's* "Yesteryear" and "The Counter-Clock Incident").

There is, however, something poignant about having what seems like the beginning of a friendship with someone suddenly turn out to be the end.

Did you know? Lisa Klink recalls, "I knew that Tim Russ could sing, so I wanted to include a Vulcan lullaby. He heard about this and called me to talk about it, and we agreed that a Vulcan lullaby would be practical and include a lesson. It turned out really well, and as an unexpected bonus, I got into *ASCAP*, the composers and performers' union."

"The Thaw": B

Voyager discovers a virtual reality world where a demented clown is holding people hostage.

Air date: April 29, 1996
Teleplay by Joe Menosky
Story by Richard Gadas
Directed by Marvin V. Rush
TV rating: 4.7

"This is my world, my festival. And you're here without an invitation." —The Clown

Star Trek does its version of the old "evil clown" horror story in a malfunctioning holodeck-like episode (minus the holodeck) with a plot that slyly avoids having to leave Voyager, save for one alternate stage set.

After beaming up the hardware for a virtual reality world gone awry (sort of a demented Cirque du Soleil), Janeway finds herself in a battle of wits and wills with a clown that has the ability to kill anyone who has wandered into his world (which, unfortunately for her, includes Ensign Kim). It's really a "how do we save the hostages without killing them" dilemma in (literally) different clothes, crossed with an exploration of the nature of fear.

Michael McKean dominates the episode as the nameless antagonist, with his character interacting with various Voyager crewmembers and even getting in the final word. His clown is basically the same idea as Q, a character with complete control over his universe (in this case, one room) and exercising a whimsical and dangerous sense of humor.

Director of Photography Marvin Rush, stepping into the director's role, gives the episode an experimental theatre feel, taking the focus off the limited set and placing it on the exotic characters that inhabit it. The result is a spirit unlike anything *Trek* has ever done, save maybe for *TOS's* "Whom Gods Destroy" or *DS9's* "Move Along Home."

The very definition of a one and done, "The Thaw" is nonetheless one of *VOY's* most memorable episodes.

Did you know? Michael McKean, a good friend of Robert Picardo's, is perhaps best known for playing Lenny opposite David Lander's Squiggy on ABC's *Laverne & Shirley* (1976–1983).

"Tuvix": B–

After a transporter malfunction, Tuvok and Neelix are merged into a single being, Tuvix.

Air date: May 6, 1996
Teleplay by Kenneth Biller
Story by Andrew Shepard Price & Mark Gaberman
Directed by Cliff Bole
TV rating: 5.0

"Don't you think that I care about Tuvok and Neelix? Of course I do! Without them, I wouldn't exist. In a way, I think of them as my parents." —Tuvix

The first *Star Trek* episode to feature something like endosymbiosis, the idea of two organisms merging to form a new one, creates one of the tougher acting jobs *Star Trek* has ever known. There is, of course, an inherent difficulty of performing the merging of two established personalities. But the even greater challenge is creating a character the audience doesn't perceive as an imposter, with an actor who convinces the audience to accept and invest in his work as if he really is a combination of two regulars. Enter Tom Wright, who creates such a compelling Tuvix, it's impossible not to feel some affection for the guy and get caught up in his "life." It's almost as if the show found someone who's a likable cross between Tuvok and Neelix and decided to write an episode around him.

The performance gives the premise its punch, allowing the story to successfully explore several interesting questions. What does this mean for Neelix's girlfriend, Kes? Is this a new life-form with individual rights? If Tuvix doesn't want to change back, do the rights of Tuvok and Neelix trump Tuvix's own wishes? The latter becomes Janeway's dilemma, and it's a no-win situation she must resolve. In the end, the questions and answers prove more interesting than any of the issues raised by the episode's antonym, *TOS's* "The Enemy Within," and provide quite a dramatic and controversial finish.

Did you know? Tom Wright would go on to appear in *ENT's* "Storm Front," where he plays an alien military officer.

"Resolutions": C–

Infected by a virus, Janeway and Chakotay must remain on a planet while the remainder of the crew searches for a cure.

Air date: May 13, 1996
Written by Jeri Taylor
Directed by Alexander Singer
TV rating: 4.5

"Why do you have to see it as a defeat? Maybe it's simply accepting what life has dealt us, finding the good in it." —Chakotay

This "Janeway and Chakotay trapped on a desert island" story (with a planet in place of a desert) is a character-based episode with Chakotay trying to turn the situation into his own Kirk-like Nexus while Janeway struggles to accept the situation.

With location shooting at the Angeles National Forest and a spider monkey guest starring as an alien, it's basically a vehicle for a romance story. There are two problems with this idea. A, the writer/producer knows she can't actually have the two do anything more than touch and hold hands because she can't change the nature of the show, and B, the audience knows the writer/producer can't actually have the two characters do anything more than touch and hold hands because it would change the nature of the show. Within these confines, the story works okay, with a few good moments, but it would work better if there was another element, perhaps a sequel to "Tattoo," with a *Lost* flashback sequence interwoven into the narrative that explores more of Chakotay's youth. As is, there's quite a bit of filler instead.

The B story fares better, with Tuvok facing a near mutiny when nearly everyone on board disagrees with his decision to give up on Janeway and Chakotay. (It's certainly rare in *Star Trek* to see a character like Ensign Kim speak up and vocally undermine the captain right on the bridge!) Unfortunately, the whole thing nonetheless ends quite predictably, because there's only one way it *can* end.

Did you know? This episode scored the lowest ratings of *VOY's* first two seasons.

"Basics, Part I": B

Voyager flies into a trap. (Season finale)

Air date: May 5, 1996
Written by Michael Piller
Directed by Winrich Kolbe
TV rating: 4.9

"It's time to reexamine our game plan." —Janeway

Following up on loose threads from "Alliances," the writers send Voyager on a chase that even the crew knows is probably not a good idea. (Writer Michael Piller, knowing Chakotay and the crew need extra motivation to take the bait, invokes a spiritual vision reminiscent of "Tattoo.")

Like the *Harry Potter* books, the real interest here isn't in whether evil will strike but in the detective story leading up to it. Piller drops clues throughout the episode, such as damage to the deflector dish and anomalous blood readings, and Voyager prepares some surprises of its own. They're all efforts by Piller to create anticipation for a secret climax which we know is coming in some shape or form, but which remains a mystery until it unfolds. And that all leads to a dramatic finish that would be a killer cliffhanger for any *Star Trek* series but works best for *VOY*, with no Federation help available.

And so as an episode itself, "Basics" works quite well, with Ensign Suder brought back for a small sequel to "Meld" and everyone giving fine performances. Unfortunately, some of the recurring alien baddies are beginning to undermine the premise of the series. The whole point of *VOY* is supposed to be that the ship has to work its way back home while discovering new frontiers and new civilizations. When the crew keeps running into the same aliens over and over, it makes it seem as if everyone is running in place.

All the same, "Basics" serves its purpose as a thrilling season finale that leaves viewers to ponder, "How will they get out of this one?"

Did you know? Prior to filming scenes where Voyager is parked on a planet, Dan Curry and visual effects supervisor Ronald B. Moore visited the shooting location and used a rope to measure out the size of the ship. "It was just Dan and I and a teamster," Moore recalls. "So we just told the guy, 'Just take the end of this rope and head out that direction, you know? We'll tell you when to stop.' This guy's taking off and we're just feeding out this rope. And eventually we could barely see the teamster at the other end! It really defined just how big the ship was, and it gave us some kind of idea with landmarks of where the ship sat."

Season Two Roundup

With the novelty of *VOY's* debut having worn off and the series struggling to hold onto its viewers amidst a sci-fi landscape that was more crowded than ever, the show's second season saw its ratings fall behind *DS9*, a series in its prime that had just added the popular Worf from *TNG* to its cast.

Yet, on the whole, *VOY's* Season Two is a solid, if unremarkable season of *Star Trek*, helped by four episodes donated from Season One. In fact, one of those holdovers, "The 37's," posted the highest ratings of the season while another, "Projections," brought a version of Dwight Schultz's popular Barclay character into the *VOY* fold. And with standouts like "Projections," "Resistance," "Death Wish," and "Deadlock," there's enough excitement to offset lesser episodes like "Threshold" and "Parturition." Meanwhile, it's also evident that the writers and the actors are becoming more comfortable with the characters, with Janeway, Neelix, and Torres being the big three at this point. There's even some leftover friction between Starfleet and the Maquis, with Seska thrown into the mix as a delicious villain.

But nagging problems still persist. Voyager seems to magically repair herself week to week, the recurring Kazon make it seem like the ship isn't going anywhere, and the Delta Quadrant seems to be awfully similar to the Alpha Quadrant...all of which caused quite a bit of grumbling from viewers back in the day. Getting less attention, but just as important, are problems with the show's character development. Neelix's jealousy and Paris's insubordination, both introduced to spice things up, go so terribly for the writers, each idea is put to bed before season's end. Meanwhile, The Doctor begins to break out as a character, but his holographic nature limits where he can be. And then there's the character no writer can figure out what to do with, Kes.

As with any series, *VOY* would continue adjusting, emphasizing what has worked while reworking (or jettisoning) what has not. For, despite all its flaws, *VOY's* second season did land it in 87th place in the overall television ratings and went on to win an Emmy for make-up, more than adequate in the growing television landscape to earn the series another season.

Season Three

Production Order
(with air date order in parentheses)

1. "Sacred Ground" (7th)
2. "False Profits" (5th)
3. "Flashback" (2nd)
4. "Basics, Part II" (1st)
5. "The Chute" (3rd)
6. "Remember" (6th)
7. "The Swarm" (4th)
8. "Future's End" (8th)
9. "Future's End, Part II" (9th)
10. "Warlord" (10th)
11. "The Q and the Grey" (11th)
12. "Macrocosm" (12th)
13. "Alter Ego" (14th)
14. "Fair Trade" (13th)
15. "Blood Fever" (16th)
16. "Coda" (15th)
17. "Unity" (17th)
18. "Rise" (19th)
19. "Darkling" (18th)
20. "Favorite Son" (20th)
21. "Before and After" (21st)
22. "Real Life" (22nd)
23. "Distant Origin" (23rd)
24. "Displaced" (24th)
25. "Worst Case Scenario" (25th)
26. "Scorpion" (26th)

The Third Season Cast

Captain Janeway: Kate Mulgrew
Commander Chakotay: Robert Beltran
B'Elanna Torres: Roxann Dawson
Kes: Jennifer Lien
Tom Paris: Robert Duncan McNeill
Neelix: Ethan Phillips
The Doctor: Robert Picardo
Tuvok: Tim Russ
Harry Kim: Garrett Wang

Notable Guest Stars

Brad Dourif
Martha Hackett
Anthony De Longis
Nancy Hower
George Takei
Grace Lee Whitney
Michael Ansara
Don McManus
Dan Shor
Becky Ann Baker
Sarah Silverman
Ed Begley Jr.
Suzie Plakson
John de Lancie
James Nardini
Alexander Enberg
Sandra Nelson
Len Cariou
Alan Oppenheimer
Jessica Collins
Wendy Schaal
Henry Woronicz
Concetta Tomei
John Rhys-Davies

"Basics, Part II": B

With the Kazon in control of Voyager, Ensign Suder and The Doctor attempt to retake the ship while the remainder of the crew must return to basics in order to survive on a harsh world inhabited by alien natives.

Air date: September 4, 1996
Written by Michael Piller
Directed by Winrich Kolbe
TV rating: 5.9

"One hologram and one sociopath may not be much of a match for the Kazon, but we'll have to do." —The Doctor

Setting science fiction, character development, or complex story ideas aside, this conclusion to "Basics" is just a good old action/adventure romp with an A story on a primitive planet and a B story aboard the stolen Voyager.

The Doctor and Suder get the latter in a small-scale version of *Die Hard*, which is really there just to tie up the stories of Suder, Seska, and the Kazon, with the latter making their final noteworthy appearance in the series. That said, Picardo, who at this point is still stuck in the sickbay set, is less Bruce Willis and more Groucho Marx, with The Doctor getting off some nice one-liners as chaos reigns around him. Meanwhile with Suder, the writers get some mileage out of the interesting idea of a killer who has "kicked the habit" who is forced back into killing again by an enemy. Brad Dourif acts his heart out, and if this was a Showtime series like *Dexter*, it would be fun to see where they could go with his character. Unfortunately, as a family friendly primetime franchise, *Star Trek* can only take things so far before tidying everything up.

The real money, however, is spent on the planet-based A story, with Chakotay serving as the writer's character of choice to follow. Despite being a bundle of clichés (a stranded crew, a monster, primitive aliens, and a Native American rubbing two sticks together to start a fire) and moving in circles, it works nonetheless, with gorgeous location shooting at Alabama Hills near the Sierra Nevada Mountains and *VOY's* first CGI monster giving the adventure story a feature film quality.

Interestingly, the script itself was a result of a civil war of sorts between departing writer Michael Piller and producer Jeri Taylor, who argued over setups and payoffs. You might say that the climax of the finished episode lacks some punch as a result, but the two-parter still comes across as a fun little TV movie.

Did you know? Starting with this episode, the name Roxann Biggs-Dawson is changed to Roxann Dawson in the credits. The "Biggs" part actually came after Dawson married Casey Biggs, who plays the Damar, a Cardassian, on *DS9*. But the two divorced before either became involved with *Star Trek*.

"Flashback": C

When Tuvok begins to suffer from a mental breakdown, a mind-meld with Janeway takes them both back to his tour of duty with Captain Sulu aboard the USS Excelsior.

Air date: September 11, 1996
Written by Brannon Braga
Directed by David Livingston
TV Rating: 5.3

"I think we may be dealing with a repressed memory." —The Doctor

Whereas *DS9's* "Trials and Tribble-ations" celebrates *Star Trek's* thirtieth birthday by revisiting *The Original Series*, this episode of *VOY* honors the milestone by revisiting the *Star Trek* movies.

In truth, the story itself—minus the movie tie-in—was conceived before the idea was proposed to do something special for *Star Trek's* birthday. But with Tim Russ having been on the Excelsior bridge for *Star Trek VI: The Undiscovered Country* and the adventures of Excelsior in that film largely occurring offscreen, the *VOY* producers figured it was better to tap into *Star Trek's* own history rather than create a backstory of their own for the sake of the plot. The result is rich nostalgia placed upon a framework of a mediocre premise, the latter causing the story to fall short of fans' expectations. but the former making it better than it would have been otherwise. (Personally, I think a better idea would be to celebrate the larger scope of *Star Trek* by doing the "All Good Things" thing with some plot device causing Janeway to skip around in time, bouncing from Voyager to Excelsior to *TOS's* Enterprise. Through original scenes and *Forrest Gump*-style insertions, she could thread her way through the time periods *Quantum Leap* style, using information from all three to solve some sort of puzzle and save the day. Such an episode would, of course, be absurdly expensive and encroach on *DS9's* "Trials and Tribble-ations" gimmick, but as a story itself, it could have been quite special.)

As is, "Flashback" honors *TOS* by filling in gaps left by its superior *DS9* counterpart, revisiting the feature films instead of the TV show and using Sulu, the only main *TOS* character who doesn't appear in "The Trouble with Tribbles" and "Trials and Tribble-ations." Bringing back some of the Excelsior bridge crew is a coup, with the actors reenacting scenes (and even camera angles) from five years before—which must have been surreal. And Nicholas Meyer and Brannon Braga form a sort of Yin/Yang relationship, with writer/director Meyer enjoying throwing odd details into his films, like Sulu's broken cup, and Braga enjoying developing such aspects into stories of their own. Yet the episode's strongest suit is its development of Tuvok, exploring his backstory in such a way that he's able to simultaneously act out bits of his past while breaking the fourth wall to explain his actions and choices. (It's sort of like a reality show with cutaway interviews, but less intrusive.)

None of this can fix the issue of the dishwater bland premise, and the ending is more of a shrug than anything else, but it is fun to see Sulu and his crew in action, and it's great to see Sulu (George Takei) and Rand (Grace Lee Whitney), who share a scene together in *TOS's* first episode, "The Man Trap," share the screen in their final appearances in *Star Trek* history.

George Takei and Grace Lee Whitney
(photos by Gage Skidmore and Larry D. Moore)

Did you know? Pieces of the original Excelsior bridge set had been used for other sets over the years, forcing the crew to rebuild the set mostly from scratch for this episode, save for the main viewscreen, the ops and conn consoles, and a few minor details.

70

"The Chute": B

Kim and Paris are imprisoned in an alien facility where the only way in or out is through a chute.

Air date: September 18, 1996
Teleplay by Kenneth Biller
Story by Clayvon L. Harris
Directed by Les Landau
TV Rating: 4.3

"They must have drugged me, because the next thing I knew, I woke up at the bottom of the chute to that welcoming party." —Paris

The second big Kim/Paris episode takes the two characters to the edge of madness in a prison story that features fine performances from the guest stars and main cast alike, but, like "Non Sequitur," is carried by Garrett Wang.

For the most part, the story is the standard prison tale, with the falsely convicted protagonists meeting various interesting characters and being laughed at for entertaining thoughts of escape. The show even finds a way to give the characters a sense of frustration, thanks to a sci-fi gadget, that usually takes weeks of sleep and food deprivation to develop.

Like Jonathan Frakes and Colm Meaney before him, Wang is great as the everyman dealing with a new reality that tests and defines his character in a way most *Star Trek* episodes don't. Robert Duncan McNeill, as always, uses Paris to make Harry more interesting than usual, but it's Don McManus giving a memorable performance as the calm but eccentric Zio that brings out Wang's best and drives the plot.

Meanwhile, Janeway deals with the stubborn, obstinate government official of the week, well played by Robert Pine, father of future *Star Trek* actor Chris Pine, in the predictable B story where she attempts to recover her missing crewmen.

Is it old hat to see an alien government wrongly convicting Starfleet officers while a Starfleet captain tries to clean up the mess? Do both stories go in circles until the conclusion? Yes and yes. But it does make for exciting television and is well worth a look. As a character piece, the episode accomplishes just what it sets out to do, and with a fun twist in the middle and some striking visuals, it's one of Season Three's finer episodes.

Did you know? Don McManus appears as a prison guard in *The Shawshank Redemption* (1994).

71

"The Swarm": C

While Voyager is attacked by a swarm of alien ships, The Doctor begins losing his memory.

Air date: September 25, 1996
Written by Mike Sussman
Directed by Alexander Singer
TV Rating: 5.1

"We seem to have a small problem. I can't remember how to perform this operation." —The Doctor

With an attack on Paris and Torres winding its way into an A story about The Doctor and a B story about the ship-in-peril, this episode delivers an uneven cross between a character piece and an atypical ship-based cat and mouse game.

The main plot features Picardo taking on a double role as both the holographic doctor as well as a holographic recreation of The Doctor's creator. With the former suffering from something similar to Alzheimer's, there's some heartbreaking pathos that Picardo plays well, even while acting with himself and developing the character of Doctor Zimmerman. But it's actually Jennifer Lien who steals the show in her finest performance of the series as she interacts with both of them. With a mixture of wisdom and determination, she finally comes into her own, using scenes without Neelix to find a niche for herself and show everyone how the character can work.

With the main plot centered on her and The Doctor, it's interesting to see the show tap into the technological issue of rebooting versus reinitialization, with the first becoming the go-to fix in the computer age while the second has become the course of last resort, forcing the user to wipe a slate clean and start from scratch. Unfortunately, there's also a distracting subplot about Voyager in peril, a misplaced idea that could be quite interesting as a developed main story but instead just gets in the way of the A story and merely serves as a showcase for some CGI.

Nonetheless, as a Doctor episode, "The Swarm" is quite good, though the consequences of the ending are mentioned in future episodes only in passing and are otherwise ignored, negating their importance.

Picardo would go on to reprise his creator some months later in a Season Five episode of *DS9*, "Dr. Bashir, I Presume," as well as some years down the line in a Season Six episode of *VOY*, "Life Line."

Did you know? From this episode onward, Foundation Imaging, best known for their work on *Babylon 5*, became the *VOY's* go-to CGI supplier. Unfortunately, the company went out of business in 2002 shortly after completing work on new effects for a director's cut of *Star Trek: The Motion Picture*.

"False Profits": C

Voyager discovers that two Ferengi have gained control of a primitive world in the Delta Quadrant.

Air date: October 2, 1996
Teleplay by Joe Menosky
Story by George A. Brozak
Directed by Cliff Bole
TV rating: 4.3

"We have to out-Ferengi the Ferengi." —Janeway

This follow-up to "The Price," a *TNG* episode which conveniently deposits some comic relief into the Delta Quadrant, is a Ferengi episode with Neelix thrown into the mix as a Ferengi impersonator in a planet-based story made in Season Two but held back for Season Three. (Got all that? There will be a test later.)

As something new and exciting, "Profits" fails miserably. Falling back on tropes long established by *Star Trek* and comedy in general, there's the classic combination of a dimwitted leader and his dimmerwitted companion, the old story idea of foreigners being mistaken by primitive people as gods, and Neelix stumbling over himself trying to be something he's not and getting in over his head in the process. Yet Cliff Bole is well aware that combining the Ferengi and Neelix is never going to lead to serious drama and presents it as a Shakespearian farce instead, fully embracing its nature. As such, Bole turns the episode into a fine piece of fluff.

Guest star Dan Shor reprises his Ferengi from "The Price," continuing to make the character dumb enough to be funny but smart enough to be dangerous. He's joined by Leslie Jordan as his sidekick, with the two being more or less *Star Trek's* version of Abbot and Costello—or maybe Gilligan and the Skipper.

Unfortunately, there's no getting around a *Gilligan's Island* ending, with the writers simultaneously sweeping the guest stars under the rug while taking away Voyager's way home. The wrap-up is, of course, a necessary evil, but even so, it's poorly written, making Voyager's crew look especially inept. Fortunately, the end is so predictable, viewers have time to prepare themselves for its awfulness before it manifests. And on the whole, the episode accomplishes what it wants to, satisfied to be harmless Ferengi comedy filler.

Did you know? Ethan Phillips was very ill when this episode was shot but refused to take time off.

"Remember": B

Lieutenant Torres experiences life as another woman through vivid, ongoing dreams.

Air date: October 9, 1996
Teleplay by Lisa Klink
Story by Brannon Braga & Joe Menosky
Directed by Winrich Kolbe
TV rating: 4.7

"Those dreams I've been having, they're getting kind of strange." —Torres

Roxann Dawson shines in this B'Elanna Torres character-driven episode that allows the actress to step into another character from the past for a Holocaust denial story. (It's sort of a redo of *TNG's* "Violations.") Ironically, "Remember" is still somewhat forgettable, featuring aliens of the week that are never seen again and seeming unwilling to step fully into its idea. (The story has one foot in a *Quantum Leap*-like premise on a planet but keeps the other foot firmly on the ship.) It's as if the episode wants to be as profound as *DS9's* "Past Tense" but doesn't want to get its hands dirty in the process, playing it safe and leaving some of its darker ideas to the imagination. It's too bad because a *Star Trek* version of *Schindler's List* (1993), perhaps as a two-parter with a B story, would be quite an episode to...well, remember.

What we do get, however, is a fine character piece that manages to take what was originally conceived as a Troi story for *TNG* and turn it into a workable Torres vehicle for *VOY* with something interesting to say.

Interestingly, *VOY* would do another plot similar to this one in Season Six's "Memorial."

Did you know? Roxann Dawson was especially happy that this episode gave her a chance to work with guest star Bruce Davison, who has been nominated for an Academy Award and an Emmy and has won two Golden Globes. "I had known of him since I lived in New York City," she later said, "and I've always wanted to work with him. He's just brilliant."

"Sacred Ground": B

When Kes is injured on an alien planet, Janeway undertakes a mysterious ritual to save her.

Air date: October 30, 1996
Teleplay by Lisa Klink
Story by Geo Cameron
Directed by Robert Duncan McNeill
TV rating: 4.6

"I cite the story of King Nevad as precedent. In the same way he pleaded for his son, I ask that Kes be restored to health." —Janeway

With McNeill sitting in the director's chair for the first time, *VOY* gives Janeway a spiritual journey that challenges her scientific background in another episode produced in the second season but held back for the third.

It's the sort of idea that must be treated with care, because *Star Trek* fans are no dummies, and if the script tries to say that science is just another kind of religion, fans will see through the ridiculousness, knowing science and spirituality are as different as *MythBusters* and *The 700 Club.* Equally problematic would be to assert or display that the scientific method is a flawed process, with most fans well aware a writer can manipulate the circumstances to "prove" (or mock) anything he or she wants. Klink, however, avoids preachy lessons in favor of a script that simply says, "Science is one approach. Let's look at this from another perspective." In the *Star Trek* world, it's a bold statement and a springboard for a refreshing story.

And who better to ask to make a leap of faith than the captain? With Janeway's scientific background and Mulgrew's acting chops, it's the perfect fit, complimented with a cast of fine geriatric guest stars who chew the scenery in abstract scenes that allow them to say much that means little. Meanwhile, Becky Ann Baker plays Janeway's spiritual guide, giving a Kathy Bates-like performance that's warm and whimsical.

For McNeill, the first *VOY* actor to direct an episode, it's the perfect bundle of ingredients to mix together into something special, and he does just such.

Did you know? Robert Duncan McNeill was given the opportunity to direct this episode after Jonathan Frakes backed out to direct *Star Trek: First Contact*—which happened only after Leonard Nimoy turned down an offer to direct the movie. McNeill also appears as Tom Paris in the episode, but he has no lines.

"Future's End": A

After encountering a Federation time-ship from the future, Voyager is flung back to 1996.

Air date: November 6, 1996
Written by Brannon Braga & Joe Menosky
Directed by David Livingston
TV rating: 5.6

"I was trying to save billions of lives! To stop a chain reaction that started with Voyager. But it's too late now. All things are set in motion. The temporal explosion will occur. The end is coming! The future's end!" —Captain Braxton

Like a cross between *Star Trek IV* (1986) and *Back to the Future* (1985), "Future's End" is a fun, fast paced time travel romp that finds something for each character to do while we see our *Star Trek* heroes run amok in the past. (It even includes a Doc Brown-like explanation, with Braxton pulling out a piece of chalk to map out what's going on with the timeline.) But whereas *Star Trek IV* and *Back to the Future* put their stamp on the 1980s, "Future's End" tackles the 1990s, with a plot developed around the computer revolution.

Sparing no expense, this installment is a CGI-filled feast with plenty of Los Angeles location work. So for fans back in the 1990s, "Future's End" was quite a treat. But for fans *of* the 1990s in today's time, it's even better, with a chance to see old computers, overly large cell phones, and news footage of UFOs from a time before YouTube and the explosion of social media changed the direction of hobbies, technology and entertainment. (Remember when soap operas dominated daytime television? So does this episode.)

Like *Star Trek IV*, "Future" breaks up the plot into committee-like substories, with the planet-based A and B stories going to Janeway/Chakotay and Paris/Tuvok while a ship-based C story uses the remainder of the regulars to give everyone something to do. Each plot also develops some memorable guest performances, with Allan G. Royal playing a 29th century time traveler, Sarah Silverman playing a spunky 90s girl, and Ed Begley Jr. playing the episode's antagonist. And with the focus on fun, everyone gets a chance to step out of the usual *Star Trek* box to ham it up. (Mulgrew even debuts another new hair style.)

"Future's End" would go on to be nominated for an Emmy for sound mixing.

Did you know? Ed Begley Jr., who plays a villain willing to destroy the future of the world for his own self gain, is one of Hollywood's most notable environmental activists. "Most people probably figured if I ever did *Star Trek*, I'd play a good guy," he says. "I liked the idea of playing someone completely unlike me, who does things I could never live with were I to do them myself."

"Future's End, Part II": B+

The Voyager crew must prevent a 1990s disaster from endangering the future.

Air date: November 13, 1996
Written by Brannon Braga & Joe Menosky
Directed by Cliff Bole
TV rating: 5.8

"Captain, the future you're talking about: that's nine hundred years from now. I can't be concerned about that right now. I have a company to run." —Starling

Tying everything up in a predictable fashion, "Part II" is a charming follow-up to its prequel, retaining the same production values and sense of fun. With ample effects and plenty of location shooting, including a car chase and an exploding semi that would seem more at home in *Knight Rider* than *Star Trek*, the second part shuffles the deck to create new character combinations, putting Janeway back on the ship and giving the Earthbound adventures to Paris/Rain, Tuvok/Doctor, and Chakotay/Torres. (The latter story, which introduces Earth radicals, pops up out of nowhere and is obviously just there to fill time. But with so few *VOY* episodes that include Earth at all, it's great nonetheless to see more of the show's characters on our planet.)

As with the first part, however, it's Ed Begley Jr.'s Henry Starling character that drives the story, and the episode is richer for it. Unlike too many antagonists who spend their time and energy on plots and actions that make no sense from their own standpoint (created by a writer merely to provide an obstacle for the protagonists), it's easy to see where Starling's coming from. He's a 20th century man who has discovered a piece of 29th century technology, and time travelers from the 24th century show up to take it from him, explaining that he'll cause irreparable damage if he uses it. Occam's razor casts suspicion on this claim. It seems more likely that the people of Voyager want the technology for themselves. (And indeed, they do end up keeping what they can, giving The Doctor a landmark acquisition that factors into almost every future episode.) Besides, if Voyager really wants to save the world, shouldn't the crew be searching for whales?

All kidding aside, "Future's End" and "Future's End, Part II" are landmark episodes that scored high ratings and remain perennial favorites among fans.

The Federation time-ship and Captain Braxton reappear in Season Five's "Relativity."

Did you know? There was talk amongst the producers of turning "Future's End" into a three or four-parter, but the studio thought it was too risky.

"Warlord": C

Kes is taken over by the mind-force of an obsessive rebel.

Air date: November 20, 1996
Written by Lisa Klink
Directed by David Livingston
TV rating: 4.7

"I've been exploring the mind of this little girl, and I've discovered some rather interesting abilities." —the obsessive rebel

As another *Star Trek* mind-possession story, this one allows Jennifer Lien to step out of Kes's usual sedateness and into a bad-boy role reminiscent of the possessed characters in *TNG's* "Power Play."

"Warlord," which spends its A story following the antagonists for a change, cuts a fast pace and keeps its vanilla plot interesting by fleshing out the villains and their culture (which would mean more if we ever saw them again). It also introduces a holographic Caribbean resort that continues to appear throughout the season. Unfortunately, despite playing against type, Jennifer Lien never develops her character into anything interesting, with her tantrums coming across more like those of a spoiled child than a psychotic alien dictator. And writer Lisa Klink does her no favors, failing to layer the scenes with any subtext for the actress to play up to create the illusion that her character is more than just talk.

All the same, as a *VOY* episode, it has enough interesting bits to remain entertaining throughout, and as a Kes episode, it succeeds better than most by being unafraid to shake up the status quo.

Did you know? This episode debuted two days before *Star Trek: First Contact* was released in theaters.

"The Q and the Grey": C

Q attempts to mate with Captain Janeway to end a civil war within the Q Continuum.

Air date: November 27, 1996
Teleplay by Kenneth Biller
Story by Shawn Piller
Directed by Cliff Bole
TV rating: 4.7

"What the Continuum needs right now is an infusion of fresh blood, a new sensibility, a new leader, a new messiah. Think of it, Kathy. Our child will be like a precious stone tossed into the cosmic lake, sending endless ripples of human conscience and compassion to wash up on every distant shore of the universe." —Q

This sequel to "Death Wish" set within a Q civil war, is another John de Lancie vehicle inspired by Shawn Piller that features Q and Janeway.

Again needing a metaphor for the Q Continuum, the writers here choose the American Civil War, putting Q and Janeway on its playing field and using a siege as a way to develop rich character interplay. It's a unique setting in which de Lancie and Mulgrew can do their thing, and their scenes amidst the gunfire are the highlight of the episode. Unfortunately, the A story ties into a technobabble-laden B story with a female Q trapped on Voyager who needs the crew's help to return home. Needing a combination of sarcasm and superiority for the guest part, *Star Trek* brings back Suzie Plakson (last seen as Worf's mate on *TNG*), filling the need but adding little originality. (She's basically *TNG's* K'Ehleyr refashioned into a Q and even gets off an inside joke about liking Klingon women.) Using a female Q (called Suzie Q by the fans) to form a love triangle is a fine idea, but here it's just a throwaway notion to give Janeway's crew something to do before the predictable resolution.

But make no mistake, "The Q and the Grey" does have its moments. In a way, it's an upgraded version of *TNG's* "Hide and Q," also directed by Bole, with a more interesting plot and far superior production values. including location shooting at Los Angeles's Griffith Park. In another way, however, it's plodding and unfocused, with the ship-based B story getting in the way of the important matters and adding nothing.

John de Lancie reprises his Q character again for a follow-up to this episode in Season Seven's "Q2." Plakson doesn't appear on *VOY* again, but she does play an Andorian in *ENT's* Season Two episode "Cease Fire."

Did you know? "The Blue and the Gray" is a Civil War poem by Francis Miles Finch (1827–1907) first published in 1867. In 1982, it became the title of a hit CBS miniseries.

"Macrocosm": A–

When viruses grow large enough to fly around and attack the crew, Janeway must find a way to eliminate them once and for all.

Air date: December 11, 1996
Written by Brannon Braga
Directed by Alexander Singer
TV rating: 4.9

"As for the larger versions of the virus, what I have termed the macrovirus, I would suggest a flyswatter." —The Doctor

A medical drama crossed with a monster story, this "Janeway as an action hero" episode is sort of an upgraded version of *TOS's* "Operation--Annihilate!" but with the danger on the ship instead of a planet.

There's something brilliant—and unbelievably creepy—about Braga's idea of a virus that grows inside us into bugs, only to eventually fly out and continue growing into flying monsters. To bring the creatures to life, the show relies on CGI, with the visual effects people pulling it off in a way that was satisfactory for 1990s television, even if it doesn't hold up today. Meanwhile, the sound department deserves an Emmy for their assist, supplying many frightening noises constantly coming from out of frame, creating the illusion of many more creatures than actually shown and heightening the suspense with the unseen danger inherently scarier than the seen.

Braga builds the tension by cleverly crafting the story out of chronological order, with the first half featuring Janeway (basically stepping into Sigourney Weaver's *Alien* role) before the second backtracks to tell the story from The Doctor's point of view to fill in the blanks. It's an effective structure that intensifies the mystery and keeps the story moving throughout.

Did you notice? Poor old Neelix is dragged away early in the story and never seen again...until the next episode.

Did you know? The plot of this episode is reminiscent of a 1987 episode of NBC's *Alf* entitled "La Cuckaracha" in which an alien cockroach grows in size each time someone sprays it with bug killer. Eventually, the creature grows to be about six feet and corners the title character, but when it's doused with perfume, it unexpectedly keels over and dies.

80

"Fair Trade": B

Neelix, worried his usefulness on Voyager might be coming to an end, turns to an old friend of questionable character for help.

Air date: January 8, 1997
Teleplay by Andre Bormanis
Story by Ronald Wilkerson & Jean Louise Matthias
Directed by Jesus Salvador Trevino
TV rating: 4.2

"I just took one step; a step that seemed perfectly reasonable. And that step led to another and another, and before I knew it, I was involved in something I didn't know how to handle." —Neelix

Of all the teleplays to come from *VOY's* science advisor, who would expect a "Leave it to Neelix" story where the Talaxian, like the Beaver, digs himself into a deeper and deeper hole?

It's actually good stuff, and it's especially nifty that it taps into the idea of Voyager finally leaving the area of space Neelix is familiar with, a necessary issue for the show to acknowledge at some point, with the sooner being the better. (Surprisingly, the writers develop this and the consequences of what it means without involving Kes, who is inexplicably absent, though the story works fine nonetheless.)

Neelix, like the Beave, starts down the path of trouble innocently enough, being more or less manipulated by an old friend, the episode's version of Eddie Haskell. It's the sort of story that's worked since sitcoms were invented and still works today because we can all identify it. James Nardini, a veteran of *Cheers* and *Married with Children*, steps into the guest part quite nicely, developing his character as someone similar enough to Neelix to feel like another of the same race but different enough to allow us to contrast the two. Unfortunately, Carlos Carrasco, better suited as "the third Klingon from the right" on *DS9*, bites off more than he can chew as Bahrat, a station manager, giving a confusing performance that leaves more questions than answers.

As the episode moves along, it's easy to sympathize with Neelix and wonder how he's eventually going to get himself off the hook. Then when the time is right, Bormanis invokes *TNG's* "First Duty" and sends the story home with a killer scene. It's an impressive debut for a writer who would go on to contribute to six more *VOY* episodes before becoming the story editor and co-producer of *ENT*.

"Fair Trade" would go on to win an Emmy for hairstyling.

Did you know? This episode marks the first appearance of Ensign Vorik, a Vulcan played by producer Jeri Taylor's son, Alexander Enberg. He would go on to appear in seven more episodes.

"Alter Ego": C–

Tuvok becomes fascinated by a holodeck character.

Air date: January 15, 1997
Written by Joe Menosky
Directed by Robert Picardo
TV rating: 4.8

"Beauty and mystery: a tantalizing combination." —Janeway

Robert Picardo, directing his first *Star Trek* episode, does what he can with this Tuvok story, an adequate character piece that gives Tuvok a mystery to solve while guest star Sandra Nelson chews the scenery as a holographic character who's more than she seems.

Unfortunately, the whole thing is just a composite of worn-out ideas *VOY* and *TNG* have tackled before, offering little new beyond developing some character interplay between Tuvok and Kim. Even the B story, about a mysterious nebula, never develops into anything unique or memorable before folding into the A story so both can crawl to an end.

All the same, writer Joe Menosky knows the characters well enough to allow the episode to run on autopilot and remain reasonably entertaining, even if the plot as a whole never quite finds a through-line, seeming uncertain of what the focus is and what the point of it all should be.

Did you know? Garrett Wang performed in this episode while suffering from the flu.

"Coda": C

After Janeway's apparent death, her journey to the afterlife leaves her with suspicions.

Air date: January 29, 1997
Written by Jeri Taylor
Directed by Nancy Malone
TV rating: 4.6

"I'm not ready to accept it. I'm not ready to go." —Janeway

With a beginning reminiscent of *TNG's* "Cause and Effect," this ship-based episode takes the concept and the mystery behind it a step further by playing around with various scenarios before ultimately forcing Janeway to deal with her own death much like La Forge and Ro in another *TNG* episode: "The Next Phase."

The idea of seeing those we love move on without us is some interesting turf, and with Kate Mulgrew getting a chance to work with guest star Len Cariou, who serves as an ambassador to the afterlife, we get to see a journey to the beyond and back with all the emotions such a journey entails, with Mulgrew playing it well and nearly making it all worthwhile.

Unfortunately, the whole "seeing people move on without us" idea is only discussed and not developed, and the goofy Cariou is a disappointment. Worse yet, rather than a unique climax explaining all, we instead get such a *Star Trek* cliché ending, it's a palm slap to the head hardly worth the wait. (Heck, it's practically the same climax as the previous episode!)

Still, the permutations of the mystery are interesting enough to pique some interest, and the main cast members give Taylor's script everything they have, layering the funeral scene with just the right emotions.

Did you know? Some details about Janeway that are revealed in this episode are drawn from *Mosaic*, Jeri Taylor's 1996 *Star Trek* novel about Janeway's life before she became captain of Voyager.

"Blood Fever": C+

B'Elanna Torres experiences symptoms similar to the pon farr, the Vulcan state of arousal.

Air date: February 5, 1997
Written by Lisa Klink
Directed by Andrew Robinson
TV rating: 4.6

"Your emotional balance has been disrupted. You may not be in control of your more aggressive instincts." —Tuvok

Just as *TOS's* "Amok Time" plays against expectations by presenting Spock in a sexualized context, "Blood Fever" takes what everybody assumes will be a Tuvok story and gives it to Lieutenant Torres instead.

The fact is that since the beginning of the series, fans and *VOY's* writing team alike have known such a story is a natural for the show. (As established in "Amok Time," once every seven years, sex becomes a biological necessity for Vulcans. Voyager is going to take decades to return home. The math is clear!) But with Tuvok firmly established as a devoted father with a wife back home, the writers opt to go with Torres instead…which makes little sense on the surface but can happen in a show like *Star Trek* where a little technobabble can get you anywhere. In the end, it serves as the beginning of the Torres/Paris relationship while Alexander Enberg's Vulcan character, Vorik, appears in a B story that seems to be included just to offer a solution to the *pon farr* issue once and for all (until it doesn't).

As an episode, it's all over the map, with spelunking, romance, aliens, and settings that include the ship, a planet set, and the cave set. But director Andrew Robinson ("Garak" on *DS9*) holds it together with *Star Trek's* version of sex and violence, often employing a handheld camera to emphasize their nature.

Is it a classic like "Amok Time"? No. But for *VOY*, it's an entertaining enough entry, and the episode even throws in a harbinger at the end that hits like a bucket of cold water while laying the foundation for the future of the series.

Did you know? This episode was originally supposed to feature Tuvok helping Torres manage her *pon farr*. The day before shooting began, the writers decided it was better to use Tom Paris in Tuvok's place. "So we were kind of reworking each scene as we were shooting," Robert Duncan McNeill recalls, "because the original script was a different story, and the writers had to deal with more sexual tension between Tom and B'Elanna."

84

"Unity": B+

Chakotay is injured and trapped on a world where the inhabitants are former members of the Borg.

Air date: February 12, 1997
Written by Kenneth Biller
Directed by Robert Duncan McNeill
TV rating: 5.4

"You want to hook up my mind to some Borg collective?" —Chakotay

Giving the Borg a personal touch and new direction, writer Ken Biller gives the Federation's most infamous enemy a fresh take that reinvigorates them on the small screen in the wake of *First Contact* (1996). (The Borg know how to stay relevant, don't they? Just when you think you have a handle on their ways, the species adapts to a new story.)

For this episode, Chakotay is the featured character, with the first officer discovering a lost colony on a planet and the story peeling back its layers over the course of the hour while Beltran works with guest stars Lori Hallier and Ivar Brogger, with the latter two playing the primary locals. Hallier and Brogger are both very good, and as the plot develops, it eventually winds its way into a dilemma and a twist as director Robbie McNeill, cutting a quick pace, balances the character interplay with action and suspense to build to an exciting climax. The collective effort makes for good television, giving *VOY's* Season Three a much-needed boost during sweeps week.

That said, don't expect anything epic in story, scope, or spirit. This one was never meant to be a gamechanger, nor is it related to the future *VOY* Borg episodes that would use recurring Borg characters to flesh out a loose narrative that takes the show to the finish line. But as a standalone episode, "Unity" is worthy of the hype the Borg always bring to the table.

Did you know? To prepare for this episode, McNeill studied the aftereffects of the breakup of the Soviet Union, considering it a parallel for what ex-Borg must go through.

"Darkling": C–

When The Doctor alters his subroutines, a hidden personality emerges.

Air date: February 19, 1997
Teleplay by Joe Menosky
Story by Brannon Braga & Joe Menosky
Directed by Alex Singer
TV rating: 4.3

"Doctor, wait. There's a problem with your program" —Torres

Taking advantage of The Doctor's unique nature, this Robert Picardo vehicle allows the actor to play Jekyll & Hyde. As a monster episode, it's sufficiently creepy, succeeding in its nature in some ways better than *TNG's* seventh season episode, "Phantasms," which attempts a similar idea with Data, albeit more creatively. As a story, however, it has little substance or importance.

Most of the episode, in fact, consists of Picardo chewing the scenery, though Jennifer Lien continues to give it a go as "wise old owl" Kes in a supporting role, with her character attempting to help The Doctor with his psychological problems. But as a talky episode with few consequences, "Darkling" is never going to be a favorite among the fans, though it does include enough fine work by the actors to be fondly remembered by the cast.

Did you know? Robert Picardo had previously played a creepy character in *The Howling* (1981). The part required him to wear a dental appliance designed to give him scarier teeth, which he subsequently saved in a drawer and pulled out to use for this episode.

"Rise": D+

Neelix and Tuvok must use a space elevator to escape a planet.

Air date: February 26, 1997
Teleplay by Brannon Braga
Story by Jimmy Diggs
Directed by Robert Sheerer
TV rating: 4.6

"I've helped rebuild a dozen mag-lev carriages. Give me a chance to get that one working." —Neelix

When people think of science fiction in *Star Trek*, they usually think of space-based ideas. And from wormholes to Dyson spheres, the franchise has explored the fictional frontiers of our known universe as well as any sci-fi franchise. But there's quite a lot of interesting sci-fi ideas right here on Earth, and more often than people realize, *Star Trek* enjoys mining this turf as well. (In fact, some of the franchise's Earth-based ideas have already found their way into reality, from advances in mobile technology to 3D printers.)

This episode, of course, does not take place on Earth, but it does provide a substitute as it tackles the idea of an orbital tether allowing a carriage to journey up into space. It's a dramatic yet pragmatic concept that will probably become reality at some point. The idea of a space elevator taking people to ships without the need for those ships to suffer the punishing effects of entering and exiting an atmosphere would be much more efficient in the long run than our current space programs that spend a fortune on hardware replacement.

In this episode, a mag-lev carriage is used as a device for a character-based Neelix episode with Tuvok in a supporting role while Janeway and the remainder of the crew engage in a B story about the asteroids striking the planet. At its heart, it's really just a glamorous "elevator episode," trapping Neelix, Tuvok, and a few other aliens in the elevator and letting their interactions dictate the story. But Ethan Phillips shines, and as a Neelix/Tuvok bonding experience, it's quite nice.

Unfortunately, the cliché script itself, borrowing ideas from *The Flight of the Phoenix* (1965), simply goes through the motions of a protagonist redemption story and contains little originality or surprise. It's like a disaster movie written by a Hollywood writer who knows how to come up with the story and plot out the beats, but doesn't know how to develop the plot into something unique enough to become a summer blockbuster. (Director Robert Sheerer doesn't do the script any favors either) What really needs to happen here is for the characters to overcome one problem at a time *Apollo 13* style and for the tension to increase along with the altitude. Neither happens, and in the end the device is wasted, with writer Brannon Braga himself disappointed with the result.

Did you know? When the pyramids of Giza were completed around 2560 B.C., the tallest stood 146 meters tall, and amazingly, it remained the tallest manmade structure in the world for 3,800 years! In the past couple hundred years, however, manmade structures have struggled to hold onto the "tallest" title for more than a couple decades. If a space elevator is ever built, however, that could change. Many engineers believe that a tether with one end attached to the surface of the Earth and the other end in space beyond geostationary orbit (22,236 miles) is a sound design that could be constructed in the next century or two.

My wife sitting at the top of the Willis Tower, the
tallest building in the world from 1973 to 1998.

"Favorite Son": D

When the crew of Voyager discovers a mysterious planet, the inhabitants claim Ensign Kim is really one of them.

Air date: March 19, 1997
Written by Lisa Klink
Directed by Marvin V. Rush
TV rating: 4.4

"Everyone here was born on other worlds. We all found our way back home like you and discovered we're not quite who we thought we were." —Taymon

In this Harry Kim planet-based episode, *VOY* does a combination of *DS9's* "Second Skin" and *TAS's* "The Lorelei Signal," albeit less subtle than either. Like "Second Skin," in which Kira awakens as a Cardassian and is told she's always been one, everything in the first half of "Favorite Son" indicates that Kim has always been a Taresian. (Most notably, a Taresian welcoming committee greets him and says, "You're Taresian!") Considering Taresia is about 60 million miles from where Harry was born, it's a lot to accept. For the record, the aliens' explanation is that a Taresian embryo was delivered to Earth where Kim's mother was secretly impregnated, and Kim has always had an instinct to return to his native land, hence his reason for joining the Voyager crew. (If this causes your B.S. meter to flash "red alert, red alert," you're not alone.) But the true point of a story of this sort is the mystery, with viewers wondering where the writers are going with it all, and what evil plan is afoot. Unfortunately, here it simply develops into a pedestrian great escape plot devoid of daring questions and creative ideas.

Despite its flaws, however, "Favorite Son" has a few good moments, even if the story itself is as predictable as a sunny day on Vulcan. Garrett Wang brings his A game, and a *Wicker Man*-ish horror aspect has a nice build. All the same, if this is your favorite *Star Trek* episode, you probably haven't seen many. The premise doesn't fit the concept of the show (no matter how hard the writers try to shoehorn it in), and *VOY* should have saved the concept for a future *Star Trek* series.

Did you know? This episode's shooting schedule was split in half by a Christmas break.

"Before and After": A

On her deathbed, Kes begins living her life backwards.

Air date: April 9, 1997
Written by Kenneth Biller
Directed by Allan Kroeker
TV rating: 4.5

"It's as though I came into existence at the moment of my own death without any memories. I've been living my life backwards ever since, jumping progressively to earlier moments in my life." —Kes

This high concept Kes story is like a lost episode of the 1980s *Twilight Zone* series. Beginning six years after "Favorite Son," Kes wakes up on her deathbed with no memories before beginning to process what's going on while she continually moves backwards in time to her birth. It's like a literary short story and the perfect episode for someone who doesn't regularly watch *VOY* because it's completely self-contained, requiring no knowledge of the series or even *Star Trek* at large to understand it.

Jennifer Lien, beginning the episode as an elderly grandmother before getting younger throughout the hour, delivers several different stages of her character that are each more interesting than the Kes we regularly know. (Seriously, if writers were to decide to have her stay a grandma for the rest of the series, it would probably be an improvement.) She even gets a new hairstyle designed to hide her ears and save the actress time in the make-up chair (which she keeps for the remainder of the season).

Unfortunately, with Kes's normal aging cycle allowing the episode to explore a lifetime of events inside just a few years, there's no need for the show to attempt any significant make-up or costume changes for anyone besides the main character...which saves money but robs the episode of the scope and originality presented in *TNG's* "All Good Things" and *DS9's* "The Visitor." And the story itself begins to lose a little momentum about halfway through as the pieces of the puzzle begin to come together and the whole thing becomes more of a standard *VOY* plot. But writer Ken Biller deserves credit for thinking outside the box and finding an area of turf, inspired by Martin Amis's 1991 novel, *Time's Arrow*, that finally gives Kes an important story, and Jennifer Lien deserves praise for expertly executing the game plan.

Season Four's "Year of Hell" would borrow several elements of this episode and expand on them in a loose sequel of sorts.

Did you know? *The X Files* does a story about someone living backwards in "Redrum," a Season Eight episode that first aired December 10, 2000.

"Real Life": B

The Doctor creates a holographic family.

Air date: April 23, 1997
Teleplay by Jeri Taylor
Story by Harry Doc Kloor
Directed by Anson Williams
TV rating: 4.4

"There is nothing wrong with your premise, Doctor. It just needs a little tweaking to bring it closer to real life." —Torres

This week on *VOY*: The Doctor gets his own Lifetime special.

Recognizing that the Emergency Medical Hologram's unique nature opens up the possibility of creating a holographic family that's real to him, even if it's fictitious to everyone else, writers Doc Kloor and Jeri Taylor assemble a poignant slice of life that begins as a cutting satire of early television before digging deeper and turning the family dynamic on its ear. For Picardo, it offers a small-scale version of the same challenge "The Inner Light" gives to Patrick Stewart, and the *VOY* star doesn't let us down. (Be sure to have a hanky ready!)

The remainder of the crew deal with space tornadoes in a B story, a short but inoffensive bit of sci-fi designed to give the episode a sense of danger. (It's basically *Star Trek's* version of *Twister*, the 1996 disaster film, with Paris stepping into the role of the tornado chaser.) Happily, however, The Doctor gets the majority of the episode's time, which allows the director to develop the dramatic scenes organically from the comedy. (I especially like seeing the Klingons used as "neighbors with another culture.") Sadly, after this episode, we never see The Doctor's family again, though the writers get just about everything they can out of them here.

Did you know? Wendy Schaal, who plays The Doctor's holographic wife, is a longtime friend of Picardo's and previously played his wife in *Munchies* (1987) and *Runaway Daughters* (1994).

Did you also know? In 1994, writer Harry Kloor became the first American to earn two PhDs at the same university simultaneously, earning his degrees in physics and chemistry at Purdue.

"Distant Origin": B

An alien scientist finds evidence linking his species' ancestry to Earth, but government officials refuse to accept his evidence because it conflicts with existing doctrine.

Air date: April 30, 1997
Written by Brannon Braga & Joe Menosky
Directed by David Livingston
TV rating: 4.4

"You'd do anything to silence me. Well, it won't work. I'll never retract my claims. I'd rather go to prison than help you perpetuate ignorance." —Gegen

Star Trek does *The Planet of the Apes* thing with anthropomorphic dinosaurs in this allegory about Galileo Galilei versus the Church.

On the surface, this plays out as more ridiculous than *VOY* perhaps intended, with actors wearing over the top make-up appliances pushing a silly, pseudo-sci-fi plot that says dinosaurs left the Earth to colonize a planet in the Delta Quadrant. But really, the whole idea is just a backdrop for an internal battle of wills among the Saurians, and on this level it works. If it has a real fault, it's that the plot tends to lose focus at times. (It's a dinosaur story! Wait no, it's a Galileo story. Actually, no, it's a "humans viewed by outsiders" story! With dinosaurs.) And the bottom line is that the whole dinosaur aspect is superfluous, seemingly only there to capitalize on the resurgent interest in the creatures in the 1990s popular culture. (*The Lost World: Jurassic Park* came out in theaters just a few weeks after "Distant Origin" first aired.) Personally, I would have gone with Mayan Civilization in their place. As intelligent creatures that developed advanced technology only to abandon their homes for unknown reasons, their real history would play into the sci-fi plot beautifully.

All the same, the Galileo story is one of history's more interesting tales, with issues of science, religion, power, and stubbornness all bound together, and it's nice to see *Star Trek* give a parallel story a try. (Heck, we've got the same thing going on today with people who study climate change or infectious diseases facing a political backlash.) Henry Woronicz is fabulous as the episode's protagonist, Concetta Tomei perfectly represents "Doctrine," and Robert Beltran nearly makes the ridiculous plot work with a three-minute soliloquy about its wonder and importance. Throw in some exquisite make-up for the aliens and David Livingston's atmospheric direction and you have one of *VOY's* most popular episodes.

Did you know? Henry Woronicz, who plays the lead character in this episode, previously guest starred as a Klingon suspected of sabotage in *TNG's* "The Drumhead," and would later be prominently featured in *VOY's* Season Four episode, "Living Witness," playing the curator of a museum.

"Displaced": C–

Voyager crewmembers begin disappearing one by one, replaced by aliens.

Air date: May 7, 1997
Written by Lisa Klink
Directed by Allan Kroeker
TV rating: 4.7

"Chakotay, I don't care how they seem. All I care about is that I've had a knot in my stomach since the first Nyrian arrived. Something about this is wrong, I can smell it. Look at us, running around the ship, checking sensors and spinning theories, while the Nyrians slowly replace our crew." —Janeway

This one begins with a ship-based mystery before meandering into a planet-based escape story that uses most of the regulars and a large group of extras. Essentially, however, Janeway, Paris, and Torres get the bulk of the action, with the captain trying to solve the episode's issue while Paris and Torres continue their relationship in a character-based B story.

As an episode, "Displaced" is not very good, though there's nothing particularly awful about it. The escape attempt is a paint-by-numbers plot that dates back to the days of *TOS* (with shades of "All Our Yesterdays") and Torres and Paris don't give us anything that's must-see TV even for fans of the duo. On the other hand, the episode moves along quickly and allows most of the characters to have a moment to shine. You can argue that it's par for the course, though it's also dull as a Ferengi pashmir and writer Lisa Klink is capable of much better.

Did you know? All the featured guest stars in this episode make an appearance in one of *VOY's* sister shows. Kenneth Tigar (Dammar) plays an alien leader in *TNG's* "Symbiosis," Mark Tyler (Jarlath) plays a colonist in *TNG's* "The Ensigns of Command," James Noah (Dr. Rislan) plays a Trill scientist in *DS9's* "Rejoined," and Nancy Youngblut (Taleen) plays a Klingon in *DS9's* "Once More Unto the Breach."

"Worst Case Scenario": B

A holodeck program depicting a Maquis mutiny is discovered by the crew.

Air date: May 14, 1997
Written by Kenneth Biller
Directed by Alexander Singer
TV rating: 4.0

"I found this holonovel. It's a kind of 'what if' story, all about a Maquis mutiny. It's completely compelling and believable. I guess it's because it's all about us."
—Lieutenant Torres

Dipping back into the show's Starfleet versus Maquis roots, *VOY* sinks its teeth into a comedic "holodeck gone awry" episode that actually works. With the writers and the cast able to step outside their usual boundaries, the characters are more flamboyant and everyone has a good time as a result.

The story itself evolves quite a bit as it progresses. Writer Ken Biller knows he can't milk the basic premise for the duration of the episode and wisely keeps the mystery aspect a moving target. First, the question is what's going on. Then it's a question of who the holonovel's writer is. Finally, it's a matter of solving the scenario. The story itself is told in a circular way, but Biller adds wrinkles to each pass, saving the biggest twist for last. The whole idea is a nice foundation for an ensemble piece, and the ending, the old sitcom trope where somebody tells a joke relating to the episode's events and everybody chuckles as we segue into the credits, actually works because it fits in with the established mood.

Unfortunately, parts of the episode do get a little talky, and the malfunctioning holodeck storytelling device that the last half of this episode exploits has been beaten into the ground. Nonetheless, "Worst Case," which even includes some writing conversations that satirize *VOY's* own writing staff, is a lot of fun and a good choice for the penultimate slot for the season, giving the show a lighthearted change of pace before we get to the serious drama of the season ending cliffhanger.

Did you notice? This episode is reminiscent of *DS9's* Season Three offering, "Civil Defense."

94

"The Scorpion": A–

When threatened by a common enemy, Janeway considers forming an alliance with the Borg. (Season finale)

Air date: May 21, 1997
Written by Brannon Braga & Joe Menosky
Directed by David Livingston
TV rating: 5.6

"A scorpion was walking along the bank of a river wondering how to get to the other side. Suddenly he saw a fox. He asked the fox to take him on his back across the river. The fox said, 'No, if I do that you'll sting me, and I'll drown.' The scorpion assured him, 'If I did that, we'd both drown.' So the fox thought about it and finally agreed. So the scorpion climbed up on his back and the fox began to swim. But halfway across the river, the scorpion stung him. As the poison filled his veins, the fox turned to the scorpion and said, 'Why did you do that? Now you'll drown too.' 'I couldn't help it,' said the Scorpion. 'It's my nature.'" —Chakotay

What could be worse than entering Borg space? Meeting an enemy that leaves a graveyard of Borg ships in its wake. It's a bold idea that simultaneously redefines the Borg, poses a new enemy threat, and opens up many new story possibilities.

Like "The Best of Both Worlds," "Scorpion" balances quiet character-based scenes (which introduce John-Rhys Davies as a holographic Leonardo Da Vinci) with action sequences the like of which *Star Trek* has never seen before. But unlike "Both Worlds," this one isn't about a one-on-one fight that redefines the quadrant. It's about making a deal with the devil. As such, "Scorpion" is to Janeway what *DS9's* "In the Pale Moonlight" is to Sisko: a story that forces the captain to sort through priorities and determine what's worth sacrificing in order to accomplish a goal. Perhaps more groundbreaking, however, the plot asks the same of the Borg, with the species suddenly faced with the necessity of cooperating with Voyager to stay alive, turning "resistance is futile" into an inward statement. The Borg answer remains a mystery for a time, but Janeway and Chakotay have one of their most intense conversations of the series to flesh out what's at stake and pinpoint Voyager's part in the tapestry.

Unfortunately, the episode is unable to sustain the tension and urgency that permeates some of the previous Borg encounters owing to "the good guys" having more of an upper-hand than we're used to. And the new aliens, Species 8472, are only vaguely defined and turn into nothing more than a story device for a season ending cliffhanger. But make no mistake: "Scorpion" is a home run for the show, a Delta Quadrant story that's finely crafted and takes advantage of the location and premise of the series while using the entire ensemble in lieu of guest stars. It's definitely a *VOY* must see.

Did you know? The teaser for this episode is one of the shortest in *Star Trek* history, clocking in at about twenty seconds. (*ENT's* "Impulse" is a hair shorter.) Interestingly, the average teaser time for *Star Trek* episodes tended to grow until the mid-1990s, when it began to decrease due to the television executives' fear of attention deficit disorder and the remote control. Here is a breakdown of the average teaser times for the first five live-action *Star Trek* shows:

TOS: 2 minutes, 57 seconds
TNG: 3 minutes, 21 seconds
DS9: 4 minutes, 3 seconds
VOY: 2 minutes, 44 seconds
ENT: 1 minute, 42 seconds

Season Three Roundup

VOY's Season Three might not seem much different than Season Two on the surface, but hidden below is an altered course, the result of both an intentional choice by producer Jeri Taylor, who issued a memo to the writers asking for a conceptual shift, and the departure of producer Michael Piller, who left to pursue other projects (including *Star Trek: Insurrection*). As a result, the Kazon are finally left behind, the quest to return home is deemphasized, and the focus on the regulars in their normal capacities takes a back seat to stories that emphasize the guest stars and showcase the regulars in altered states of mind.

Looking more closely, some of this can be attributed to Lisa Klink, a young talent who attended a writer's workshop with Ron Moore before becoming a *Star Trek* intern. After contributing a teleplay to *DS9*, "Hippocratic Oath," and two teleplays to *VOY*, "Resistance" and "Innocence," she became *VOY's* new story editor (after Kenneth Biller was promoted to co-producer), penning Season Three's "Remember," "Sacred Ground," "Warlord," "Blood Fever," "Favorite Son," and "Displaced." But the staff saw another significant change as well, with *TNG* vet Joe Menosky joining the show as a producer and teaming up with Brannon Braga to help write some of the season's best episodes as well, such as "Future's End" and "Scorpion, Part I."

The resulting alchemy gives us arguably *VOY's* strongest season, with memorable stories that give us a little bit of everything, from the introduction of The Doctor's mobile emitter to the reappearance of the Borg. Behind the scenes, we even have some castmembers who direct, with Robert Duncan McNeill overseeing "Sacred Ground" and Robert Picardo helming "Alter Ego."

Like Season Two, the third campaign benefits from the inheritance of four episodes from the season before. Unlike the year prior, this time it was planned all along, allowing the show to prepare "Basics, Part II" and "Flashback" well ahead of time for their specific purposes of opening the season and paying homage to thirty years of *Star Trek* respectively. With that out of the way, Season Three proper delivers a wallop, with "Future's End" taking us back home, "Real Life" pushing the boundaries of holographic emotions, "Macrocosm" and "Worst Case Scenario" allowing for some campy fun, and "Distant Origin" making up for an absurd premise with a powerful allegory. We even get guest appearances from John de Lancie and Jonathan Frakes in "The Q and the Grey," even if Frakes's inclusion amounts to a superfluous ratings ploy. "Fair Trade," meanwhile, would go on to win an Emmy for hairstyling.

In a way, it feels like *Star Trek* getting back to its roots, with the episodic stories about time travel, monsters, and allegorical fables reminiscent of *TOS* (which attempted its own guest star ratings stunt by enlisting super attorney Melvin Belli to play Gorgan, the evil spirit). But there's something very *VOY* about it all as well, with episodes like "Fair Trade" and "Before and After" emphasizing the show's exclusive early strengths before "Scorpion" comes along to change everything yet again to lay a foundation for the second half of the show's life.

97

Season Four

Production Order
(with air date order in parentheses)

1. "Scorpion, Part II" (1st)
2. "The Gift" (2nd)
3. "Nemesis" (4th)
4. "Day of Honor" (3rd)
5. "Revulsion" (5th)
6. "The Raven" (6th)
7. "Scientific Method" (7th)
8. "Year of Hell" (8th)
9. "Year of Hell, Part II" (9th)
10. "Random Thoughts" (10th)
11. "Concerning Flight" (11th)
12. "Mortal Coil" (12th)
13. "Message in a Bottle" (14th)
14. "Waking Moments" (13th)
15. "Hunters" (15th)
16. "Prey" (16th)
17. "Retrospect" (17th)
18. "The Killing Game" (18th)
19. "The Killing Game, Part II" (19th)
20. "Vis à Vis" (20th)
21. "The Omega Directive" (21st)
22. "Unforgettable" (22nd)
23. "Living Witness" (23rd)
24. "Demon" (24th)
25. "One" (25th)
26. "Hope and Fear" (26th)

The Fourth Season Cast

Captain Janeway: Kate Mulgrew
Commander Chakotay: Robert Beltran
B'Elanna Torres: Roxann Dawson
Tom Paris: Robert Duncan McNeill
Neelix: Ethan Phillips
The Doctor: Robert Picardo
Tuvok: Tim Russ
Harry Kim: Garrett Wang
Seven of Nine: Jeri Ryan
Kes: Jennifer Lien

Notable Guest Stars

Alexander Enberg
Leland Orser
David Anthony Marshall
Nikki Tylor
Mickey Cottrell
Rosemary Forsyth
Kurtwood Smith
John Loprieno
Gwynyth Walsh
Wayne Péré
John Rhys-Davies
Nancy Hower
Brooke Stephens
Andy Dick
Tiny Ron
Tony Todd
Clint Carmichael
Mark Deakins
Virginia Madsen
Henry Woronicz
Ray Wise
Jack Shearer

"The Scorpion, Part II": B+

Voyager and the Borg fight Species 8472.

Air date: September 3, 1997
Written by Brannon Braga & Joe Menosky
Directed by Winrich Kolbe
TV rating: 6.5

"Species 8472 has penetrated matrix 010, grid 19. Eight planets destroyed. 312 vessels disabled. 4,000,621 Borg eliminated. We must seize control of the Alpha Quadrant vessel and take it into the alien realm." —the Borg

VOY introduces a new regular, Seven of Nine of the Borg, in a tense thriller balancing the alliance with the Borg with the threat of Species 8472. Using Seven as a spokesperson for the Borg in much the same way Picard is used in "The Best of Both Worlds, Part II," this episode explores the issues stemming from Voyager and the Borg working together with different agendas. It's new territory for everyone, and Janeway and Chakotay (alternately in command) are in complete disagreement over how to handle it, creating an internal conflict as interesting as the external one and serving as a clear illustration of the differences between the individualistic human command structure and the hive mind of the Borg.

Jeri Ryan is fantastic, playing a cold and dispassionate creature in full Borg make-up with such confidence and ease, she instantly throws Seven of Nine into the category of "most interesting *Star Trek* characters" founded by Spock. With the plot built around her, the other regulars have it easy; and with Seven, Janeway, Kes, and Torres adding their estrogen to each scene, it represents a rare time in *Star Trek* when the number of female regulars nearly equals the number of men. (Not that this would last!)

As the episode progresses, it quickens its pace and builds an edge of the seat excitement that's complimented by some expensive CGI effects, including Species 8472's "fluidic space." Meanwhile, ace director Winrich Kolbe holds everything together with a sure hand, allowing the episode to navigate through each twist and turn without losing its cohesiveness. Unfortunately, resolving a near death experience from "Part I" and setting up a command change late in "Part II" is a little too much ground for this episode to cover, forcing the writers and director to rush the recoveries of the two characters involved. (The writers try to cover this up with humor, having The Doctor wryly note, "I'm two for two.") But it's a minor issue that doesn't diminish the exquisite job Braga and Menosky did combining all the story threads into a satisfying climax while organically bringing Seven into the fold with a dynamic introduction that continues to pay off for the remainder of *VOY's* run.

Species 8472 would return one last time in Season Five's "In the Flesh."

Did you know? When Jeri Ryan was cast as Seven of Nine, she wasn't familiar with *Star Trek*. The producers had her watch "The Best of Both Worlds", *First Contact*, and *VOY's* own "Unity" to help catch her up to speed.

Jeri Ryan (photo by Gage Skidmore)

101

"The Gift": B

Seven of Nine deals with her new individuality while Kes's psychokinetic powers endanger the ship.

Air date: September 10, 1997
Written by Joe Menosky
Directed by Anson Williams
TV rating: 5.6

"I've got an Ocampan who wants to be something more and a Borg who's afraid of becoming something less." —Janeway

An A story with Seven intersects with a B story about Kes to allow the writers to swap one character for the other in the main cast.

The heart of the matter is Seven having to deal with individuality even while Janeway takes away her freedom of choice. ("You are no different than the Borg," gripes Seven.) Along the way, the story also allows Jeri Ryan to lose most of her Borg appliances, with the writers counting on her acting to carry the part forward in much the same way that Leonard Nimoy, appearing mostly human, created Spock through performance as opposed to prosthetics. The idea here is that Seven is addicted to the Borg, and Janeway is attempting an intervention—which is important because if Seven returns, she'll lead the Borg to Voyager and everyone will end up assimilated. Storywise, it's similar to what Hugh goes through in *TNG's* "I Borg," but because we're dealing with a regular here, there's no hidden escape hatch allowing the characters to suddenly solve their dilemmas. Instead, Menosky plays up her plight, and there are times when it's hard not to feel sincerely sorry for her, even while we simultaneously feel sympathy for Janeway, who must make difficult decisions as a captain and as the ship's community leader.

Meanwhile, reminiscent of *TNG's* "Transfigurations," Kes is evolving beyond existence as we know it (or something like that) and begins to realize it's time to say goodbye. Unfortunately, there's not much to this story, and Kes's departure is somewhat underwhelming as a result.

Lien returns for one last appearance in Season Six's "Fury."

Did you know? Before joining the cast of *VOY*, Ryan was a regular on *Dark Skies*, a sci-fi show on NBC. For her last episode of the series, she worked with Don Most, best known as Ralph Malph from *Happy Days*. "When I saw the call sheet for 'The Gift,'" she recalls, "and saw that it was going to be directed by Anson Williams, I realized that I was working my way through the *Happy Days* cast."

"Day of Honor": B

Torres struggles to express her feelings on a day the Klingons are supposed to observe as a holiday.

Air date: September 17, 1997
Written by Jeri Taylor
Directed by Jesus Salvador Trevino
TV rating: 4.5

"Welcome to the worst day of my life." —Torres

Jeri Taylor cleverly weaves together three plotlines in this subdued B'Elanna Torres episode that finally sees a breakthrough in the half-Klingon's relationship with Paris.

Borrowing a title and the Klingon holiday it represents from a four-volume *Star Trek* book series, this episode might seem like paint-by-numbers *VOY*. The ideas of Torres struggling with her emotions, Seven struggling to fit in with the rest of the crew, and aliens twisting Janeway's arm to get their way are more than *Star Trek* staples; they're part of *VOY's* DNA. Yet amidst new visuals that include a breathtaking shot of the warp core being ejected (an effect created by Foundation Imaging that would be right at home inside a *Star Trek* movie) and a couple crewmembers stranded in space (utilizing environmental suits borrowed from *Star Trek: First Contact*) the contemplative episode finds a rhythm and remains engaging throughout its duration before paying off each of its story-threads with satisfying conclusions. Unfortunately, the performances of the actors in the bulky EV suits—with the nature of the suits forcing them to rerecord their dialogue in a studio at a later time—are less organic than usual, robbing the climax of some of its power.

Did you know? Guest star Alan Altshuld, who plays an alien beggar, is no stranger to the *Star Trek* make-up chair. He appears in *TNG's* "Starship Mine" as an alien mercenary, reappears in *TNG's* "Gambit, Part I" as a Yridian who informs Riker of Picard's apparent death, and also guest stars in *VOY's* "False Profits" as a Takarian sandal maker.

103

"Nemesis": B–

After being stranded on a planet, Chakotay finds himself recruited by a band of soldiers to fight an enemy.

Air date: September 24, 1997
Written by Kenneth Biller
Directed by Alexander Singer
TV rating: 4.5

"If we greet the nemesis in the trunks, you'll fire like the rest. As long as you're with us, you do my tellings." —Brone

Not to be confused with *TNG's* fourth feature film with the same name, this Chakotay planet-based adventure features Robert Beltran and a guest cast for the entire first half before finally involving the remainder of the regulars in the later acts. Shot partly on location and partly on stage sets, a jungle environment serves as the setting for a confrontation between two rival factions, with Chakotay attempting to piece together the meaning of his situation with only incomplete information to rely on. Unfortunately, this leads the first officer to walk right into the central theme of the story: the effect of propaganda.

Co-producer/writer Kenneth Biller handles most of the story well, allowing the audience to bond with the human-like Vori while keeping the ugly Kradin more than an arm's length away. He also shrewdly incorporates a stylized language into the narrative, giving the Vori a familiar yet distant way of speaking that gives Chakotay a verbal distance to traverse while he becomes indoctrinated into their way of thinking. When the first officer finally begins talking like the Vori, it illustrates exactly where his heart lies, allowing the true nature of the plot to kick into gear.

Unfortunately, Biller gives it all a somewhat weak ending, using another character's explanation to diffuse the episode's tension rather than letting the drama build to a breaking point and having Chakotay figure things out himself. It's a disappointing climax, and all the worse for being more about an illusion than a cognitive distortion, undermining the original point of the episode.

Still, with guest stars Michael Mahonen, Matt E. Levin, and Nathan Anderson giving fine performances as Vori soldiers, and Booth Colman and Megan Murphy capably guest starring as the most noteworthy members of a village—with all making the only *Star Trek* appearances of their careers—"Nemesis" has enough elements to remain an engaging piece of entertainment.

Did you know? Jeri Ryan does not appear in this episode. She does however, appear in every subsequent episode of the series.

"Revulsion": C+

Torres and The Doctor answer a hologram's call for help.

Air date: October 1, 1997
Written by Lisa Klink
Directed by Kenneth Biller
TV rating: 5.0

"I think there's a problem with our isomorph, and I'm not talking about his emitters." —Torres

Kenneth Biller pivots from writing to directing in this horror-based episode featuring Leland Orser as a violent hologram with a mental disorder. Like a John Carpenter film, "Revulsion" is more about style than the substance, with the dialogue carrying the day as Torres and The Doctor interact with the hologram on a ship littered with the remains of its deceased crew. Meanwhile, Kim and Seven are paired up in a B story that allows each to learn a little more about the other.

If there's one common denominator for both plots, it's that they're each played intentionally awkwardly, with Orser exhibiting a socially impaired personality and Kim and Seven unsure how to interact. The actors are all good enough to pull it off in an entertaining way, giving us a perfectly adequate character-based episode, but as a filler offering with few surprises, "Revulsion" never becomes remarkable or memorable enough to stand out from the crowd.

Did you know? The day after finishing his work for this episode, Orser flew to England to join the cast of *Saving Private Ryan.* "I get on the plane, fly to London, and turn on the TV at the hotel," Orser remembers, "and I look at the screen and what comes on, but Bob Picardo's face! *Voyager* was on. It was so strange."

"The Raven": C

Seven of Nine experiences flashbacks and believes that she is being called back to the Borg Collective.

Air date: October 8, 1997
Teleplay by Bryan Fuller
Story by Harry Doc Kloor & Bryan Fuller
Directed by LeVar Burton
TV rating: 4.8

"It's as if I were aboard a Borg vessel, but I was frightened. I felt fear. Each experience is similar. I'm being pursued by the Borg. They want to assimilate me. I'm running from them, and then, and then, each time I see a bird." —Seven

This Seven episode is essentially a mystery story with a chase reminiscent of the hunt for Data in *TNG's* "Brothers" and a capture sequence reminiscent of Data's capture at the beginning of *Star Trek: Insurrection* (minus the sing-along). Seven's suddenly having flashbacks, and she thinks she's being called back to the Borg, but all isn't as it seems. In reality, what we have here is a story that serves as an opportunity for Seven to take the next step in her human journey while simultaneously giving the writers a chance to flesh out a little more of her backstory. Unfortunately, to give the episode some tension and a faux-jeopardy climax, some cliché xenophobic aliens are tossed in to serve as an obstacle and a threat. (Voyager is in their space, and they're a cross between obstinate diplomats and trigger-happy law enforcement officers.)

Director LeVar Burton, with help from an uncredited David Livingston, plays up the episode's surreal imagery, and he ensures that the pace moves along appropriately, with introspective dialogue-driven scenes getting enough time to develop before the more action-oriented scenes move along at a faster clip. Meanwhile, Kate Mulgrew gives another fine performance as Janeway, serving as the glue that holds the episode together.

Overall, however, it's just another vanilla *VOY* offering, and while the ending enriches Seven's character, there are better Seven episodes to come. The teleplay, nonetheless, earned Bryan Fuller a job on the staff.

Did you know? Inspired by *Citizen Kane's* "rosebud," Brannon Braga came up with this episode's title and its meaning.

"Scientific Method": C+

Invisible aliens perform experiments on the crew without their knowledge.

Air date: October 29, 1997
Teleplay by Lisa Klink
Story by Sherry Klein & Harry Doc Kloor
Directed by David Livingston
TV rating: 4.6

"They seem to be conducting experiments on the crew and monitoring the results." —Seven

This ensemble piece, reminiscent of John Carpenter's *They Live* (1988), starts off as part whodunnit, part medical mystery, beginning somewhat uncomfortably with X-ray-like voyeur scenes. When we jump into the second part, the cinematography gets even creepier to show what's hidden from most of the crew's visual spectrum, giving us a better idea of what's going on and ratcheting up the tension tenfold. (Thank goodness the ship has a Borg as part of its crew! If there's one species that can handle what's hidden below the surface, it's them, giving us a good use of Seven of Nine.) But this only sets the stage for a third part, in which the crew has finally had enough and takes action. It's all a little disjointed but also includes enough elements to keep the viewer engaged.

Still, longtime Trekkers have seen this sort of thing before on *TNG* ("Schisms" "Phantasms") and the cookie cutter solutions (being part technobabble, part Jim Kirk) overwhelm much of what it has to say about the ethics of experimental medical testing on non-consenting subjects.

The episode does, however, accomplish what it sets out to do and is one of the more memorable episodes of *VOY's* run.

Did you know? For Kate Mulgrew, playing a cranky Janeway in this episode was easy. "That was shot when I had just stopped smoking, and it showed in my performance. I just let go. Actually, I allowed my feelings to play, I think very nicely, into Janeway's personality the whole season. Janeway was under a lot of pressure, as was I."

Season Four Roundup

Television is always evolving, but in the late 1990s, the industry was changing in ways that hadn't been seen since color televisions swept over America in the 1960s, with the old days of watching sitcoms on boxy sets giving way to audiences watching reality TV in widescreen. For *Star Trek*, this was concerning, because the franchise was increasingly beginning to look like a dinosaur. So by 1997, Rick Berman was under direct orders from Paramount to shake things up. But what to do? Go widescreen? With some sci-fi shows, such as *The X-Files* and *Stargate SG-1*, beginning to shoot that way, it was something to consider. But Berman ultimately decided it wasn't worth doing for *DS9* and *VOY*. Meanwhile, high definition was on the horizon, but the technology to bring it into the average viewer's home wasn't yet in place. So in the end, *Star Trek* would have to adapt to a new age of television in *Star Trek's* own way. *DS9* had already pulled a coup by adding *TNG's* Worf to the show. *VOY* would have to come up with something of its own. So when Brannon Braga proposed adding a Borg character to the show, Berman had a suggestion/order: make her a Borg babe. Inspired by the success of the Borg Queen in *Star Trek: First Contact* (1996), he thought that adding a sexy Borg bombshell to *VOY* might help bring a new audience to the show and add some tension to the stories.

Enter Jeri Ryan, the former Miss Illinois and *Dark Skies* star, who won the part of Seven of Nine, a human assimilated by the Borg before being rescued by *VOY*, a metaphor for a child raised by wolves before being rescued by society.

Unfortunately, with the budget only allowing for nine castmembers, someone had to go. So the producers prepared to say goodbye to Garrett Wang, whose death was written into the "Scorpion" two-parter. But between Seasons Three and Four, Wang landed on People Magazine's "50 Most Beautiful People in the World" list (with the magazine making a conscious effort to find lesser-known actors of various ethnicities) and was suddenly deemed unexpendable by the producers. That led to Plan B. Jennifer Lien, who, like most of the other regulars, had originally signed a three-year contract, was set free while the others renegotiated their deals.

In truth, Lien's character, through no fault of the actress, never finds a niche, and replacing Kes with Seven indisputably breathes new life into the show, giving the writers many new story opportunities while bringing out Mulgrew's best as mentor/captain, with standout episodes like "Scorpion, Part II" and "Prey" showcasing the Janeway/Seven relationship. Happily, the other characters still get their time in the sun as well, with memorable episodes ranging from The Doctor-centric "Living Witness" (directed by Tim Russ) to the Torres-centric "Day of Honor," while a couple of two-parters, "The Year of Hell" and "The Killing Game," use the whole ensemble. (We even get one last good Kes episode with "The Gift.")

Unfortunately, behind the scenes as the episodes were being shot, not all was so rosy. Ryan had to endure the grumbling of her castmates—most notably Kate Mulgrew—who felt Ryan's addition was a message from the studio that the rest of the actors weren't good enough. There was other drama as well, with

131

"Year of Hell": A

When aliens tinker with the timeline in an attempt to restore their empire, Voyager suffers the effects.

Air date: November 5, 1997
Written by Brannon Braga & Joe Menosky
Directed by Allan Kroeker
TV rating: 4.7

"Time is patient, so we must be patient with it." —Annorax

Braga and Menosky craft a bold plot into this long-form ensemble piece with a story that, in conjunction with its concluding part, takes place over the course of a year. (Today a show would take such a concept and run with it for a whole season.) The key to what makes it special is the creative use of time as an experimental weapon. Aliens are tinkering with the past in an attempt to shape the present more to their liking, but they can't seem to get it quite right, turning their butterfly effect experiments into more of a deviant artform than a scientific achievement. And it's especially fascinating to reflect upon how Season Three's "Before and After," which starts in the future before going back in time, works with this episode as an abstract prequel or sequel, depending on your view of timespace.

For the show's lighting and design teams, "Year of Hell" offers an opportunity to create a seemingly new show, with dark and gritty visuals giving the Voyager new looks that go even further than *TOS's* "Mirror, Mirror" and *TNG's* "Yesterdays' Enterprise." (Janeway even breaks out another hairstyle.) Meanwhile, Braga and Menosky give the crew quite a journey, taking us from a beginning in which The Doctor brags about the crew's unity to a middle where Chakotay floats the idea of breaking up the family, to a finale where it actually happens. It's all played brilliantly and poignantly, with tragedies adding up throughout the hour that change how the crew thinks and behaves while altering the nature of the show (if only for a little while).

Kurtwood Smith, after previously appearing as the Federation president in *Star Trek VI: The Undiscovered Country* and Odo's counterpart in *DS9's* dystopian thriller, "Things Past," plays Annorax, the alien with the keys to a Death Star-like time weapon. A combination of arrogant and vulnerable, the character provides the episode with its only constant, setting up a second part in which we hope for his defeat.

Did you know? In the middle of shooting "Year of Hell," an additional scene for "Revulsion" was filmed to help pad out that episode.

"Year of Hell, Part II": B+

With Voyager in danger, the ship's remaining crew risks everything to stop an alien from tampering with the timeline.

Air date: November 12, 1997
Written by Brannon Braga & Joe Menosky
Directed by Mike Vejar
TV rating: 5.2

"Time's up." —Janeway

This concluding episode is surprisingly quieter than the first, filled with conversations which, while less noisy than bombast and battles, are still compelling, with some internal conflicts lacing the discussions as Voyager's usual command structure and rules are tossed out the window.

This time, Kurtwood Smith gets even more time to flesh out his time-meddling bad guy, Annorax, with Chakotay and Paris on board his ship asking the tough questions. "I've been studying your previous incursions," Chakotay says. "No matter how close you get to restoring the timeline, one component is always missing: Kyana Prime. Who was on that colony? Who did you lose?" This, of course, cuts to the heart of the matter: Annorax has made a mistake, and his attempts to undo it by further tinkering with time only dig him and everyone else into a deeper hole. It's like he's trying to solve a Rubik's cube without the proper expertise. The more he tries to move pieces around to solve one side, the more he inadvertently moves pieces out of position on the other sides.

Janeway, meanwhile, forms an alternate plan to end this all, even if it means going down with the ship by herself. Her part in the episode is a study of obsession, with the captain simply unwilling to take no for an answer, whether it comes from her enemies or her friends.

Unfortunately, "Year of Hell" doesn't quite reach the bar set for these sort of stories by *TNG's* "Yesterday's Enterprise" and "Parallels," mainly because it plays it too safe, with fewer elements and less of a "wow" factor than its time-tinkering predecessors or even "Part I." There are no wildcards such as the appearance of Kes or an unexpected demise throwing a wrench in someone's plan. For such a time travel puzzle, it all plays out in quite a linear and predictable fashion. Nonetheless, it is a satisfying conclusion to another successful two-parter and even includes a poignant "Time in a Bottle" coda that makes it all the more worthwhile to watch.

"Part II" was nominated for an Emmy for visual effects.

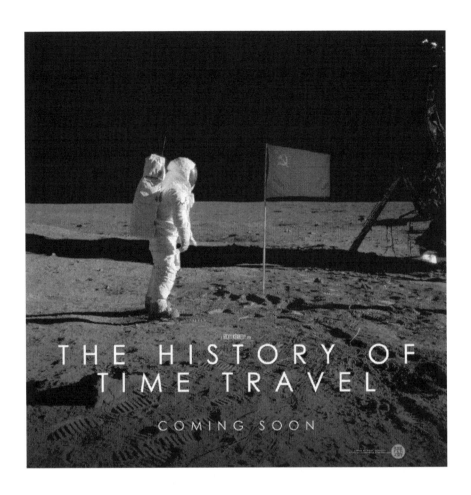

Did you know? In 2014, a low-budget fictional documentary was released called *The History of Time Travel* which features interview subjects discussing "The Indiana Project," a supposed time travel invention that began as a government effort before being secretly completed by one of the project's team-members and his son(s). Throughout the documentary, history subtly changes as the family tinkers with time, with the people being interviewed changing the details of their stories without even being aware of it. On the whole, the documentary shares many cosmetic similarities to *VOY's* "Year of Hell," with both even concluding in much the same way.

"Random Thoughts": B–

When Torres is imprisoned for having violent thoughts on a planet of peaceful telepaths, Tuvok investigates the situation.

Air date: November 19, 1997
Written by Kenneth Biller
Directed by Alexander Singer
TV rating: 4.7

"From what I've learned, crime here is a result of exposure to violent thought."
—Tuvok

Set on a planet of telepaths, this allegory for violence in the media meanders into a Tuvok story where he sticks his Vulcan nose into a black market for violent thoughts that takes on almost sexual overtones.

In a way, it feels like the offspring of "Ex Post Facto" and "Meld," though it's also the sort of story that would have been right at home on *TNG*. But *VOY*, having learned quite a few lessons in its first few seasons, is mature enough by this time to present the story more properly than it might have in seasons past, laying out enough well-paced exposition before getting to the heart of the matter in a meaningful way. And while the plot's key alien is played by Wayne Péré, an actor of limited talent who never appears in *Star Trek* again, it's Gwynyth Walsh, who previously played one of the Duras sisters on *TNG*, who steals the show, playing a Chief Examiner who ends up in over her head.

Still, Biller leaves some loose threads. (Paris is given a mini-story that works its way up to an assigned task before the matter simply disappears from the story at large.) And in the latter acts, the writer deliberately gives Tuvok a poor plan to enhance the drama. All the same, as a study of what happens when a society dictates what a person can and can't think, it's quite an interesting story with some significant things to say.

Did you know? Gwynyth Walsh, who previously played B'Etor in three episodes of *TNG*, one episode of *DS9*, and *Star Trek: Generations*, was relieved that for this episode, she did not have to wear much make-up. "It was so nice not to have to spend three hours having it applied every day," the actress says. "There had been a few attempts to have me do another guest spot, and I always said, 'I'll come back, but I want to be someone vaguely human!'"

"Concerning Flight": C

When pirates steal the ship's main computer, Captain Janeway must track down the missing equipment with the help of a holographic Leonardo da Vinci.

Air date: November 16, 1997
Teleplay by Joe Menosky
Story by Jimmy Diggs & Joe Menosky
Directed by Jesus Salvador Trevino
TV rating: 4.1

"There are things in this world that I understand and you don't." —Janeway

Star Trek's most abstract writer, Joe Menosky, gives us one of his more pedestrian outside the box stories, bringing back John Rhys-Davies ("Scorpion") as a holographic Leonardo da Vinci to team him up with Kate Mulgrew so their characters can run amok on an alien planet.

Truth be told, I find Janeway's English gothic holodeck adventures ("Cathexis," "Learning Curve," and "Persistence of Vision") a little more exciting than her interactions with da Vinci because her governess adventures are more unique to *Star Trek*. But a representation of the most famous Italian Renaissance man, particularly with John Rhys-Davies bringing the character to life, is probably more appealing to the masses, and it's fun to see the dialogue throw in a tongue and cheek reference to *TOS's* "Requiem for Methuselah," an episode which proposes that Methuslelah, Brahms, and da Vinci are all the same ageless person.

With Chakotay and the gang keeping tabs on the planet in a B story that's little more than a framing device, Janeway, with da Vinci in tow, gets to play Indiana Jones down on the planet, which is brought to life by the design team via a village stage set, location shooting, and some optical effects. That makes it one of the most visually diverse episodes of the season, with a feeling of freedom playing into the thrill of flying for the first time, the episode's central theme.

Unfortunately, the aliens themselves are underdeveloped, and as a viewer, it's difficult to invest too heavily in a Janeway/holographic da Vinci relationship that is never touched on again. As a harmless hour of entertainment, however, the episode adequately serves its purpose.

Did you know? Da Vinci was fascinated with the idea of flight for much of his life, producing more than 35,000 words and 500 sketches dealing with flying machines, the nature of air, and bird flight. Most of his aeronautical designs were ornithopters, a name derived from the ancient Greek words for "bird" and "wings," with his most sophisticated plans allowing a pilot to use hand levers, foot pedals, and a system of pulleys to operate them. Da Vinci, however, was probably aware that his design was too heavy to take off from the ground and was best suited to be used as a glider. But glider technology eventually proved more important to powered flight than any competing ideas, such as steerable balloons. It was 19th century glider technology, after all, that evolved into 20th century airplanes. And while steerable balloons evolved into flying airships, airplanes proved faster, safer, and, of course, eventually became the most common way for humans to fly.

"Mortal Coil": B–

After being killed and revived, Neelix finds himself facing an existential crisis, questioning his beliefs after his death was not what he expected.

Air date: December 17, 1997
Written by Bryan Fuller
Directed by Allan Kroeker
TV rating: 3.9

"I died, and there was nothing. There was no one there." —Neelix

What happens when you discover that your cornerstone beliefs, taught to you since birth by the people you love, turn out to be false, and the great mystery of death turns out to be simply a void? *VOY*, after mining similar territory in Season One's "Emanations," returns to the subject and makes it more personal by forcing Neelix to deal with these questions head-on. It's the perfect character choice, as Neelix wears his heart on his sleeve, and when he begins questioning if there's any reason for his own existence, his usual cheer and optimism give way to a more troubled side that's all the more dramatic for being so genuine.

This time, ace director Allan Kroeker is at the helm, giving the episode the perfect pacing while handling a vision quest, which Neelix partakes in under the guidance of Chakotay, particularly well. And with the teleplay by writer Bryan Fuller (polished by the uncredited Brannon Braga and Joe Menosky) giving the plot little more substance, the directing and acting prove the key to the episode's success, with Kroeker, Ethan Phillips, and Robert Beltran carrying the day. For in the end, unlike "Emanations," the episode isn't really about death and the great mystery that surrounds it. It's about what it means to live.

All the same, you'd think that the events in this episode would forever change Neelix, and the show couldn't simply go on to the next episode as if nothing meaningful has happened. But this is *VOY*, not *DS9*, and the series isn't up to the challenge of sticking with such a significant character arc.

Did you know? The title of this episode comes from William Shakespeare's *Hamlet*, in which the title character, in his famous "To be, or not to be" soliloquy, says, "For in that sleep of death what dreams may come when we have shuffled off this mortal coil must give us pause."

"Waking Moments": C–

The crew begins to experience vivid nightmares, all containing the same mysterious aliens.

Air date: January 14, 1998
Written by Andre Bormanis
Directed by Alexander Singer
TV rating: 3.7

"I'm still asleep." —Chakotay

VOY's science consultant, Andre Bormanis crafts this Chakotay episode that foreshadows *Inception*, a 2010 sci-fi film that explores the concept of lucid dreaming and the issues of losing yourself in a dream within a dream. (Both "Waking Moments" and *Inception* also owe a debt to *TNG's* "Ship in a Bottle," a holodeck story that pioneers a similar concept.)

As a creative endeavor, it works okay, but as a Chakotay episode, it's underwhelming. Reminiscent of "Displaced," the aliens of the week are paper-thin caricatures, with Bormanis keeping them secondary to the plot device. Meanwhile, the main beats of the story, intended to play with our minds, are too predictable to accomplish their purpose. By the time the story morphs into *Nightmare on Elm Street* in its later stages, there simply aren't enough compelling ingredients for the episode to effectively pull it off.

All that said, "Waking Moments," filled with surreal moments and a few unique visuals, has enough to it that it's worth watching once.

Did you know? Starting with this episode, Roxann Dawson begins wearing an over-jacket to hide her pregnancy.

"Message in a Bottle": B+

The crew finds an alien relay system that has the ability to send The Doctor to the Alpha Quadrant.

Air date: January 22, 1998
Written by Lisa Klink
Directed by Nancy Malone
TV rating: 4.2

"When I requested more away missions, this isn't exactly what I had in mind."
—The Doctor

Andy Dick teams up with Roberto Picardo in this offbeat story featuring two holographic doctors on board a commandeered Starfleet vessel interacting amidst a backdrop of intrigue. Voyager's found a way to use an alien array to send its Doctor to the Alpha Quadrant, but not only does he end up on a ship full of Romulans, the Hirogens, the aliens who built the array, become upset with Voyager for using their technology and attempt to stop things before The Doctor can return to his crew. It all leads to an exciting episode with everything getting more and more out of control with every act, making you wonder how the good guys—and the writer—will ever set things right.

The interiors of the Starfleet vessel itself include a brightened redress of the original *Star Trek* movie bridge set, giving The Doctors a suitable playground, and Dick, a friend of producer Brannon Braga, works especially well with Picardo, with his EMH character sharing enough similarities with The Doctor to pass as another of his kind while also having enough differences for the two to develop a ying and yang relationship. In fact, the two actors are so adept at bringing the snappy, fast-paced dialogue to life, they almost appear to be a comedy duo from a lost sitcom.

The Doctor
Stop breathing down my neck!

EMH 2
My breathing is merely a simulation.

The Doctor
So is my neck.

The B story, on the other hand, is a little more serious, with Seven and Torres still struggling to get along even as the crew is introduced to their next alien threat. (We'll be seeing more of the Hirogen in the next episode.) But it's intruded on by a companion C story with Paris played for laughs. Asked to fill in for The Doctor, he says he's a patient, not a doctor, dammit, and he wants Kim to create another holographic doctor to do the job instead.

116

All in all, it adds up to a lot of elements for one single *VOY* episode to develop and balance, and yet writer Lisa Klink and director Nancy Malone somehow pull it off, giving us one of the most successful episodes of the season, and one that would continue to be referenced in future episodes.

Did you know? Before becoming a director, Nancy Malone was an actress who appeared on *The Twilight Zone* and *The Outer Limits*. She died in 2014 at age seventy-nine.

"Hunters": C+

Voyager receives a message from Starfleet containing letters from the crew's friends and family.

Air date: February 11, 1998
Written by Jeri Taylor
Directed by David Livingston
TV rating: 3.8

"You shouldn't get your hopes up, Harry. No hopes, no disappointments."
—Paris

Despite initially airing after a rerun, "Hunters" picks up right after the events in "Message in a Bottle," with Starfleet attempting to communicate with Voyager through an alien array.

Most of the episode is quiet and poignant as various crewmembers deal with letters from home, which range from "You're a grandfather!" to "I found someone else to marry." Each letter is personally delivered by Neelix, who aptly demonstrates how to be the worst mailman in the world by announcing to everyone which crewmembers are receiving private mail and then lingering to try to read each letter over the recipient's shoulder. And following up on the last episode's mention of the Dominion, there's even a little more *DS9* news that comes out as well, with the crew learning some of what's been going on in the Alpha Quadrant since they've been away. (Back in the 1990s, this sort of crossover information was rewarding for fans who were loyally watching both shows, though today, it can be a bit awkward for someone streaming one series at a time.) The news itself lays the groundwork for Season Five's "Extreme Risk."

Eventually, the action picks up, culminating in one of *Star Trek's* most technobabble-laden battles, though Voyager's new adversary, the Hirogen, is more cartoonish than Neelix's mail delivery service, and the sequence doesn't come together as well as hoped.

What's most disappointing, however, is that Jeri Taylor, whose strengths as a writer lie in developing relationships among the crew and exploring humanity in space, couldn't come up with a better script as a whole, despite the main subject matter being right in her wheelhouse.

Did you know? The Hirogen look was loosely modeled after the look of American football players.

"Prey": B+

When a member of Species 8472 hides aboard Voyager, the crew and the Hirogen team up to find it.

Air date: February 18, 1998
Written by Brannon Braga
Directed by Allan Eastman
TV rating: 3.8

"You want to be part of the hunt? Now's your chance." —Janeway

For this monster episode, Brannon Braga takes a "Devil in the Dark"-like story and turns it into a battle of wills between Janeway and Seven.

The Hirogen are back, but this time they've bitten off more than they can chew. A member of Species 8472, a group of aliens last seen in the opening episode of the season, gets the better of them, and Voyager gets entangled in the fight. The real battle, however, turns out to be between the Janeway and Seven, with viewers caught in the middle, able to see both their viewpoints. Janeway, looking at the situation from a captain's perspective, wants Seven to recognize a chance to reach out with compassion to a helpless being so she'll have a chance to grow as a person and perhaps understand the reasons and origins of human values. Seven, on the other hand, views the situation from a Borg perspective, believing that helping a dangerous alien is a tactical risk that must be avoided.

Throughout it all, there's a lot of action and suspense, with Allan Eastman, directing his first *Star Trek* episode, giving it a cinematic quality with long, uncut shots that make you feel like you're right there on the ship as the crew deals with a dangerous intruder. Meanwhile, Tony Todd, better known for playing Worf's brother and an elderly Jake Sisko on *TNG* and *DS9*, guest stars as the new face of the Hirogen, finally bringing some gravitas to a race that would continue to appear from time to time.

But even as all the other elements compete for attention, the focus of the episode continually returns to the simmering conflict between Janeway and Seven as it brews throughout the episode before bubbling over at the end. It's exactly the kind of thing the producers were hoping for when they brought Seven aboard.

Did you know? After finishing his work on this episode, Allan Eastman immediately began work on *DS9's* "Honor Among Thieves."

"Retrospect": C+

When Seven believes she's been assaulted, the crew conducts an investigation.

Air date: February 25, 1998
Teleplay by Bryan Fuller & Lisa Klink
Story by Andrew Shepard Price & Mark Gaberman
Directed by Jesus Salvador Trevino
TV rating: 4.2

"There's no doubt that Seven was the victim of a brutal assault." —The Doctor

With Seven serving as the accuser, this Doctor episode is basically a rape accusation allegory with an investigation and a chase after Seven recalls being secretly captured by an alien, with memories reminiscent of Riker's experiences in *TNG's* "Schisms" forcing the crew to figure out whether she's remembering the truth or has had some sort of dream. (The Doctor, who has been developing a psychiatric subroutine to his program, believes her at once and serves as her advocate.)

Michael Horton plays the accused, coming off as smarmy and defensive but also somewhat cowardly, giving the story its legs. But he's undermined by the fact that most people won't care nearly as much as The Doctor and Janeway about the fate of his character, since we've never seen him before, and we know we'll never see him again whatever happens. Fortunately, the writers are able to make up for this by playing up The Doctor's feelings about the investigation and turning it all into a lesson about confirmation bias and patient manipulation. Still, the whole thing would be stronger if it were to end more ambiguously, with the crew forced to let a possibly dangerous man go because he could not be proven innocent or guilty. Instead, the writers take an easier way out, cleaning up their mess while leaving the characters to ponder the meaning of it all.

Did you know? Michael Horton also plays an Enterprise-E crewman, Lieutenant Daniels, in *Star Trek: First Contact* and *Star Trek: Insurrection.*

"The Killing Game": B

The Hirogen alter the memories of the Voyager crew and force them to play out a violent holodeck simulation.

Air date: March 4, 1998
Written by Brannon Braga & Joe Menosky
Directed by David Livingston
TV rating: 4.3

"This has been going on for nineteen days. Dozens of battle scenarios, one more brutal than the next."—The Doctor

Like *DS9's* "Our Man Bashir," this ambitious ensemble episode provides some of the *Star Trek* actors with new parts to play in a holodeck simulation, but this time the story preserves the essence of the characters and their relationships with each other even in their new roles.

What we have here is basically a precursor to HBO's adaptation of *Westworld*, with characters unaware of their past lives and the true nature of their world while they are forced to navigate a violent simulation. In this case, however, the setting isn't the Wild West but World War II, with the exteriors brought to life courtesy of Universal Studio's "Little Europe" backlot set.

Meanwhile, The Doctor and Kim must serve the Hirogen, with The Doctor healing the wounds of the unconscious and Kim in charge of keeping the holodeck running properly. The point of it all, of course, is to enable a period piece without the headaches of time travel, and in this regard the episode succeeds, with the new settings and costumes serving as a refreshing change of pace from what we're used to seeing. (The episode would go on to be nominated for an Emmy for hairstyling too.) On the other hand, the plot itself remains somewhat simplistic, content to remain obvious and shallow with bad guy Nazis/Hirogen on one side and good guy resistors on the other and offering virtually no mystery or science fiction. The writers try to add some complexity by throwing in some conflict among the Hirogen soldiers themselves, but when there's a life and death war going on, such squabbling seems a secondary issue, even if it will become more important in the next episode.

"The Killing Game" concludes in "The Killing Game, Part II."

Did you know? Surprising *VOY's* cast and crew, UPN initially aired "The Killing Game" and "The Killing Game, Part II" back-to-back on the same night as a single two-hour presentation.

121

"The Killing Game, Part II": B

The Voyager crew, trapped in a deadly simulation staged by the Hirogen, must find a way to retake the ship.

Air date: March 4, 1998
Written by Brannon Braga & Joe Menosky
Directed by Victor Lobl
TV rating: 4.3

"No wonder the system breached. You've turned Voyager into one big holodeck." —Janeway

Utilizing Janeway as its focal character, this concluding episode starts off a little slow but kicks into gear about halfway through before finishing with a shoot-em-up climax befitting a blockbuster movie, complete with a cinematic score.

With the crew regaining their memories, the plot here merges an attempt to kick the Nazis out of France with an attempt to kick the Hirogen off the ship. To help facilitate this, the writers employ a bit of a cheat: Voyager itself is essentially turned into a giant holodeck, allowing the World War II simulation to spill into the ship at large.

It's all exciting stuff, and it gives the writers another opportunity to find something for each character to do, even if the plot itself never develops into anything more significant than an action-adventure story.

Ultimately, however, the Hirogen fail to satisfy as antagonists, which is probably why they never appear again as a collective alien threat. They do, however, return in "Flesh and Blood," a sequel to "The Killing Game" where the Hirogen become the prey.

Did you know? While shooting on location at Universal Studios' European Street backlot, the cast and crew had to deal with torrential downpours because of El Niño, a Pacific Ocean climate phenomenon, with the rain unexpectedly becoming incorporated into the episode itself.

"Vis à Vis": C

A genome thief switches physical forms with Paris..

Air date: April 8, 1998
Written by Robert J. Doherty
Directed by Jesus Salvador Trevino
TV rating: 3.1

"The alien seems capable of some sort of selective DNA exchange." —Daelen

This Paris identity theft episode, reminiscent of *TOS's* "Turnabout Intruder," *TNG's* "The Schizoid Man," and *TAS's* "The Survivor," is a perfectly acceptable old-school sci-fi story, though it never develops into anything unique or memorable, unwilling to dig beneath the superficial.

The meat and potatoes of the plot lie with Robert Duncan McNeill, first playing Paris himself before playing an alien pretending to be Paris. Dan Butler, better known as Bob "Bulldog" Briscoe from *Frazier*, guest stars as his counterpoint: first playing the alien before playing Paris in the alien's guise. (Butler is rather awful as Paris, with no recognizable mannerisms, but his B story, where he meets up with another victim, Daelen, and tries to put things back to normal, is thankfully short.)

In the end, the episode simply serves as a budget-saving placeholder while the show attempts to recoup the money spent on "The Killing Game," though it remains watchable enough to avoid most fans' criticism.

Did you know? Robert J. Doherty joined the *VOY* writing staff in his early twenties after he graduated from Colgate University in 1996 with a degree in creative writing. He went on to create and produce CBS's *Elementary*, a contemporary reimagining of *Sherlock Holmes*.

"The Omega Directive": C+

Captain Janeway must carry out a top secret directive to save the Delta Quadrant from the most dangerous substance known to exist.

Air date: April 15, 1998
Teleplay by Lisa Klink
Story by Jimmy Diggs & Steve J. Kay
Directed by Victor Lobl
TV rating: 3.7

"Omega destroys subspace. A chain reaction involving a handful of molecules could devastate subspace throughout an entire quadrant. If that were to happen, warp travel would become impossible." —Janeway

This is one of those episodes with a backstory more interesting than the episode itself. Apparently, years ago, Starfleet had a Manhattanish project go terribly wrong, and now there's a secret directive to detect this sort of activity and put a stop to it. Unfortunately, this is all conveyed with a clandestine discussion in the briefing room rather than a Genesis-like presentation. But this is a TV show and not a feature film, so we have to settle for some talk and then a scaled-down echo of the incident when some aliens have the same thing happen to them.

As the plot continues to develop, Janeway is determined to follow Starfleet's directive in the A story while Seven becomes convinced that the Omega molecules have spiritual significance and should be harnessed in a tangent B story. This allows writer Lisa Klink to flesh out another conflict between the two characters, but the problem is the playing field is tilted because Janeway outranks everyone on the ship and, as Kirk has said, a starship isn't a democracy. (I don't usually advocate bringing in a guest star to take the spot of a regular, but in this case, the drama would work better if Janeway and an alien captain were to have the disagreement, allowing both to be on equal footing.)

Still, there's enough logic and danger in all facets of this one to make it intriguing enough to watch once or twice.

Did you know? B'Elanna Torres is largely absent from this episode because during its shoot, Roxann Dawson went into labor and gave birth to her first daughter, Emma.

"Unforgettable": D+

An alien who claims to have had a relationship with Chakotay requests asylum.

Air date: April 22, 1998
Written by Greg Elliot & Michael Perricone
Directed by Andrew J. Robinson
TV rating: 3.4

"The memories of my people can't be held in the minds of other races. When we encounter others, which we do infrequently, they remember us for a few hours, but then the memories fade away." —Kellin

Using a lot of technobabble, the writers here craft a ship-based story in the spirit of *Logan's Run* about a woman, weakly played by Virginia Madsen, who's attempting to escape from others of her kind. The twist? She was aboard Voyager recently and even had a relationship with Chakotay, but due to the nature of her species, no one on the ship can remember her.

The execution of the concept itself is a little clunky, with the writers simultaneously making her "forgettable" nature both biological and technological, which is a lot to swallow. (She comes from a race of isolationists. Wouldn't it just be simpler to make it all a technological thing?) More than that, however, the writers and director just don't know how to present the idea, with such a high concept needing a cleverly layered script and creative execution to succeed but not getting either.

At its heart, "Unforgettable" is a romance story. The alien has returned to continue her relationship with Chakotay, but of he doesn't remember her, of course, and isn't sure what to make of her advances. As the story progresses, it's all presented from his perspective to allow the viewers to see it take shape through his eyes, almost backing into a story akin to *The Notebook*, though what the writers really needed to do here was to once again tap into the future *Lost* formula, crosscutting back and forth between the past and the present with parallel plotlines before they converge into a single meaning at the end. Instead, we get a couple wooden flashback scenes and a somewhat poorly developed romance through the lens of a half-baked science fiction idea.

True to the aliens' nature but contrary to the episode's title, the whole thing comes across as rather forgettable, though at least it has enough creative touches to remain unique.

Did you know? At a 2001 fan convention, Robert Beltran cited "Unforgettable" as his favorite *VOY* episode.

"Living Witness": B+

Many centuries in the future, a backup version of The Doctor attempts to rebut the claims of war crimes supposedly committed by Voyager.

Air date: April 29, 1998
Teleplay by Bryan Fuller, Brannon Braga & Joe Menosky
Story by Brannon Braga
Directed by Tim Russ
TV rating: 3.9

"I never meant to throw your beliefs into doubt, but I can't deny what I know to be true." —The Doctor

VOY's take on Rashomon is a little more creative than *TNG's* more on-the nose version, "A Matter of Perspective," with debuting director Tim Russ turning it into the closest *VOY* comes to a mirror universe episode.

The frame for it all takes place in a museum beyond the year 3000, giving the writers a chance to look at Voyager from a new angle: revisionist history, where the stories of the true events have been altered over time with people filling in the gaps of their knowledge with conjecture mostly based on what they want to believe. This allows the writers and design team to sprinkle in many variations—some obvious, some subtle—as we witness the events aboard Voyager in a couple of different simulations. But the true beauty of the episode's script itself lies in how the petty conflict between two sets of aliens serves as a through-line, merging their issues of the past with the present.

With all of this serving as a backdrop, the centerpiece of the drama is a backup version of The Doctor, which has been discovered and activated by the Museum's curator, played by Henry Woronicz. The idea of a "backup Doctor" seems a bit contrived considering *VOY* has previously gone out of its way to say the possibility of a backup Doctor is a technological impossibility, but the writers needed some way to present a living witness here, so it's something that we just have to accept as a temporary bit of artistic license. This allows Picardo and Woronicz to develop an interesting relationship between their characters, with The Doctor having to deal with the fact that his shipmates, whom he remembers seeing the day before, are all gone, and Woronicz's character, Quarren, having to deal with the fact that the history he's passionately believed in his whole life isn't actually true. It's as if one of the Twelve Apostles was to wake up like "Rip Van Winkle" today and was like, "Hey, y'all got Jesus wrong."

Unfortunately, it all ends with a bit of a writer's cheat, with a twist serving as a way to clean up the whole situation in seconds. But considering we're unlikely to see any of these characters ever again—including the backup version of The Doctor—it's something the show can get away with this one time.

126

Did you know? The museum framing device in this episode is reminiscent of the framing device in the *Space Museum* comic book series published in the late 1950s and early 1960s by National Comics (now DC Comics) in its flagship science fiction title *Strange Adventures*. The concept of this episode is also reminiscent of *Babylon 5's* Season Four episode, "The Deconstruction of Falling Stars," which first aired October 27, 1997.

"Demon": C+

Voyager, desperately low on fuel, must mine an energy source on a highly hostile "Demon class" planet.

Air date: May 6, 1998
Teleplay by Kenneth Biller
Story by Andre Bormanis
Directed by Anson Williams
TV rating: 3.8

"I've been thinking. With Tuvok's shield modifications and a few tweaks to an environmental suit, I could take a shuttle to the surface and mine the deuterium from there." —Kim

This *Body Snatchers* ensemble piece is quite the offbeat episode of *VOY*, but it works okay on its own merits, with some unique visuals and engaging character banter.

The A story, with Kim and Paris finding their bodies seemingly adapted to the atmosphere of a hostile planet, is reminiscent of *TAS's* "The Ambergris Element," where Kirk and Spock are "bioformed" into water breathers. "Demon," however, takes a bizarre twist in another direction, ultimately leading to a surprise ending.

Meanwhile, the B story with Neelix is even stranger, with the Talaxian moving into sickbay as part of a temporary relocation. Serving partly to add some comic relief and partly to allow for the development of the relationship between Neelix and The Doctor, the subplot might bring a smile to anyone who's had to put up with a nocturnal college roommate, but there's not much depth to it.

In a way, the two halves feel like a throwback to the days of old sci-fi when style mattered more than substance. For *VOY*, however, it's just another day at the office.

Interestingly, the show does a direct sequel to this episode the following season with "Course: Oblivion."

Did you know? This episode features Voyager landing on a planet for the first time since Season Two. Back then, the CGI team accidentally made the ship too small. This time, the effects team spent extra time to make sure the ship would be the exact size it should be according to the published specifications.

"One": C+

After the rest of the crew is placed in suspended animation to protect them from dangerous radiation, the immune Seven is placed in control of the ship.

Air date: May 13, 1998
Written by Jeri Taylor
Directed by Kenneth Biller
TV rating: 3.9

"Once when I was a drone, I was separated from the collective for two hours. I experienced panic and apprehension. I am feeling that way now." —Seven

This attempt at a mind-bending Seven episode is more pedestrian than it wants to be but serves as a nice character piece for *VOY's* resident Borg nonetheless.

Based on a pitch by Jim Swallow, a writer for various *Star Trek* magazines, the idea here is sort of a sanitized adaptation of *The Shining*, with Seven having to deal with being alone while simultaneously suffering from hallucinations. The latter mostly manifests itself in the form of people, allowing the regulars and guest star Wade Williams to play parts that voice Seven's own internal thoughts and fears while Jeri Ryan acts up a storm, running the gamut of Borg emotions.

Unfortunately, the story itself doesn't quite reach the bar set by *TNG's* "Frame of Mind," but the plot does give Ryan a good chance to develop her character further, and Taylor and Biller help her successfully mine the territory to make the episode a worthwhile endeavor.

ENT does a similar story in its Season Three episode "Doctor's Orders," in which Doctor Phlox must put the crew in stasis and pilot the ship himself to traverse a transdimensional disturbance.

Did you know? Jim Swallow began submitting unsolicited scripts to *Star Trek* as soon as he heard about the open submissions policy. The pitch for "One" was his first sale. He would go on to sell another, leading to Season Six's "Memorial."

"Hope and Fear": C+

When the Voyager crew discovers a ship that might be able to take them home, Janeway becomes suspicious. (Season finale)

Air date: May 20, 1998
Teleplay by Brannon Braga & Joe Menosky
Story by Rick Berman, Brannon Braga & Joe Menosky
Directed by Winrich Kolbe
TV rating: 4.1

"All of this is just a little too perfect. The alien genius with the answers to all our problems. A message from Starfleet telling us everything we want to hear. A starship delivered right to our doorstep. What more could we ask for? They even turned down the beds. The only thing missing was chocolates on the pillows."
—Janeway

Employing a loose thread from "Hunters," the *VOY* writing staff once again teases the ship's crew with an opportunity to get back home in this standalone season finale featuring guest star Ray Wise.

As in several previous episodes, a conflict between Janeway and Seven takes center stage before they must find a way to work together—this time to foil an evil genius's convoluted revenge plot. (Janeway initially frames the possible way home as something to hope for while Seven defines it as something to fear, causing each to develop different agendas until a plot twist forces them to redefine their priorities and learn about themselves in the process.)

With this being the final episode of the season and with Rick Berman's name in the credits for the first time since the first episode of the series, there was initially a lot of anticipation for this episode, with some fans speculating Voyager would finally get back to the Alpha Quadrant. (This is even teased in the episode's preview.) However, in truth, Berman's name is only in the credits because Braga and Menosky were having trouble with their story and took some of Berman's advice to help complete it. And with the low-budget episode as a whole failing to live up to the high expectations fans have for a season finale, "Hope and Fear" is often labeled a disappointment. But as a Janeway/Seven character piece, it's not so bad.

Did you know? Ray Wise previously appeared in *TNG's* Season Three episode "Who Watches the Watchers" as a Mintakan who believes "The Picard" is a god.

130

Roxann Dawson's pregnancy forcing the directors to find ways to disguise her growing baby bump, and the male actors (minus Robert Picardo) gaining weight as well, thanks to an on-set buffet table, with Brannon Braga slyly adding some dialogue to acknowledge the situation.

But the train rolled on, nonetheless, with everyone working hard to keep up with the weekly schedule. To help keep this train on its tracks, Kenneth Biller was promoted to producer and made his directorial debut with "Revulsion" before also directing "One," while Bryan Fuller, who had sold a couple stories to *DS9*, helped shore up the writing staff and Lousie Dorton was promoted to art director.

In the end, the season was vindicated with a ratings boost thanks in part to increased press coverage and thanks to many fans tuning in specifically to see the new character in her numerous form-fitting catsuits. Meanwhile Mulgrew won two significant awards, beating out Gillian Anderson (*The X-Files*), Kim Delaney (*NYPD Blue*), Julianna Margulies (*ER*), and Ally Walker (*Profiler*) for Best Actress in a Drama Series at the second Golden Satellite Awards, and topping Gillian Anderson, Ally Walker, Sarah Michelle Gellar (*Buffy the Vampire Slayer*), Peta Wilson (*La Femme Nikita*), and *VOY's* own Jeri Ryan for Best Genre TV Actress at the 24th Saturn Awards. Robert Beltran and Roxann Dawson also saw their good work recognized, with both being nominated in separate categories at the American Latino Media Arts Awards. At the same time, the show's crew was nominated for two more Emmys, one for hairstyling and another for visual effects.

For *VOY*, the success meant the show would continue. But this would have to happen without the day-to-day efforts of co-creator Jeri Taylor, who decided to step down as showrunner after Season Four and pass the baton to someone else, though she would remain a creative consultant for the show's final three seasons.

Season Five

Production Order
(with air date order in parentheses)

1. "Night" (1st)
2. "Drone" (2nd)
3. "Extreme Risk" (3rd)
4. "In the Flesh" (4th)
5. "Once Upon a Time" (5th)
6. "Nothing Human" (8th)
7. "Timeless" (6th)
8. "Thirty Days" (9th)
9. "Infinite Regress" (7th)
10. "Counterpoint" (10th)
11. "Gravity" (11th)
12. "Latent Image" (11th)
13. "Bride of Chaotica!" (12th)
14. "The Fight" (18th)
15. "Bliss" (14th)
16. "The Disease" (16th)
17. "Dark Frontier" (15th)
18. "Course: Oblivion" (17th)
19. "Think Tank" (19th)
20. "Juggernaut" (20th)
21. "Someone to Watch Over Me" (21st)
22. "11:59" (22nd)
23. "Relativity" (23rd)
24. "Warhead" (24th)
25. "Equinox" (25th)

The Fifth Season Cast

Captain Janeway: Kate Mulgrew
Commander Chakotay: Robert Beltran
B'Elanna Torres: Roxann Dawson
Tom Paris: Robert Duncan McNeill
Neelix: Ethan Phillips
The Doctor: Robert Picardo
Tuvok: Tim Russ
Harry Kim: Garrett Wang
Seven of Nine: Jeri Ryan

Notable Guest Stars

Martin Rayner
Ken Magee
Steven Dennis
J. Paul Boehmer
Alexander Enberg
Ray Walston
Kate Vernon
Nancy Hower
Scarlett Pomers
Wallace Langham
LeVar Burton
David Clennon
Alissa Krämer
Heidi Krämer
Warren Munson
Mark Harelik
Randy Oglesby
Nancy Bell
Joseph Ruskin
Lori Petty
W. Morgan Sheppard
Susanna Thompson
Musetta Vander
Jason Alexander
Kevin Tighe
John Savage
Titus Welliver

"Night": C+

When Voyager enters a void devoid of reference points, the crew struggles to adapt.

Air date: October 14, 1998
Teleplay by Brannon Braga & Joe Menosky
Directed by David Livingston
TV rating: 3.7

"I guess mass murder doesn't factor into your profit margin." —Torres

Braga and Menosky throw a lot into this episode, though they're unable to find a direction for anything until the second half. We have Paris trying to interest others in a black and white sci-fi serial holodeck program, Janeway, regretful of her decision in "Caretaker" and unwilling to socialize with the crew, Neelix suffering from panic attacks due to nihiliphobia, and some dark-matter-like aliens suffering when another group of aliens, the Malon, dump toxic waste in their space.

The backdrop for it all is a region of space with seemingly nothing in it, which the writers treat as a metaphor for a sailing ship on a calm sea with no wind—the scariest weather of all. It's not a very good metaphor, since Voyager doesn't require anything to propel it, and Janeway and company are far better off self-entertaining than dealing with an attacking ship, whatever comments they make in this episode to the contrary. But the concept probably scares the writers plenty, since the show itself does rely on good stories to keep it going.

When Braga and Menosky finally do find a direction, thanks to the aliens' "not in my backyard" squabble, the two writers are able to take all the different threads and weave them into the plot in a respectable way that pays off each story in one way or another. But you still have to wonder why such an episode needs a hodgepodge of so many different elements. The whole thing comes across as seeming more like the writers experimenting with different ideas as opposed to everyone coming together to present a polished product that honors a core concept.

Regardless, "Night" has enough in it to remain engaging throughout and only becomes more interesting as it progresses, making up for whatever flaws it has in design. In particular, the idea of an alien waste industry being afraid of technology that could put it out of business, regardless of the good it would do for a culture as a whole, makes for compelling drama, with guest star Ken Magee giving the episode just what it needs, playing a character that serves as the focal point of the issue.

Did you know? For *TNG's* "The Big Goodbye," the writer and director wanted Picard's Dixon Hill holodeck scenes to be shot in black and white, but Rick Berman wouldn't allow it, arguing that the holodeck couldn't change the colors of the real crewmembers. By the time of *VOY*, Berman felt it was an artistic license *Star Trek* could get away with.

"Drone": C+

A transporter malfunction results in the creation of a Borg..

Air date: October 21, 1998
Teleplay by Bryan Fuller, Brannon Braga & Joe Menosky
Story by Bryan Fuller and Harry Doc Kloor
Directed by Les Landau
TV rating: 3.7

"A drone, but unlike any I've ever seen." —Seven

J. Paul Boehmer guest stars as the titular character, a newborn Borg, in this suspenseful Seven episode that comes across as a hybrid of *TNG's* "The Offspring" and "I Borg."

The idea here is that Seven and The Doctor, with the unwitting help of an ensign, accidentally have a child, thanks to a mishap that merges some of Seven's Borg nanoprobes with The Doctor's mobile emitter and the ensign's DNA. After discussing the possibility of aborting the new life-form, the Voyager crew, led by Seven, instead attempt to raise the Borg drone and teach him right from wrong.

Boehmer, who previously appeared as a German Schutzstaffel officer in "The Killing Game," is quite good as a blank page, with his Borg character both curious and confused as a frightened crew learns how to interact with him while simultaneously attempting to keep the collective unaware of his presence. Meanwhile, the writers deserve credit for fleshing out the drone's story in a unique way, realizing he's not a true Borg, and taking advantage of opportunities to set him apart from the drones we've met in the past. (The make-up people drive home the point as well, since they don't have to worry about putting the poor guy in the same prosthetics ever again and can go all out designing a unique look.)

In the end, however, like the best *Star Trek* episodes, the whole purpose here is to hold up a mirror to allow us to view humanity through outside eyes, with this episode using a literal version of the mirror as its bookends.

Did you know? Boehmer would go on to play a Cardassian in *DS9's* "Tacking into the Wind," a Vulcan in *VOY's* "Carbon Creek," and another SS officer in *ENT's* "Zero Hour" and "Storm Front."

"Extreme Risk": B+

While the crew races to build a new shuttle, Torres immerses herself in dangerous holodeck programs.

Air date: October 28, 1998
Teleplay by Kenneth Biller
Directed by Cliff Bole
TV rating: 3.6

"According to the holodeck logs, you've been spending a lot of time there over the last few months. If I were to check, would I find that you've been running other programs without safety protocols?" —Janeway

VOY expertly balances a miniature space race ensemble story with a self-harm individual story in this Torres episode about the engineer becoming increasingly apathetic amidst another encounter with the Malon, the toxic waste dumpers introduced in "Night."

Of the two stories, the mini space race gets going the quickest and is most likely to excite the audience. When the aliens attempt to steal one of Voyager's probes, it gets stuck in the atmosphere of a gas giant, and the aliens and Voyager both race to complete a shuttle that's capable of retrieving it. With most of the main characters contributing something to the design of Voyager's version, the Delta Flyer, it leads to some rich character interplay from just about everyone...everyone except for Torres, who's an old stick in the mud. (Viewers can be forgiven if they become frustrated with her, since it seems as if the crew has stumbled upon a great idea, and Torres, the chief engineer, doesn't want to involve herself in it.) This, of course, leads to the introduction of the Delta Flyer itself, with its exterior look and interior set both being welcome additions to the show.

But it's the Torres plot that sneaks up on you and gives the episode greater meaning when Janeway begins to figure out what's going on and Chakotay is forced to conduct an intervention. The climax itself, a faux jeopardy mission that simultaneously ties up both plots, is nothing more than a paint-by-numbers action sequence similar to what we've seen many times in the past, with shades of "The Galileo Seven," not to mention *MacGyver*. But the idea of a *Star Trek* regular suffering through so many losses that she begins to shut down to shut out any more grief is new, and it's well played by Dawson, who gives perhaps her best performance of the series.

Did you know? This episode's opening sequence, featuring Torres skydiving from space, is similar to a scene cut from the beginning of *Star Trek: Generations* in which Captain Kirk does the same. In fact, Roxann Dawson uses the space suit costume originally made for William Shatner for that film. In 2012, Felix Baumgartner needed a real space suit for his jump from what the media described as "the edge of space," though this was not really correct. (NASA and the Federal Aviation Administration both consider space to begin about 330,000 feet, or 62 miles, above sea level.) Baumgartner's capsule, however, did achieve an altitude of 128,000 feet, allowing him to break Colonel Joseph Kittinger's 52 year old record for highest jump. Baumgartner's record, however, was surpassed in 2014 by Alan Eustace, who jumped from 135,908 feet.

(Photo courtesy of Felix Baumgartner)

139

"In the Flesh": C+

Voyager finds a planet in the Delta Quadrant with a recreation of Starfleet Command and Starfleet Academy.

Air date: November 4, 1998
Teleplay by Nick Sagan
Directed by David Livingston
TV rating: 4.2

"Back in the twentieth century, the Soviets used to build American towns to train their agents to infiltrate the United States. Species 8472 could be doing the same thing." —Paris

Ray Walston steals the show in this Chakotay episode set amidst an alien copy of Starfleet Academy & headquarters, with Walston playing a copy of his groundskeeper character first seen in *TNG's* "The First Duty."

The premise itself allows *VOY* to revisit familiar elements, with the look of Starfleet Academy once again brought to life courtesy of location shooting at the Tillman Water Reclamation Plant. But the plot itself is a Cold War standoff reminiscent of several episodes of *TOS*, with no one trusting each other until an unexpected romance forces everyone to look at the situation through new eyes. In this case, Chakotay and an alien imposter are the centerpiece, carefully dancing around each other's suspicions like James Bond and one of his girls while secretly growing to admire each other.

However, it's Ray Walston, formerly the title character of *My Favorite Martian* (1963–1966), who proves the real treat, playing Boothby's doppelgänger with his usual pragmatic sincerity and eventually engaging in negotiations with Janeway herself, allowing Walston and Mulgrew to show off their chemistry, with Janeway and "Boothby" proving as good a pairing as Boothby and Picard.

Unfortunately, the plot as a whole undermines the previous efforts to establish Species 8472 as a special kind of threat. (The writers would have been wiser to use different aliens intended to be seen only in this episode.) The attempt to humanize the species effectively neuters the race, turning its members into nothing more threatening than Elvis impersonators. As a result, they don't appear in any subsequent episodes of the show.

Walston returns to play yet another incarnation of Boothby later in the season in "The Fight."

Little America (Photo courtesy of Clamshack)

Did you know? When Paris said the Soviets used to build American towns to train their spies, he was correct. During the Cold War, because the Soviet Union had significant travel and entertainment restrictions, most of the people in the country knew little about what life in America was like. To teach potential agents about American culture, the Russian government created spy schools located in specially constructed towns, giving recruits a chance to learn everything from American English to how to use a parking meter before they were sent to the U.S. to pose as Americans and advance a Soviet agenda.

Today, Russia's attempt to infiltrate America continues, though most spies are not sent overseas. Many now use the internet, posing as Americans on social media and spreading misinformation and propaganda from the comfort of their home country in an effort to destabilize the United States culture from within.

"Once Upon a Time": B–

Neelix tries to distract a child while her mother is in danger.

Air date: November 11, 1998
Teleplay by Michael Taylor
Directed by John Krechmer
TV rating: 3.8

"Your mission was to keep her occupied, not to lie to her." —Janeway

VOY pairs Ethan Phillips with child actor Scarlett Pomers in this offbeat episode written by new staff writer Michael Taylor, the author of *DS9's* "The Visitor."

In another disaster plot reminiscent of "The Galileo Seven," the crew of the Delta Flyer crashes into a planetoid, and there doesn't seem to be any way for them to escape. But in a delightful change of pace, that's just the B story. The main plot lies with Neelix and Naomi Wildman, the half-human, half-Ktarian girl born in Season Two. As her mother struggles to survive in the B story, Naomi, now played by Pomers, is given very little information, with Neelix believing it's better to hide the truth from her than to cause her to worry. But being an intuitive, bright child, she worries anyway, and the strategy backfires as her fears manifest in a void with no one to turn to for help.

Tucked inside this plot is a new holodeck program, this one aimed at kids, with elemental characters in a fairytale world such as Flotter, played by William Langham from *The Larry Sanders Show* (1992–1998) and Trevis, played by future *Stargate Universe* star Justin Louis.

Pomers herself would go on to appear in fifteen more episodes of *VOY*, starting with "Infinite Regress," before landing the part of one of the kids in WB's *Reba* (2001–2007).

Did you know? Naomi's Flotter doll, created for this episode, reappears later in the season in "Bliss." In 2006, it sold at auction for $1,560.

"Timeless": A

Kim and Chokatay attempt to undo a mistake that caused Voyager to crash into a frozen planet, killing everyone on board.

Air date: November 18, 1998
Teleplay by Brannon Braga & Joe Menosky
Story by Rick Berman, Brannon Braga & Joe Menosky
Directed by LeVar Burton
TV rating: 4.3

"Mr. Kim, did you ever stop to think about what you're trying to do here? Altering the timeline may make things worse. At least you and Chakotay survived. Why tempt fate?" —The Doctor

This ambitious Harry Kim story, representing *VOY's* 100th hour of television, would be a fantastic season finale and even has enough story to be spread out over two parts—but it works fine as a self-contained episode and remains one of *VOY's* most memorable offerings.

The core concept itself isn't a plot so much as a visual: sometime in the future, Voyager is buried under several meters of ice, and Chakatay and Kim, both visibly older, seek out its resting place, like Bob Ballard searching for the Titanic. From there, the story branches off in two directions, flipping back and forth between Chakotay, Kim, The Doctor, and Chakotay's girlfriend, Tessa, in the future, and Janeway and the crew in the show's present.

The beauty of the hook, of course, is that we get to see an all new look for Voyager, with the different lighting and set dressings completely selling the idea that we're visiting the interior of a frozen, wrecked ship many years after a catastrophic accident. (When Chakotay sits in the command chair and reflects that he hasn't been there for fifteen years, it feels so authentic, it makes for one of the episode's most poignant moments.) Meanwhile, the set for the Delta Flyer, which is still in use in the future, is altered to appropriately reflect the passage of time as well.

But the emotional center of it all lies with Harry Kim, with Garrett Wang giving future-Harry a makeover, showing off a grittier attitude after Kim has endured years of survivor's guilt. (Future-Chakotay also gets a short plot of his own, as he and his girlfriend deal with the fact that their plan to change the past would break up their relationship before it ever begins. This, however, is kept quite short, with the single episode not allowing the writers enough time to develop it into anything significant.) There's also a cameo by the director, with LeVar Burton reprising Geordi La Forge, though his part could have been filled by any other actor playing any Starfleet captain.

Nonetheless, the pieces of the episode, including some stunning special effects, are confidently put together, giving the whole thing an "All Good Things" quality, if on a smaller scale. *VOY* would go on to mine a similar story for its finale.

"Timeless" would go on to be nominated for an Emmy for visual effects.

Did you know? The show's crew spent a week preparing Voyager's frozen bridge while the actors were given the time off. After three days of shooting scenes set in the future, the bridge set was returned to normal and the sequences set in the show's present were completed. "There were some serious challenges in terms of freezing some of the permanent sets and then having to turn them around and shoot them normal," LeVar Burton recalls. "That was really hard on the art department and set dressers."

"Infinite Regress": C–

The discovery of a piece of Borg technology causes Seven to develop multiple personalities.

Air date: November 25, 1998
Teleplay by Robert J. Doherty
Story by Robert J. Doherty & Jimmy Diggs
Directed by David Livingston
TV rating: 3.3

"Seven, you were a Borg drone who's now becoming an individual. That's practically unheard of. There's bound to be rough spots along the way. We just have to get past them." —The Doctor

This vehicle for Jeri Ryan sees Seven develop a dissociative identity disorder, allowing the actress to play several different characters throughout the course of the hour. Less abstract than *TNG's* similarly themed "Masks," this one uses former victims of the Borg to flesh out its idea, including a Klingon, a Ferengi and a human. Unfortunately, the idea, which probably could have been done on its own without the need of a tech explanation due to Seven's Borg nature, is saddled with Jimmy Diggs's idea of a Borg vinculum—a Borg processing device that interconnects the minds of all the Borg drones, disseminating information relevant to the Collective. This newly introduced concept supplies the episode with an overload of technobabble (ghost-written by Brannon Braga) and leads to a squabble with some random aliens, ultimately becoming more important to the plot itself than Ryan's good work, which is a shame.

Did you know? "Infinite regress" is a term for a sequence of reasoning or justification which can never come to an end, with a skeptic (or child) asking "why?" after every explanation. One of the more humorous examples of infinite regress escape is a famous anecdote. When a scientist gave a public lecture on astronomy, a little old lady at the back of the room got up and said: "What you have told us is rubbish. The world is really a flat plate supported on the back of a giant tortoise." The scientist replied, "What is the tortoise standing on?" "You're very clever, young man," she replied, "but it's turtles all the way down."

"Nothing Human": C–

When a wounded alien creature attaches itself to Torres, The Doctor creates a hologram of a notorious Cardassian exobiologist to assist in its removal.

Air date: December 2, 1998
Written by Jeri Taylor
Directed by David Livingston
TV rating: 4.1

"I had a bad feeling about that hologram the second I saw him." —Torres

So this week on *VOY*, we meet a new type of alien in a scaled down version of the alien space-baby plot from *TNG's* "Galaxy's Child." But the real story here is about The Doctor and his new holographic created to help him with the situation: a representation of a Cardassian specialist who, much like Nazi Josef Mengele, did unspeakable things to his patients to learn more about medicine. Inside this dual framework, the writers unpack a number of uncomfortable questions about medical ethics, including the morality of present people benefiting from inhumane medical testing from the past and the question of overriding a patient's wishes, with Janeway and The Doctor forced to choose whether to use the knowledge of the holographic Cardassian to save Torres's life over her objections—which leads to quite an argument in the briefing room as well, allowing everyone else to weigh in.

David Clennon, best known for his Emmy-nominated portrayal of Miles Drentell in ABC's *Thirtysomething* and also known for playing lunar geology instructor Lee Silver in HBO's *From the Earth to the Moon*, plays the holographic character with his distinctive tenor voice and compelling mannerisms. But there's not much more to this one that sets it apart from the other medical dilemma episodes that pepper *Star Trek's* history.

Did you know? David Clennon and Robert Picardo had been good friends for many years before working together here.

"Thirty Days": B–

While spending thirty days in the brig, Paris reflects upon the events that led him to his imprisonment.

Air date: December 9, 1998
Teleplay by Kenneth Biller
Story by Scott Miller
Directed by Winrich Kolbe
TV rating: 4.2

"Lieutenant Thomas Eugene Paris. You are guilty of insubordination, unauthorized use of a spacecraft, reckless endangerment, and conduct unbecoming an officer. Do you have anything to say?" —Janeway

Like *TNG's* "Suspicions," this Paris episode uses a framing device to allow a character to reflect upon a sequence of events that led to an insubordinate decision.

This time, the issue is an ecological problem on an artificial world of water that some aliens have commandeered. This gives us some interesting science fiction paired with some beautiful visuals, but the plot really kicks into gear when it becomes more about the dichotomistic reactions to the situation. To keep it all a ship-based episode with minimal characters, the writers limit the planet's visible inhabitants to two representatives who visit Voyager to ask for help: Burkus, a deputy consul played by prolific TV guest star Benjamin Livingston, and Riga, a meek scientist played by the equally prolific Willie Garson. But that's enough to flesh out the conflict. The politically savvy Burkus wants to postpone a response to the problem to avoid disrupting anyone's lives, but Riga fears they don't have the time. As the conflict develops, it's Paris, of course, who gets mixed up in it all.

Along the way, Biller weaves in another appearance of Paris's black and white Captain Proton holodeck program, using it to finally introduce the oft-mentioned Delaney sisters, played by former Doublemint twins Alissa and Heidi Krämer. (They do not appear again.) But with the episode ending at just about the same point where it begins, the main story can't deliver any more sense of danger or surprise than the holodeck simulation itself, dampening what's otherwise a good offering.

"Thirty Days" went on to be nominated for an Emmy for visual effects and won the International Monitor Award for electronic effects.

Did you know? The framing device was added to this episode after its initial run time fell ten minutes short of what was necessary.

"Counterpoint": B–

While Voyager smuggles telepathic refugees through hostile space, Janeway becomes involved with the alien whose job it is to find them.

Air date: December 16, 1998
Written by Michael Taylor
Directed by Les Landau
TV rating: 3.4

"Your culture has many contradictions. Violence and beauty, science and faith, all somehow mingled harmoniously. Like the counterpoint of this music."
—Kashyk

In this episode that's part underground railroad and part spy story, Kate Mulgrew teams up with Mark Harelik to create a romantic relationship between Captain Janeway, hell-bent on smuggling a persecuted group of aliens to freedom, and Kashyk, the inspector in charge of finding them, amidst a backdrop of their shared love of classical music.

With Voyager in Kashyk's space, it allows the show to create a Nazi-like region with surprise inspections that no Federation ship in the Alpha Quadrant would have to tolerate. The fact is, Voyager is alone and while resistance might not be futile, it must be done with care—subtly and quietly. Inside this framework, Janeway and Kashyk grow closer while carefully dancing around their suspicions, never really winning each other's trust or tipping their full hands. Mulgrew is at her best, giving a multi-layered performance that sees her doing what must be done while simultaneously attempting to open a door for Kashyk to escape the totalitarian state he lives in. But does he really want to leave, or is it all a ruse?

Unfortunately, Mark Harelik is no Piers Brosnan and is unable to equal Mulgrew's performance, lacking the suave ambiguity his character really needs to make the plot unpredictable and truly compelling.

Did you know? Mulgrew has cited this as her favorite *VOY* episode, and it is even included in a DVD set celebrating the *Star Trek* captains.

"Latent Image": B–

The Doctor discovers his memory files have been tampered with.

Air date: January 20, 1999
Teleplay by Joe Menosky
Story by Eileen Connors, Brannon Braga & Joe Menosky
Directed by Mike Vejar
TV rating: 3.8

"You're conspiring against me. All of you. Why?" —The Doctor

Reminiscent of *TNG's* "Clues," "Latent Image" begins as a mystery episode where it seems something has been covered up, and when the truth is discovered, the crew finds itself back in the same dilemma the cover-up was meant to solve.

At its heart, "Image" is a Doctor episode about a quasi-human computer program asked to make a choice with no right answers, and the feedback loop that can develop after such an event. It's a story that could have been done with Data on *TNG*, or maybe in Spock on *TOS*, but it probably works best with The Doctor on *VOY* because of the three, he's easily the most willing to wear his heart on his sleeve.

Picardo makes the most of it, running the gamut of distressed emotions throughout the hour before an ambiguous ending. As a mystery, it's not quite as rich as "Clues." As a character study, however, it's one of the better Doctor episodes.

Did you know? Most of the cast and crew felt Joe Menosky's original, less ambiguous ending to this episode was better than Brannon Braga's rewrite.

"Bride of Chaotica!": B–

Lieutenant Paris and his shipmates must play out a Captain Proton holodeck scenario to save the day.

Air date: January 27, 1999
Teleplay by Bryan Fuller & Michael Taylor
Story by Bryan Fuller
Directed by Mike Vejar
TV rating: 4.0

"And so, my dear, the day you have always dreamed of has arrived. The day you become Bride of Chaotica!" —Chaotica

Star Trek pays homage to Flash Gordon in this malfunctioning holodeck episode, complete with old style bass-free music, in a story featuring Paris's alter-ego, Captain Proton, first introduced in "Night."

Proton himself is almost a periphery character in it all, but with almost everyone getting in on the fun, this is the holonovel's most substantial and memorable appearance in the series. There are even some new "photonic" aliens who get mixed up in it all, with the writers using ample technobabble to tie everything together.

In the end, however, like the old 1930s installments of Flash Gordon, the charm of it all is in the main plot's simplicity and predictability, with Captain "Flash Gordon" Proton doing what he does best.

Did you know? This episode was written to allow time for the bridge set to be repaired after a fire.

"Gravity": B

When Voyager's away team crashes on a planet, Tuvok meets an alien woman who takes a liking to him.

Air date: February 3, 1999
Teleplay by Nick Sagan & Bryan Fuller
Story by Jimmy Diggs, Bryan Fuller & Nick Sagan
Directed by Terry Windell
TV rating: 4.0

"I am sorry. I cannot return your affection." —Tuvok

This Tuvok episode, like a mashup of *TOS's* "The Galileo Seven" and "All Our Yesterdays," sees Tuvok, Paris and The Doctor stranded on a planet of mercenaries, forcing them to accept the help of a young alien lady.

Lori Petty, best known for her distinctive parts in *Point Break* (1991) and *A League of Their Own* (1992), plays Noss, the shy loner who struggles with an unrequited crush on Mr. Vulcan. Petty, who has a quirky quality to her, is certainly one of the more memorable one-off guest stars on the show, imbuing her character with an infectious enthusiasm laced with vulnerability. Meanwhile, Russ, McNeill, and Picardo honor their lanes, with Russ playing out the philosophical crisis, McNeill giving him a buddy to talk to, and The Doctor intermittently appearing to offer a detached outsider's perspective. In a way, it's all paint-by-numbers *VOY*, but the producers help them by filling out the character-based hour with plenty of location shooting at the Vasquez Rocks to help break up the inherent claustrophobia on a show primarily set aboard a spaceship, with freshman director Terry Windell proving himself worthy of the extra expense.

As for the ship itself, Janeway gets a B story that's simply there to serve as a countdown clock, with some obstinate aliens, who seem to have attended the Tholian school of alien adversity training, giving Janeway only so much time to mount a rescue mission.

Did you know? In flashback sequences that appear throughout the episode, Joseph Ruskin plays a Vulcan master. Ruskin previously appeared in *TOS* ("The Gamesters of Triskelion), *DS9* ("The House of Quark," "Improbable Cause," and "Looking for par'Mach in All the Wrong Places,") and *Star Trek: Insurrection* (1998). He would go on to guest star on *ENT* in "Broken Bow." He passed away in 2013 at age 89.

"Bliss": C

While the rest of the crew celebrates the discovery of a possible shortcut home, Seven suspects it might be a trap.

Air date: February 10, 1999
Teleplay by Robert J. Doherty
Story by Bill Prady
Directed by Cliff Bole
TV rating: 3.9

"I believe the crew is being deceived by false telemetry as well as overly-optimistic correspondence." —Seven

Like a combination of *TNG's* "The Game" and *TOS's* "The Immunity Syndrome," this Seven episode is part psychological thriller and part monster story.

The central idea here is that it's easier to fool people than to convince them they've been fooled—especially once they've bought into something they want to believe is true. When all evidence points to the fact that the *VOY* crew is about to return home and its members will have everything they want, Seven faces an uphill battle trying to inject a little skepticism into it all. Worse yet, she can't even trust herself! When it turns out that the whole thing is an interstellar Venus fly trap, she begins questioning her own senses when they attempt to mislead her as she tries to escape.

Unfortunately, writer Robert Doherty merely scratches the surface of these issues, failing to dig deep enough to create a truly meaningful episode, though guest star W. Morgan Sheppard, after appearing as Data's "Grandpa" in *TNG's* "The Schizoid Man" and a Klingon Commandant in *Star Trek VI: The Undiscovered Country* (1991), gives the story some depth with a fine performance as Qatai, a Captain Ahab-like pilot obsessed with killing the creature. (Even Qatai, however, is shortchanged by Doherty, getting little more to do than to spout some exposition and serve as a helping hand.)

In the end, it's all just another day at the office for Seven and the *VOY* gang, which is unfortunate because it could have been more.

Did you know? London-born W. Morgan Sheppard would go on to play a Vulcan science minister in 2009's *Star Trek* film. He died ten years later at age 86.

"Dark Frontier": B

Captain Janeway devises a plan to steal a transwarp coil from a damaged Borg sphere.

Air date: February 17, 1999
Written by Brannon Braga & Joe Menosky
Directed by Cliff Bole & Terry Windell
TV rating: 4.7

"I think it's time to do a little assimilating of our own." —Janeway

This two-hour special—with the first half directed by Bole and the second half directed by Windell—is a big-budget Borg episode featuring a power struggle between Janeway and the Borg Queen over Seven's soul. And while it's not as groundbreaking as "The Best of Both Worlds" or as ambitious as *Star Trek: First Contact*, as a *VOY* episode, it carefully balances enough intriguing elements to stand out from the crowd.

Similar to "Gravity," where the writers intercut scenes from Tuvok's youth with his present, this episode give us a complete portrait of Seven, with the writers cleverly creating a narrative that weaves scenes from her youth, chronicling her parents' secret observations of the Borg, with her present dilemma, which stems from Voyager's plan to attempt a daring heist to steal Borg technology. The two stories, sharing clandestine overtones, parallel each other nicely before metaphorically folding in on one another as push comes to shove and Seven has to choose whom to help and whom to betray.

Unfortunately, with Alice Krige unavailable to reprise the Borg Queen, we get Susanna Thompson, who unsuccessfully auditioned for the same part for *Star Trek: First Contact*. Thompson, who had some bit parts on *TNG* and played Dax's former wife in an episode of *DS9*, is an adequate actress but lacks the same vitality Krige brings to the Borg. On the other hand, anime voice artist Kirk Baily and sci-fi character actress Laura Stepp are both fantastic as Seven's parents, even if the writers are forced to reinvent Federation/Borg history to accommodate their story. (And there's more where that came from! The Borg Queen declares that Seven is the first Borg to regain her individuality, though several episodes of *TNG* and *VOY's* own "Unity" would beg to differ.) But "Dark Frontier" succeeds nonetheless, thanks in part to some of the greatest ship battles of its time and a feature film-like score to back them up.

"Dark Frontier" won an Emmy for visual effects.

Did you know? The idea of airing a special two-hour episode in the middle of a season was inspired by the success of "The Killing Game." Season Seven would follow suit with "Flesh and Blood."

"The Disease": C+

Harry Kim breaks Starfleet regulations when he falls in love with an alien woman.

Air date: February 24, 1999
Teleplay by Michael Taylor
Story by Kenneth Biller
Directed by David Livingston
TV rating: 3.4

"You make it sound like a disease!" —Kim

As Voyager attempts to assist a xenophobic generational ship, the writers unpack a couple issues stemming from the interactions between the two ships.

Foremost, we have Harry Kim, who ignores all that he learned at Starfleet Academy during his semester of interspecies protocol and all that's in the three-centimeter-thick Starfleet Handbook on Personal Relationships—most notably that all Starfleet Personnel must obtain authorization from their commanding officer, as well as clearance from their medical officer, before initiating an intimate relationship with an alien species. (These are some very specific regulations that have curiously never been mentioned before this episode.) Anyway, after getting it on with an alien-lady, Kim becomes "biochemically linked" to her, and now the two of them must stay together forever, or they'll become ill. (Next time, use protection, Harry!)

Meanwhile, both ships fall victim to saboteurs from the generational crew who don't like the life they've been forced into. (And guess who the head saboteur is?)

The whole thing creates a rare conflict between Kim and Janeway, with Wang and Mulgrew playing up the delicious drama. But the idea of pairing a multi-species love story with a ship-in-peril plot is *Star Trek* at its most vanilla, and the episode never breaks out of the usual mold for stories of this kind.

Did you know? The first *Star Trek* actor I ever met was Garrett Wang, and it was almost by accident. I was at a somewhat poorly run convention shortly after *Star Trek: Voyager* had started up, and because of problems with autograph lines in years past, the convention organizers were trying out something new: giving out a limited number of autograph tickets to fans who wanted them, rather than just asking fans to wait in line and take their chances. Thus, the convention staff would no longer have to cut off the lines at some point, angering people who had waited hours to meet their favorite celebrity. The way it worked was like this: the tickets were given at random times to kiosks located throughout the convention hall, and when a fan asked for a ticket at the kiosks, he or she was given one if any were available. When I got to there, I was excited about the idea of meeting the cast of *Mystery Science Theater 3000*, which was already preparing to meet their fans as I arrived. But when I approached a kiosk to ask if any tickets were available, the woman working the station said, "No, there aren't any left. But would you like a ticket for Garrett Wang? I just got them in." I said, "Sure!" and got one of those. Then the woman, who was very nice, said, "You know, sometimes our guests will hang around and sign extra autographs. If you want to wait until the line is clear and ask the person in charge if you can meet them, you might get lucky." I thanked her, and I did just as she recommended. After the *MST3K* line had cleared, I said to the convention volunteer in charge, "I'm sorry, I don't have a ticket, but I was wondering if..." and before I could get any further, she started yelling at me. "If you *don't* have a ticket, I can't do anything for you!" And then, continuing to yell as if I was fifty feet away, rather than right next to her, she said, "And you've got to get out of here *right now* because I'm starting the line for Garrett Wang." I said (almost to myself), but I have a ticket to see Mr. Wang." And simultaneously, since everyone within a stone's throw could hear her and there were a lot of people with tickets lurking about waiting to get the best place in line, suddenly about fifty people were jockeying for position, lining up behind me. At that point, the woman scowled at me and proceeded to walk down the line checking to see if everyone else had a ticket. She was then replaced by a very nice woman who took charge of the front of the line, ultimately being the one to tell us when it was time to step up to Mr. Wang's table. Of course, it took a few minutes for Wang and his helper to appear and prepare for the fans, so this woman and I chatted in the meantime. She told me that the guy helping Wang was Mike Russ, the brother of Tim Russ, and that everyone always ignored him so it would be nice if I could say hi. I promised her I would, and then when everything was ready, the first thing I did was walk up to Mike, seated alongside "Harry" and said, "Hello, Mr. Russ!" And he...did nothing. He just kept looking over my shoulder at the people lined up. At first, I wasn't sure if he was ignoring me, but I figured I'd move on, so I then turned to Garrett Wang and said, "Hello, Mr. Wang!" That's when Wang elbowed Russ and said, "Hello, Mr. Russ, he's talking to you!" Russ, who apparently was just zoning out, said, "What?" and Wang said, "He said, 'Hello, Mr. Russ!'" The great thing is that it served as a bit of an icebreaker, with Wang having a laugh over it and the three of us enjoying a bit of banter before Wang gave me his autograph and we said goodbye. It was all a lot of fun, and all the better for not having to wait in line! (Unfortunately for the convention itself, the kiosk idea proved highly unpopular and was dropped in the future, ultimately replaced by a new fangled technology called the internet.)

155

"Course: Oblivion": B

As Voyager crewmembers begin dying, they make a startling discovery about their true identities.

Air date: March 3, 1999
Teleplay by Bryan Fuller & Nick Sagan
Story by Bryan Fuller
Directed by Anson Williams
TV rating: 3.7

"I guess the honeymoon's off." —Torres

Anson "Potsie" Williams, director of Season Four's "Demon," returns to direct a sequel in which a duplicate of Voyager's crew comes to grips with the fact that they aren't the real deal.

As a bottle episode with no guest stars, Williams relies on the regulars to anchor the drama, and they come through with fine performances, as each of the characters reevaluates who they are and what their relationships with each other really mean. ("But you're not really a captain! You're a biomimetic life-form created in Janeway's image.") Meanwhile, the writers, enjoying a rare opportunity for carte blanche, have fun taking the script in unexpected directions and killing off crewmembers at will. The real star of the day, however, might be the make-up artist, with Suzanne Diaz, a former *DS9* make-up lady who joined *VOY* in Season Five, taking the crew from healthy to goo inside an hour.

All in all, "Course" is the rare sequel that surpasses its prequel—though some fans might find it underwhelming to see so little of the real Voyager crew.

Did you know? Suzanne Diaz, who began her career as a model, went on to do the make-up for *The Hunger Games* (2012).

"The Fight": C–

When Voyager is caught in chaotic space, Chakotay hallucinates that he's having a boxing match.

Air date: March 24, 1999
Teleplay by Joe Menosky
Story by Michael Taylor
Directed by Winrich Kolbe
TV rating: 4.1

"I'm filing a grievance with the Delta Quadrant Boxing Commission. This bout came out of nowhere." —Neelix

This Chakotay episode is basically a redo of *TNG's* "Night Terrors" but with boxing matches in place of "one moon circles" as *VOY* attempts to escape the anomaly of the week with some help from some abstract aliens.

Inside Taylor and Menosky's offbeat story, Ray Walston plays another version of Boothby, the Starfleet groundskeeper, serving as Chakotay's cornerman in the fights, which gives the former *My Favorite Martian* actor the opportunity to impart life lessons between each round while Chakotay attempts to interpret the advice to save the ship.

There's something intriguing about the idea of an alien species so far outside mankind's frame of reference that it takes a surreal journey inside one's self just to learn to communicate with them, and Chakotay's the perfect choice for such a quest. Unfortunately, the episode fails to develop this core idea into anything new (other than the idea of boxing), content to be more about imagery than substance, and falls somewhat flat as a result.

Did you know? Ray Walston makes his final *Star Trek* appearance in this episode. Walston died on New Year's Day in 2001 at 86 years old.

"Think Tank": C–

A group of intelligent aliens offers to help Voyager escape from a race of bounty hunters in exchange for Seven of Nine.

Air date: March 31, 1999
Teleplay by Michael Taylor
Story by Rick Berman & Brannon Braga
Directed by Terrence O'Hara
TV rating: 3.7

"Our think tank is nearby. A modest vessel. I have come to offer our help with your Hazari paradox." —Kurros

Jason Alexander of *Seinfeld* fame guest stars as the spokesperson for a group of aliens who roam the Delta Quadrant solving people's problems in exchange for something they want. And wouldn't you know it? The Voyager crew has a problem, and the ship has something they want: Seven of Nine.

Alexander, who won an Emmy for his portrayal of the neurotic George Constanza, plays Kurros, an intellectual who is everything George is not. As the cerebral character attempts to negotiate with an uncooperative Janeway, the plot weaves together several familiar elements. We get some hostile, hardheaded baddies who refuse to listen to reason, we're introduced to an interesting bit of holographic technology reminiscent of that seen in *DS9's* "For the Uniform," and we even have Seven once again having to make a decision whether to stay with the ship or not. What's unique this time is that all these elements are packaged inside a battle of wits between Voyager and the "think tank" aliens, which gives the episode the potential to step outside *VOY's* usual box and give us a witty matchup filled with mind games and one-up-manship.

Unfortunately, the writers aren't up to the task, mailing in the story's development and failing to give the aliens the shrewdness they deserve. The concept itself is still good enough to make the episode watchable, but with a lack of complexity this kind of story demands, the episode's grasp fails to meet its reach, and Voyager might as well be in simple shootout with the Hirogen or the Malon instead.

Did you know? At one point, Jason Alexander was having such trouble with his technical dialogue, he slipped back into his George Constanza persona, yelling, "Jerry!"

"Juggernaut": C–

Voyager must stop a damaged freighter from contaminating an entire sector with deadly radiation.

Air date: April 26, 1999
Teleplay by Bryan Fuller, Nick Sagan & Kenneth Biller
Story by Bryan Fuller
Directed by Allan Kroeker
TV rating: 1.7

"If we can't outrun your ship, maybe we can disable it." —Janeway

This Torres episode allows Roxann Dawson to cut loose with her character's edginess and frustration while simultaneously bringing back the polluting Malon for a "Nightmare at 20,000 Feet"-like story that proved to be a ratings dud.

With much of the action taking place on the heavily damaged Malon vessel, director Allan Kroeker stresses style over substance, filling the frame with a lot of smoke, steam, dirt, and grime as the characters move about the sets with weapons at the ready like action heroes. This gives Dawson plenty of opportunities to bring out Torres's Klingon side as Torres sorts through her emotions while she's forced to work with the Malon to prevent an environmental disaster. Meanwhile, Ron Canada, who previously guest starred in *TNG's* "Masterpiece Society" (butting heads with Picard) and *DS9's* "Rules of Engagement" (butting heads with Sisko) finally gets to play a sympathetic character here, embodying a working class alien who's just trying to do a difficult job to help his family and his homeworld.

Still, we've seen Torres's internal battle before, and nobody's asking for more Malon stories. (They do not appear again.) So while "Juggernaut" is an acceptable *VOY* episode for what it is, it can safely be skipped.

Did you know? For this episode, Alexander Enberg, who normally plays the Vulcan Vorik, guest stars as a Malon engineer.

"Someone to Watch Over Me": B+

When The Doctor teaches Seven about dating and romantic relationships, he begins to have feelings for her.

Air date: April 28, 1999
Teleplay by Michael Taylor
Story by Brannon Braga
Directed by Robert Duncan McNeill
TV rating: 3.4

"This could be an important stage in your social development. It's worth exploring." —The Doctor

Seven and The Doctor sing, dance, and date when The Doctor takes Seven under his wing and teaches her about relationships in this character-rich rom-com with strong performances from *VOY's* two breakout stars.

For Robbie McNeill's first Seven episode, the director draws inspiration from *My Fair Lady*, creating a portrait of social experimentation that's simultaneously intriguing, comedic, and sincere. With the usual spatial anomalies and attacking aliens taking the day off, "Someone" counts on the actors to carry the plot, with the subtle nuances in their performances giving the story its zing. This even spills over into a B story where Neelix has his hands full trying to keep a visiting ambassador (played by *Kids in the Hall* alumni Scott Thompson) from over-indulging in pleasure and making a fool of himself.

But it's the chemistry between Robert Picardo and Jeri Ryan that gives the bottle episode its strength, with their comedic talents making each scene a joy to watch even while they develop an undercurrent of poignancy to drive the episode to its emotional conclusion. In fact, by the end, it has arguably surpassed all other *Star Trek* episodes of the type, such as *TNG's* "In Theory" and *VOY's* "Lifesigns," and still stands out today as a Season Five gem.

Did you know? Between his previous *VOY* directorial assignment, "Unity," and this episode, McNeill began directing outside of *Star Trek*, something he felt helped his work here. "It helped me be more comfortable and relaxed on set. It also helped the whole crew and the cast, since they felt, 'Okay, he's a real director, not just an actor on our show who is trying to direct.'" McNeill would go on to direct for many shows, including *Dawson's Creek*, *Desperate Housewives*, *Supernatural*, *The Orville*, and *The Gifted*, as well as *Star Trek's* own *ENT*.

160

"11:59": B+

Captain Janeway reminisces about one of her ancestors.

Air date: May 5, 1999
Teleplay by Joe Menosky
Story by Joe Menosky & Brannon Braga
Directed by David Livingston
TV rating: 3.2

"Shannon O'Donnel inspired me when I was a girl. She had an influence on my imagination, on my goals." —Janeway

This outside the box episode, which features a 400-year-old flashback, joins *TNG's* "The Inner Light" and *DS9's* "Far Beyond the Stars" as one of *Star Trek's* most unique offerings. While Janeway shares a story about the ancestor who inspired her to become a Starfleet captain, we witness the real events, with Kate Mulgrew playing the woman herself, Shannon O'Donnel.

This allows *VOY*, as *TOS* did before it in "Tomorrow is Yesterday," to step into a future which would shortly become the past: December of 2001. The result today plays like an unintended period piece: a look at a world still populated by books, old telephones, and a pre-social media internet with people mass communicating online through chain e-mails. (The only part that's off? The idea that after a big millennial celebration to recognize the year 2000, we would all decide 2001 represented the true start of the millennium and do it all over again. The writers, however, redeem themselves by tucking in a joke about Y2K that would prove to be right on the money.)

But such details are mere minutiae. What's really important is the story, which explores the same theme as Season Four's "Living Witness": that old stories aren't always true. As we see the real events unfold, Mulgrew works with Kevin Tighe and kid actor Bradley Pierce to shape a more pragmatic narrative than Janeway's understanding while John Carroll Lynch plays an adversary who's actually not such a bad guy. Tighe, who has a Gene Roddenberry quality to him, might be better known as John Locke's father from ABC's *Lost*. Pierce's claim to fame at this point was serving as the voice of Chip the teacup for Disney's 1991 *Beauty and the Beast*. And Lynch is best known as Drew Carey's brother, Steve, on ABC's *The Drew Carey Show* (1995–2004). They're all tossed into a unique environment, with a California backlot standing in for a Midwestern town in winter, forcing the set dressers to import something not normally seen in *Star Trek*: snow! (They do such a great job, you can almost feel the cold permeating through your television set.) Just as convincing is an interior set you'd swear is the real deal: a giant bookstore built specifically for the episode. Within these playgrounds, Mulgrew and the guest stars lay out the groundwork for a self-contained story while the regular cast provides them with a frame with scenes set aboard the ship. (*ENT* would later borrow a similar idea for its Season Two offering, "Carbon Creek," which features Jolene Blalock playing an ancestor of her Vulcan character, T'Pol, who visits Earth in 1957.)

To say it's left of center for a franchise more famous for Klingons and space battles would be an understatement. Some viewers might not even recognize it as *Star Trek*. But for *VOY*, the daring departure from the norm pays off, with "11:59" standing out as one of the show's most memorable episodes.

Did you know? Many years after Jeri Taylor, a native of Bloomington, Indiana, chose her birthplace to be the hometown of Captain Janeway, a group called The Bloomington Collective organized a campaign to create a monument for the city to recognize one of their future own. It was officially unveiled on October 24, 2020.

(Photo courtesy of J.W. Braun)

"Relativity": C+

Seven is recruited by a starship from the future to save Voyager from being destroyed.

Air date: May 12, 1999
Teleplay by Bryan Fuller, Nick Sagan & Michael Taylor
Story by Nick Sagan
Directed by Allan Eastman
TV rating: 3.3

"We've brought you here to help us solve a mystery. Someone—we don't know who—has planted a weapon aboard Voyager. It's designed to fracture space-time within a radius of one hundred and fifty meters." —Braxton

This loose sequel to "Future's End" sees Captain Braxton and his ship's crew borrow Seven of Nine for a time traveling mission that allows her to visit Voyager at various points in the past to stop a saboteur from destroying the ship.

This allows the writers, including an uncredited Brannon Braga, to borrow a page from *TNG's* "All Good Things" and show us the events leading up to the pilot episode. And it's not only interesting to see from a character standpoint, it proves a visual feast as well, with our first real look at the Utopia Planitia Fleet Yards.

But as the episode progresses, it increasingly tries to be another time-tinkering escapade similar to "Year of Hell" (with a dash of *TNG's* "Timescape" as well). The problem with "Relativity" is that doesn't have a through-line to ground it, and as the episode approaches its climax, the plot spins out of control as a result. In fact, if there is an anchor, it's Captain Braxton, a returning character played by a new actor, Bruce McGill, a solid performer with an everyman look that has won him many supporting roles over the years in film and television. But as a hero or a villain, this Braxton has all the charisma of a McDonald's manager, and having three of him trapped inside a time travel puzzle isn't a tenth as much fun as watching Picard in "All Good Things." (Truth be told, I'm not even sure why they brought Braxton back for this episode rather than create a new captain. His story wraps up rather nicely at the end of "Future's End," leaving no room for a sequel, but we're asked to disregard this to make sense of Braxton's multi-part role here.)

Still, Jeri Ryan is game and gives another fine performance as Seven, and Kate Mulgrew is once again right there by her side, with the writers providing us with a healthy dose of Janeway. Together, they make it worth viewing.

Did you know? For scenes set in the past, Josh Clark reprises Lieutenant Joe Carey, an engineer who appears in several Season One episodes.

"Warhead": C

A smart bomb takes over The Doctor's body.

Air date: May 19, 1999
Teleplay by Michael Taylor & Kenneth Biller
Story by Brannon Braga
Directed by John Kretchmer
TV rating: 3.3

"The only thing I want to accomplish is the destruction of my target." —The bomb

This Doctor/bomb episode plays out like another *TOS*-inspired throwback. The look of the featured technology is reminiscent of Nomad, the "body-borrowing," allowing a regular to play another part, is akin to "Return to Tomorrow," and the overall theme echoes "The Doomsday Machine." And while there are certainly episodes of non-*TOS Trek* shows, including past *VOY* episodes "Darkling" and "Dreadnought," that mirror similar themes, "Warhead" somehow packages them all in a more *TOS* way, with everything boiling down to heart-to-heart talk with a machine that Jim Kirk would be proud of.

Roberto Picardo, thanks to the sci-fi plot device, essentially plays the episode's guest star, a paranoid weapon of mass destruction that threatens to detonate its original body anytime it doesn't get its way. But like V'Ger, somewhere inside there's also a hint of humanity, and there's something gratifying about seeing its character arc played out over the course of the hour.

Unfortunately, like *TOS's* "The Changeling," it all plays out on a small-scale, with the only off-ship sequence taking place on a planet stage set, and John Kretchmer, directing his fourth and final *Star Trek* episode, relying almost entirely on the dialogue to carry the day. It's something *TOS* was better equipped to pull off because the show has a tone that makes up for its shortcomings. *VOY's* attempt, in contradistinction, comes across as more pedestrian, lacking the vital element it needs to stand out from the crowd of similar Trekkian tales.

Did you know? "Warhead" allows all nine regulars to contribute to the story in substantial ways, something unusual for *VOY's* shortform stories.

164

"Equinox": B+

Voyager encounters a Federation starship with a dark secret. (Season finale).

Air date: May 26, 1999
Teleplay by Brannon Braga & Joe Menosky
Story by Rick Berman, Brannon Braga & Joe Menosky
Directed by David Livingston
TV rating: 3.2

"If Janeway's any indication, these people will never understand." —Captain Ransom

This episode, which introduces another Federation ship trapped in the Delta Quadrant, is reminiscent of *TNG's* "Yesterday's Enterprise" in tone and structure, with Voyager and the other ship, the Equinox, working together against a common enemy while an undercurrent of mystery and doubt complicates the situation. This time, however, the real plot that develops doesn't have anything to do with time travel but is an internal conflict between the two crews, with the two captains having two different philosophies of how to run their ships and get home, and the Delta Quadrant not big enough for the both of them.

John Savage, best known for his breakthrough role in 1979s *The Deer Hunter* and who would go on to star in Fox's *Dark Angel* (2000-2002), plays Captain Ransom of the U.S.S. Equinox, instilling the character with an earnestness and conviction befitting a Starfleet captain while adding enough Clint Eastwood-esque rough edges to keep the viewer on his or her guard. He's joined by Titus Welliver, a master of playing shady characters, as his first officer, and Olivia Burkelund, a former soap opera star, as the engineer. Together, along with a background cast to help fill out their ship, they bring a new energy to the show, giving it a different vibe, destabilizing *VOY's* usual comfort level, and holding up a mirror to Janeway and her crew, showing us what they could have become had they chosen a different way or not had such luck.

And then there are the aliens. Brought to life by CGI reminiscent of Season Three's "Macrocosm," they show up from another dimension through "interspatial fissures," attacking for a short time like piranhas before returning to their own universe like a marine creature returning to the sea.

But it's the brewing conflict between the ambitious Ransom and no nonsense Janeway that drives the story, giving *VOY* a grittier feel and pleasing some fans enough for "Equinox" to routinely rank as one of the show's best episodes in polls.

Did you know? It was only after John Savage accepted the part of Captain Ransom that the writers built a story around the character.

Season Five Roundup

As *VOY* began its fifth campaign, the show found itself in an unusual position: almost an afterthought in the *Star Trek* world. With *DS9* entering its final season and racing toward an epic conclusion, and *TNG* returning to the big screen, the attention of the average *Star Trek* fan was often elsewhere.

But *VOY* soldiered on, with Season Five featuring a new showrunner while charting a course that would lay the groundwork for the show's remaining years.

With the departure of series co-creator Jeri Taylor, Brannon Braga took the reins, overseeing a writing staff that included Bryan Fuller and Nick Sagan as story editors and a team of contributors that included Ken Biller, Joe Menosky, and Jimmy Diggs. Under their watch, the show, while still an ensemble production, would begin to shift its focus largely to three characters: Janeway, Seven, and The Doctor.

The result is a slightly darker, more brooding season, with characters openly expressing self-doubt while the crew explores more bizarre areas of the Delta Quadrant than ever before. With episodes like "Night," "Infinite Regress," "Nothing Human," "Dark Frontier," "The Disease," "Course Oblivion," "The Warhead," and "Equinox" popping up every other week, Janeway and company never have much of a chance to get comfortable. But there's also some fun tossed in, with "Bride of Chaotica!" paying homage to the pulp sci-fi films of the 1930s, "11:59" giving us a fictional history lesson about the year 2000, and "Timeless" taking us fifteen years into *VOY's* future. (We are also introduced to a new shuttle with a throwback feel: The Delta Flyer.)

The shooting of the episodes themselves was often difficult. There was still tension among the actors, with Mulgrew still not happy about the addition of Seven and Beltran particularly displeased about the direction of the show. Meanwhile, a fire caused by studio light led to smoke and water damage to the sets, forcing the stage crew to make repairs, including the reupholstering of the bridge chairs. But with a stable writing staff and four years of prior experience, Season Five finds an equilibrium nonetheless, providing fans with a consistent quality of episodes while giving the show three more Emmy nominations and a win, all for visual effects, with "Dark Frontier" beating out "Thirty Days" and "Timeless" for the award. Other accolades from the time period include a win for Jeri Ryan at the third Golden Satellite Awards for Best Actress in a Drama Series, a win for Scarlett Pomers for Best Supporting Actress at the Youth in Film Awards, and an award for Jay Chattaway, Dennis McCarthy, and David Bell from The American Society of Composers, Authors, and Publishers for *VOY's* music.

So *VOY* had somehow found a way to stay relevant amidst all the *Star Trek* hoopla of 1998 and 1999. The only question left was how it would fare as the only new *Star Trek* on television for the remainder of the show's life.

Season Six

Production Order
(with air date order in parentheses)

1. "Equinox, Part II" (1st)
2. "Survival Instinct" (2nd)
3. "Barge of the Dead" (3rd)
4. "Tinker Tenor Doctor Spy" (4th)
5. "Dragon's Teeth" (7th)
6. "Alice" (5th)
7. "Riddles" (6th)
8. "One Small Step" (8th)
9. "The Voyager Conspiracy" (9th)
10. "Pathfinder" (10th)
11. "Fair Haven" (11th)
12. "Tsunkatse" (15th)
13. "Blink of an Eye" (12th)
14. "Virtuoso" (13th)
15. "Collective" (16th)
16. "Memorial" (14th)
17. "Spirit Folk" (17th)
18. "Ashes to Ashes" (18th)
19. "Child's Play" (19th)
20. "Good Shepherd" (20th)
21. "Fury" (23rd)
22. "Live Fast and Prosper" (21st)
23. "Life Line" (24th)
24. "Muse" (22nd)
25. "The Haunting of Deck 12" (25th)
26. "Unimatrix Zero" (26th)

The Sixth Season Cast

Captain Janeway: Kate Mulgrew
Commander Chakotay: Robert Beltran
B'Elanna Torres: Roxann Dawson
Tom Paris: Robert Duncan McNeill
Neelix: Ethan Phillips
The Doctor: Robert Picardo
Tuvok: Tim Russ
Harry Kim: Garrett Wang
Seven of Nine: Jeri Ryan

Notable Guest Stars

John Savage
Titus Welliver
Vaughn Armstrong
Scarlett Pomers
Eric Pierpoint
Karen Austin
Jay M. Legett
Phil Morris
Dwight Schultz
Richard Herd
Marina Sirtis
Fintan McKeown
Daniel Dae Kim
Jeffrey Combs
J.G. Hertzler
The Rock
Manu Intiraymi
Marley S. McClean
Kim Rhodes
Tracey Ellis
Kaitlin Hopkins
John Schuck
Jennifer Lien
Nancy Hower
Susanna Thompson

"Equinox, Part II": C+

Janeway seeks revenge against a renegade captain.

Air date: September 22, 1999
Teleplay by Brannon Braga & Joe Menosky
Story by Rick Berman, Brannon Braga & Joe Menosky
Directed by David Livingston
TV rating: 3.8

"You're right, I am angry. I'm damned angry. He's a Starfleet captain, and he's decided to abandon everything this uniform stands for." —Captain Janeway

With the same writers, director, and guest cast as the Season Five finale, you might expect "Equinox, Part II" to be more of what we saw in its prequel. This installment, however, plays against expectations, swapping its captains' characterizations, with Janeway consumed by an obsession while Ransom becomes more sympathetic and heroic. It's a questionable decision that leads to a muddled episode that's not quite sure of what it's trying to say.

John Savage is back as Ransom, working with rest of the guest cast, as well as Jeri Ryan, in a substory aboard his ship. His character wants Seven's cooperation but she's unwilling to help. Meanwhile, Janeway summons her inner Khan, ignoring the advice of her first officer and hunting down a captain she can't forgive. Along the way, we're treated to some pretty sights, with some location shooting on a beach and in a forest. It all makes for an ambitious episode, with the interpersonal relationships seemingly fracturing beyond the point of return. But this isn't *DS9*, where consequences from one episode spill

169

over into the next, and the whole thing ends up somewhat unsatisfying as a result. (The CGI aliens introduced in "Part I" get the shortest end of the stick, with the writers treating them as an afterthought before sweeping them under the rug.)

Regardless, "Equinox" as a whole remains an exciting two-parter, temporarily injecting the series with a tension the Maquis were designed to bring, before, like that idea, fizzling out.

"Part II" was nominated for an Emmy for sound editing.

Did you know? This episode would seem to set the stage for some of Ransom's crewmembers to return in future episodes, but none do.

"Survival Instinct": B

Seven must help three of her former Borg relatives break free from a shared link.

Air date: September 22, 1999
Written by Ronald D. Moore
Directed by David Livingston
TV rating: 3.9

"We need to find out what happened eight years ago after the crash."
—Four of Nine

Ron Moore's first *VOY* script, featuring Seven and three other ex-Borgs and including flashbacks from a time when they were stranded from the Borg Collective, is essentially a mystery story before developing into a moral dilemma.

For this one, Moore takes the idea of the Collective and downsizes it to boil the group nature down to its essentials. To help Jeri Ryan flesh out the mini-Borg party, *VOY* employs three *Star Trek* veterans. Vaughn Armstrong, who plays the eldest of the group, previously guest starred on *TNG*, *DS9*, and *VOY* in various parts. Tim Kelleher, who plays the most uncertain of the foursome, previously guest starred as a lieutenant in *TNG's* "All Good Things." Bertila Damas, a female Borg, previously guest starred in *DS9's* "The Maquis" two-parter as a Romulan gun runner trying to purchase weapons from Quark. (Armstrong and Kelleher would also go on to guest star on *ENT* as an admiral and lieutenant respectively.)

With flashback sequences taking place on the planet stage set, and the other scenes taking place on the ship, the story gives the actors plenty of opportunity to show off their characters' Borg sides in full Borg make-up as well as their human sides and a bridge between the two. For Seven, who unexpectedly ends up defining the episode's ambiguous title before the whole thing winds to a conclusion, it's quite an interesting character study, tying nicely into her reluctance to embrace her humanity in her early episodes.

Yet for all its positives, "Survival Instinct" doesn't really stand out amongst *VOY's* many Seven/Borg episodes, content to stay small and play it safe. Nonetheless, it's one of the show's more successful explorations of group versus individual thought.

Did you know? The preview for this episode misleadingly makes it seem as though Seven is considering returning to the Collective. To do this, it takes one of Seven's lines, "I will not return them to the Borg," and edits it so she says, "I will return to the Borg."

171

"Barge of the Dead": B

Following a shuttle accident, Lieutenant Torres finds herself in an afterlife for dishonored Klingons.

Air date: October 6, 1999
Teleplay by Bryan Fuller
Story by Ronald D. Moore & Bryan Fuller
Directed by David Livingston
TV rating: 3.8

"This is the Barge of the Dead. Our dishonored souls are being taken to Gre'thor." —Hij'qa

This episode, with a story idea originally conceived by Ron Moore for *DS9's* Worf, has Klingon flowing out of its pores like bloodwine. *Star Trek* has touched upon the internal visualizations of near-death experiences before with *TNG's* "Tapestry" and "Birthright," but this one gives us our first visit to Klingon Hell, with Torres, after rejecting her people's beliefs, taking a spiritual journey that may or may not be real.

From a story standpoint, it's similar to what Janeway goes through in Season Three's "Sacred Ground," where the captain undergoes an abstract test and must take a leap of faith to save Kes. Here, Torres must go through a similar trial to save her mother's soul. But this one is even more about style over substance, with Moore finally getting his wish for a full-on visualization of the Klingon afterlife. Meanwhile, the writers also employ metaphorical afterlife sequences on the ship, with the director even using a Dutch tilt at one point to enhance the effect.

In the end, all the elements come together to produce a compelling Torres character study, making for one of the best Klingon episodes of the series.

Did you know? This is the last *Star Trek* episode with credited contributions from writer Ron Moore.

"Tinker Tenor Doctor Spy": B+

Aliens attempt to spy on Voyager by tapping into The Doctor, but they mistakenly access his new "daydream" program.

Air date: October 13, 1999
Teleplay by Joe Menosky
Story by Bill Vallely
Directed by John Bruno
TV rating: 3.5

"I have to save the ship!" —The Doctor

Like *TNG's* "Hollow Pursuits," *VOY* borrows from "The Secret Life of Walter Mitty" for this lighthearted Doctor episode about his new daydream subroutine and some alien mischief.

This one taps into the spirit of "Walter Mitty" even more so than "Pursuits," opening with a hilariously over the top musical number reminiscent of the "Mitty" stage play before giving us several more scenarios in which The Doctor saves the day, gets the girl, and wins the admiration of the crew. Amidst the frivolity, evil aliens attempt to add a backdrop of intrigue and danger, but it's hard to take them seriously, with the aliens, played by actors who don't appear anywhere else in the *Star Trek* universe, being as cartoonish and over the top as The Doctor's fantasies. In fact, the whole thing, from its plot to its tone, is almost a precursor to the movie *Galaxy Quest*, released just a couple months after this, with the episode, much like the beloved film, even finding a way to hide some depth inside the comedy, with The Doctor's fictitious world illustrating a heartfelt ambition to improve himself and his position on the ship, something Janeway can initially dismiss when it's expressed in just words but which she must take more seriously when it's demonstrated through action.

The aliens return for two episodes in Season Seven, starting with "The Void."

Did you know? *Tinker Tailor Soldier Spy* is a 1974 spy novel by British author and former intelligence operative, John le Carré, based on the premise of uncovering a Soviet double agent in the Secret Intelligence Service. It spawned two sequels: *The Honourable Schoolboy*, published in 1977, and *Smiley's People*, published in 1979.

"Alice": C

Paris is manipulated by the feminine persona of a mysterious alien shuttle.

Air date: October 20, 1999
Teleplay by Bryan Fuller & Michael Taylor
Story by Julliann DeLayne
Directed by David Livingston
TV rating: 3.5

"She can't fly herself. She needs a pilot, a biological entity to work in tandem with her programming." —Abbadon

Tom Paris gets in over his head when he acquires a one-seater ship with the personality of a possessive female before it tries to whisk him away from Voyager.

The sci-fi idea here, which is similar to Stephen King's Christine and only one or two steps removed from the plot of *2001: A Space Odyssey*, has merit. But the writing is as vanilla as it comes, with the writers taking the story from point A to B to C in such a predictable fashion, most viewers will be ahead of them at every stage.

John Fleck, a veteran *Star Trek* guest star who has played Romulans, Cardassians, and other watchamcallits, guest stars as Abbadon, an alien trader who sets the plot in motion, and Claire Rankin, who would later go on to play Dr. Kate Heightmeyer on *Stargate: Atlantis* (2004–2009), guest stars as a human manifestation of the ship, helping to give it some personality. Together, with good performances by Robbie McNeill and Roxann Dawson, they manage to make it all enjoyable enough for a ship-based filler episode, even if it all adds up to just another day at the office for Paris.

Did you know? As of this writing, David Livingston, who served as a supervising producer for *TNG*, *DS9*, and *VOY*, has directed more *Star Trek* episodes than anyone else, with a total of sixty-two directorial credits.

174

"Riddles": B

After an attack by mysterious aliens, Tuvok develops a new personality.

Air date: November 3, 1999
Teleplay by Robert J. Doherty
Story by Andre Bormanis
Directed by Roxann Dawson
TV rating: 3.4

"When is a Vulcan no longer a Vulcan?" —Neelix

VOY does its own version of *Regarding Henry* (1991) with Tuvok in this character piece that's really a Neelix episode, with the latter character serving as the Vulcan's rehab partner and cheerleader.

Freshman director Roxann Dawson, who does not appear on camera at all, plays up the character chemistry shared by a smiling Tuvok and his new best buddy, Neelix, showing the characters bonding in almost a nephew/favorite uncle kind of way. And it turns out it works a whole lot better than the usual Mr. Vulcan/Neelix fare, with the character banter coming across as less predictable and less cringe-worthy than normal, being more organic and interesting.

As Tim Russ develops the new persona for his character, Ethan Phillips generously lets him take center stage, though it's Phillips who does most of the heavy lifting that makes the episode worth watching, carefully coloring in the edges of the story to give the plot its depth. And yet all the same, the writers avoid digging too deep into the moral issue of whether Tuvok, living out the reverse of "Flowers for Algernon," can be forced to return to his old state of being if he doesn't want to. (They probably didn't want to double up on the similar issue raised in Season Two's "Tuvix.")

Still, what begins as a tease of tedium turns into what's easily the best Tuvok/Neelix pairing of the series.

Did you know? Mark Moses, who plays an alien investigator in this episode, would go on to play Captain Archer's father in the pilot of *ENT*.

"Dragon's Teeth": B

When Voyager seeks refuge from alien attackers, they find a small army with a mysterious past.

Air date: November 10, 1999
Teleplay by Michael Taylor, Brannon Braga & Joe Menosky
Story by Michael Taylor
Directed by Winrich Kolbe
TV rating: 3.6

"An old Greek myth. After a dragon was killed in a war, its teeth were spread out over the battlefield. They took root and warriors sprung from the ground to continue the fighting." —Chakotay

This mini-war story plays out like an upgraded version of *TOS's* "Let That Be Your Last Battlefield" with hostile alien races fighting amidst impressive planet visuals while just about everyone in the core cast contributes in some way.

Beginning slowly before developing its plot, this is one of those episodes that's somewhat difficult to get a handle on early in the go, with the audience left wondering where the story is going until about halfway through. (And even then there's a lot left up in the air since the original idea was to do a two-parter.)

The glue that holds the episode together is guest star Jeff Allin, who previously appeared in *TNG's* "Imaginary Friend" (as the father of the girl with the imaginary friend). Here, he plays an alien who has woken after 900 years in stasis and who is part of a race that holds the key to fast travel through "subspace corridors," shortcuts through space that allow ships to move great distances otherwise unachievable. There's also a guest spot for Robert Knepper, who previously guest starred as Troi's would-be husband in Season One's "Haven," playing an alien who wants to seize Voyager.

With questions of trust versus caution mixed in with moral dilemmas and pivoting alliances, it all has a *TNG* quality to it. But all the same, the story never breaks out of its box, content to shape itself into just another *VOY* filler episode, leaving little mark on the *Star Trek* universe.

"Dragon's Teeth" was nominated for an Emmy for hairstyling.

Did you know? Footage from this episode is included in the opening credit sequence of *ENT's* "In a Mirror, Darkly."

"One Small Step": B

Voyager discovers a spatial anomaly that's carrying a module from the first manned mission to Mars.

Air date: November 17, 1999
Teleplay by Mike Wollaeger, Jessica Scott, Bryan Fuller & Michael Taylor
Story by Mike Wollaeger & Jessica Scott
Directed by Robert Picardo
TV rating: 3.7

"Remember, when you set foot in that module, you'll be stepping into history."
—Chakotay

Robert Picardo directs his first *VOY* episode since Season Three's "Alter Ego," bringing to life an ambitious script written by several different people that simultaneously honors the groundwork for space travel while enriching the show's characters.

Like *TOS's* "Space Seed," *VOY* marries a story set in humanity's near future with events in the show's present, allowing some members of ship's crew to revel in their newfound connection to a piece of history they've always heard about.

This one layers in a story about a Mars mission gone wrong, with Phil Morris guest starring as a command module pilot in the 21st century who was lost in space after encountering an unusual phenomenon—basically an interstellar hurricane. (This gives the design team an opportunity to create 21st century space technology, which they do magnificently, presenting hardware that's similar enough to the Apollo missions to be familiar to 20th century space buffs but futuristic enough to look like something astronauts would use for interplanetary travel.) When Voyager encounters the same phenomenon, everyone—save Seven—becomes excited about the possibility of learning more about what happened to this guy. And that sets up the heart of the episode: another lesson for Seven about humanity, as she goes from disinterested in the past to ultimately, by accident, becoming the foremost character to forge a connection with it, something that profoundly affects the character, as expressed by Jeri Ryan's superb performance.

Contrived? Sure. The odds of Voyager running into an anomaly that swooped by Mars are probably less than a trillion to one, and if you know the 21st century history established by the show, it's hard to imagine Mars missions happening during such a timeframe. Furthermore, there's no mistaking that this was made on a 1990s TV budget, with *The Martian* (2015) and National Geographic's *Mars* series (2016, 2018) both bringing us 21st century Mars missions in more spectacular ways. But it's still fun and meaningful to see *Star Trek* do this sort of an episode.

TOS's "Miri," with Phil Morris far left

Did you know? Phil Morris literally grew up in *Star Trek*. As the son of Greg Morris, who starred on *Star Trek's* sister show, *Mission: Impossible*, he appeared as one of the children in *TOS's* "Miri." Later, he played an uncredited part in *Star Trek III: The Search for Spock* (1984) as a cadet who asks Admiral Kirk if there will be a reception when they return to Earth. (Kirk replies, "A hero's welcome, son? Is that what you'd like?") He later appeared in two *DS9* episodes as a Klingon and a Jem'Hadar before landing the role of the lost astronaut in "One Small Step."

Morris in Star Trek III: The Search for Spock

"The Voyager Conspiracy": B

Seven investigates a possible conspiracy involving the Federation, the Cardassians, the Caretaker, and numerous other alien races.

Air date: November 24, 1999
Written by Joe Menosky
Directed by Terry Windell
TV rating: 3.6

"The Captain and Tuvok were involved in a Federation conspiracy. They're in collusion with the Caretaker and possibly the Cardassians." —Seven

Like today's YouTube and Facebook conspiracy believers, Seven allows assumptions and confirmation bias to lead her down a rabbit hole, building theories like houses of cards while refusing to believe how precarious they stand in this ship-based episode.

What's interesting is that "The Voyager Conspiracy" actually predates the social media revolution by three or four years. With Facebook, YouTube, Twitter, and other forums on the internet giving people the power to prune news, facts, and friends to fit into a belief system they want to sustain, conspiracy theories have gained traction like never before. Sure, there have always been people who have doubted that Lee Harvey Oswald killed John F. Kennedy or that Neil Armstrong landed on the Moon, finding it easier to believe the public was duped by shady *X-Files*-like characters working outside the public spotlight to create a false history. But thanks to social media, today an alarming number of people believe the Earth is flat, Australia doesn't exist, and the Israeli government has a pack of evil, GPS-equipped sharks that they use against their enemies. (Seriously, that theory is a thing!)

And yet somehow, before this all proliferated into its modern form, Menosky wrote a prescient allegory, with Seven taking many pieces of information and, without even realizing she's doing so, connecting them by filling in the blanks between them with assumptions that may or may not be true to reach a grand unifying conclusion. It's the perfect sort of story for her, and one that wouldn't work so well with any other *Star Trek* character. (Spock and Data would never be so illogical and paranoid, and The Doctor could never throw away his innate trust of the crew.) On the other hand, having Janeway and Chakotay buy into Seven's theories might be taking the premise a step too far.

Nonetheless, for Season Six, "The Voyager Conspiracy" proves yet another winner.

Did you know? Albie Selznick, who guest stars as an alien in this episode, is not just an actor but a movement coach. He plays a juggler in *TNG's* "Cost of Living."

"Pathfinder": B

Lieutenant Barclay becomes obsessed with contacting Voyager and turns to Counselor Troi for help.

Air date: December 1, 1999
Teleplay by David Zabel & Kenneth Biller
Story by David Zabel
Directed by Mike Vejar
TV rating: 4.0

"Well I suppose it all started in the holodeck. Doesn't it always?" —Barclay

Much like *TNG's* "Hollow Pursuits," this episode sees Dwight Schultz and Marina Sirtis playing Barclay and Troi in a holodeck episode. This time, in a story conceived by future *ER* executive producer David Zabel, Barclay has programmed a simulation of Voyager to allow him to join the crew as an admired and beloved shipmate. But unlike his previous programs on the Enterprise, his interest in Voyager actually has a productive purpose. Barclay is part of the "Project Pathfinder" team, an effort by Starfleet to communicate with the lost Voyager starship; but he has his own ideas and his superiors won't listen to him. This forces Barclay to become the 24th century version of Robert Goddard, a stubborn man willing to go against the grain and even go rogue if necessary to defend and prove his beliefs. And the lieutenant uses the holodeck as a way to escape the doubters and test his theories in an environment where he's trusted and respected.

As an episode of *VOY*, this one's certainly unique, with Schultz and a few guest stars seemingly getting their own show while the *VOY* cast serves as secondary characters. (It's especially fun to see the differences between Barclay's holoprogram and the present Voyager, with the program appropriately including a Season One look and wisely excluding characters Starfleet doesn't have much knowledge of.) As in "Distant Origin" and "Living Witness," Voyager isn't so much the episode's subject as the object; though the emphasis remains on the lost ship. The supporting cast includes Richard Herd as Admiral Paris (replacing Warren Munson), who plays the part somewhat as previously established, and Richard McGonagle as Barclay's boss, giving an uninspiring performance. (His character has too little intelligence and too few leadership skills for someone in his position. About the only thing he has in common with Captain Picard is his lack of hair.) Together they manage to fill out the corners of a story about a man's obsession that's either going to pay off for everyone or land someone in the brig.

Sirtis, on the other hand, only appears minimally, serving as an audience surrogate as Barclay tells his story. And yet no one other than Troi could fill this position so well, making it feel more like an organically developed framing device than a ratings stunt. Regardless, her treatment of Barclay here represents some of her best work as a therapist, with reactions that come across as those of a real, trained counselor as opposed to a writer pretending to be one.

Unfortunately, Zabel and Biller aren't so successful at tying the episode into *VOY's* established history. They choose to ignore aspects of Season Two's "Projections" (where The Doctor interacts with a holographic version of Barclay), and they don't seem to remember that Janeway once served Admiral Paris's science officer (a relationship that, if acknowledged, would make the climax all the more emotional). But they're probably more concerned about a thorny issue in the present: just how does Barclay know where to send his signal, given all the course changes Voyager has made? (They wisely ignore the question to avoid drawing attention to it, but it still looms over the action.)

Regardless, as a change of pace and an outside the box *VOY* episode, "Pathfinder" is a breath of fresh air.

Sirtis and Schultz reprise their characters later in the season in "Life Line" before returning together for a sequel to "Pathfinder" in Season Seven's "Inside Man."

Did you know? "This episode was the last new *Star Trek* episode to first air in the 1990s.

Dwight Schultz (photo courtesy of Corey Bond)

"Fair Haven": C+

Captain Janeway falls for a holographic character in an Irish village on the holodeck.

Air date: January 12, 2000
Written by Robin Burger
Directed by Allan Kroeker
TV rating: 3.4

"Michael Sullivan is exactly my type: attractive, intelligent. We share the same interests. And if there's something I don't like, I can simply change it."
—Janeway

VOY returns to Universal's "Little Europe" backlot for this story that introduces Fair Haven, a fictional 19th century Irish village. The idea here is that Janeway discovers that dating a holographic character comes with a power many people wish they had: she can instantly change anything about her beau she wants. Want him to be taller? Want him to stop snoring? Just ask the computer. But this only reinforces the fact that she's in an artificial relationship, and she's not sure how to handle that.

Irish actor Fintan McKeown, who would go on to appear in HBO's *Game of Thrones*, guest stars as Michael Sullivan, the local pub owner Janeway takes a liking to, intentionally underplaying the character to give him a more cerebral nature. Meanwhile, there's also a faux-jeopardy B story about the ship traveling through a storm in space.

Unfortunately, writer/producer Robin Burger is unable to dig too deep into her story...because there's nothing too deep to dig into. But at least Janeway isn't getting it on with the family ghost.

Sullivan and the Fair Haven program get a sequel later in the season with "Spirit Folk."

Did you know? Richard Riehle, who guest stars as Seamus the beggar, previously appeared in *TNG's* "Inner Light" as Batai, Picard's best friend in an alternate life. He would go on to reprise Seamus in "Spirit Folk" and appears in two episodes *ENT* as a physician.

"Blink of an Eye": A

Voyager becomes stuck in synchronous orbit of a world where time passes far more rapidly than on the ship.

Air date: January 19, 2000
Teleplay by Scott Miller & Joe Menosky
Story by Michael Taylor
Directed by Gabrielle Beaumont
TV rating: 3.7

"For each second that passes on Voyager, nearly a day goes by on the planet."
—Seven

Borrowing liberally from *Dragon's Egg*, a 1980 science fiction novel by American physicist Robert L. Forward, this *VOY* episode is sort of a hybrid of *TOS's* "Wink of an Eye" and *TNG's* "Who Watches the Watchers," with Voyager inadvertently becoming a part of the heavens of a rapidly evolving populace while simultaneously witnessing the culture evolve from a primitive people to an advanced culture capable of space travel.

It's a killer premise, with the SimEarth approach creating a clear line of demarcation between the different timeflows on the ship and on the planet, which in turn allows the episode to escape the logistic timeline headaches from "Wink of an Eye." For the people on the planet, *VOY* becomes the equivalent of the Earth's Moon, albeit one that accidentally shakes the planet from time to time. It gives the culture a constant object to observe, wonder about, and ultimately reach for. And by doing so, "Blink" actually backs into the profoundness "One Small Step" strives for, showing us what it means to have pioneers touch the heavens for the first time. Meanwhile, the plot device permits those on the ship to witness the evolution of the aliens, with The Doctor even sent down for a visit, giving him his own "Inner Light"-like story, though the actual visit happens off-screen. (Picardo, nonetheless, sells the meaning of the experience with his acting.)

This is all quite a lot for just one episode, but Michael Taylor, author of *DS9's* "The Visitor" and "In The Pale Moonlight," Joe Menosky, cowriter of *VOY's* "Distant Origin" and "Year of Hell," and Scott Miller, the visionary behind *VOY's* "Thirty Days," have the experience to package all the elements together in a coherent way that preserves an overall meaning.

All the same, there are still some issues with the details. Tuvok claims the planet rotates like a quasar, which is a luminescent object powered by gas falling into a black hole, but it would make more sense to compare the planet to a pulsar, a rapidly rotating neutron star. More noticeably, the writers' Earth-centric thinking gives us the jarring visual of an alien writing in English and has the crew of Voyager, without evidence, assuming the life-forms on the planet live the same length of time as people on Earth. Another issue, which is less avoidable, is due to budget. Rather than seeing an entire community evolve from

183

a village to a city to a metropolis, the show limits the scenes on planet to a small set and limits the guest stars to two for each time period, with their interactions all coming across like something out of a stage play, complete with overly theatrical acting. And by the latter acts, scenes from the planet surface disappear entirely, giving the climax a deus ex machina quality that doesn't feel entirely earned.

Nonetheless, the episode itself has too many exceptional elements for such minutia to weigh it down. Most notably, what money isn't spent on the planet is invested in a space capsule and scenes on Voyager where the crew is moving so slowly, they appear to be frozen in time. And in concert with these sequences, Daniel Dae Kim, a relatively unknown actor who would go on to play Jin-Soo Kwon on ABC's *Lost*, gives an especially strong performance as an astronaut who makes first contact. (Kim would later appear in Season Three of *ENT* as Corporal D. Chang, an operations soldier.)

As such, "Blink" is almost always a staple of the "top ten" *VOY* episode lists and there's a strong argument it's one of the best offerings of any *Trek* series.

Did you know? For this episode, Gabrielle Beaumont directed her husband, English actor Olaf Pooley, who was cast as an elderly cleric. Pooley died in 2015 at the age of 101.

"Virtuoso": B–

When The Doctor introduces music to an alien world, he turns himself into a beloved celebrity to its inhabitants.

Air date: January 26, 2000
Teleplay by Raf Green & Kenneth Biller
Story by Raf Green
Directed by Les Landau
TV rating: 3.7

"I'm glad you're enjoying yourself Doctor, but this is getting a little excessive."
—Janeway

Like the Beatles introducing themselves to America on *The Ed Sullivan Show*, The Doctor finds himself the center of attention on a planet after knocking out its masses with something they've never imagined the like of before. In this case, however, that something isn't a song or a style but music as a whole.

The idea of introducing a culture to something most of us have taken for granted nearly all their lives is irresistible, which is why it pops up from time to time in different forms, such as in *The Invention of Lying* (2009) and *Yesterday* (2019). Even *Galaxy Quest* (1998) has some fun playing around with the idea of a race of aliens who have never heard of fiction before. Here, "the invention of music" serves as a gateway to examine the issues of celebrity, something of a meta-exercise/parody considering the inherent fame of everything and everybody that appears in a *Star Trek* episode.

Picardo, of course, is fabulous as the "it boy," even if some of his opera singing is dubbed in by Agostino Castagnola. By balancing The Doctor's excessive ego with raw vulnerability, the actor creates a textured character study as The Doctor grapples with what he really wants out of all this and what he's actually getting.

Unfortunately, the aliens of the week, the Quomar, are a complete flop. The fault doesn't lie with the writers, who give them a love of math that's hilarious. (The Doctor has them in stitches when he says, "You may also notice some fascinating trigonometric functions in the counterpoint, but I suppose I'm going off on a tangent, aren't I?") It's the casting and direction that team up to make their debut worse than the Ferengis', with the Quomar seemingly incapable of having any likeable mannerisms. (The Ferengi recover, but the Quomar are never seen again.)

Fortunately, the aliens themselves are secondary to the episode, with Picardo and the subject matter being enough to carry it.

Did you know? None of "Virtuoso's" five credited guest stars appear in any other episode of *Star Trek*. However, one of the alien extras, Leonard Crofoot, appears in *TNG*'s "Angel One" and "The Offspring."

"Memorial": C−

Voyager crewmembers begin having horrific flashbacks of an atrocity.

Air date: February 2, 2000
Teleplay by Robin Burger
Story by Brannon Braga
Directed by Allan Kroeker
TV rating: 3.8

"I dreamt I was on a planet in the middle of a battle. I have no idea how I got there. I can't remember." —Paris

Reminiscent of "Remember," this is supposed to be a mystery episode, though the title somewhat spoils things.

It's basically built around the idea of post-traumatic stress disorder, with flashback sequences on a planet inspired by aspects of the Vietnam War. The Doctor, to give the story its power, makes it very clear early on that the crewmembers are not going crazy. "These are real memories," he states, "not mere dreams or hallucinations."

But as is often the case in *Star Trek*, there are more layers to the story, and to get to the core of the onion, Janeway and her crew have to begin peeling away, with everything eventually leading to a moral dilemma.

Unfortunately, as either a social commentary or a compelling piece of drama, "Memorial" fails, with its stress of style or substance giving the audience mixed messages. The problem is the writers and director want to share a puzzle with us, but they're unwilling to give us the right pieces in the right order, and the overall picture on the box—the supposed point of it all—becomes an afterthought.

Did you know? Like "One," this episode was based on a pitch by journalist Jim Swallow, who will never forget when he got confirmation of the sale. "It was a late Friday night, and I was with my friends. When the phone rang, I thought, 'Who's calling me at this time of night?' So I answered, saying, 'Who the hell is this?' And the voice on the other end of the phone said, 'Please hold for Brannon Braga.' And I was like, 'What?!?' Meanwhile, my buddies were like, 'Hey Jim, where's the beer?' I just handed them a six-pack and went 'Take the beer and go!' And then Bran and I were on the phone for an hour or so having story conference about how he wanted to see the story evolve. Afterwards, I told the other guys, 'You're never gonna believe what just happened to me!'"

"Tsunkatse": C+

Seven of Nine is abducted by an opportunistic ringmaster who forces her to participate in Tsunkatse, a hand-to-hand combat sport.

Air date: February 9, 2000
Teleplay by Robert Doherty
Story by Gannon Kenney
Directed by Mike Vejar
TV rating: 4.1

"I know your opponent. I know his weaknesses. I can train you to defeat him."
—Hirogen warrior

While this episode was originally hyped as "Seven versus Dwayne 'The Rock' Johnson," and along with *That '70s Show* and *Saturday Night Live* helped jumpstart the latter's acting career, the meat and potatoes of the story actually features two former *DS9* guest stars, with Jeffery Combs playing an alien fight promoter and J.G. Hertzler playing a grizzled Hirogen warrior.

A lot of the episode is a patchwork of old *Trek* ideas. We've seen crewmembers abducted before only to have them reappear in another capacity to the surprise of their shipmates (such as in *TNG's* "Face of the Enemy" and "Gambit.") Seeing the *Trek* characters forced into gladiator combat is almost as old as the franchise itself (with *TOS's* The Gamesters of Triskelion" and "Bread and Circuses" both built around the idea.) And the notion of a mentor taking someone under his wing, as Hertzler's character does with Seven, is something that pops up time and time again in 1990s *Trek* (perhaps most prominently in *TNG's* "Preemptive Strike" and *DS9's* "Honor Among Thieves").

Somehow, however, "Tsunkatse" weaves the ideas together in a new and fresh way, giving it *VOY's* unique spin. With the ship and her crew so far from home, there's less of an emphasis on the righteousness of Starfleet and the need to teach others the errors of their ways. What matters here is where the mentor/student relationship goes, with the writers ultimately creating a moral dilemma out of it.

Nonetheless, the show is content to play it safe, with a cheat used to allow Seven to have her cake and eat it too, and the whole thing is satisfied to be just another filler episode, even if it's one of the more memorable.

Did you know? "Tsunkatse" was part of a special World Wrestling Federation-themed week of programming on UPN (home of the WWF's Thursday night show, *SmackDown!*). In addition to Dwayne Johnson on *Voyager*, wrestler Triple H appeared on *Grown Ups*, and the network aired a made-for-TV movie, *Operation Sandman: Warriors in Hell*, co-starring Bob "Hardcore" Holly.

"Collective": C

Voyager is threatened by a Borg cube controlled by adolescent drones.

Air date: February 9, 2000
Teleplay by Robert Doherty
Story by Gannon Kenney
Directed by Mike Vejar
TV rating: 3.5

"Mature Borg are predictable. They'll ignore you or assimilate you. But these juveniles, they're unstable." —Janeway

This kiddie-Borg show plays out as a simple hostage crisis, but it doesn't have the teeth of *TOS's* "Miri" or *TNG's* "Power Play." The fundamental problem is that the Borg-kids are in over their head on all fronts, unable to properly run their Borg cube or truly threaten Janeway, who has way too many cards at her disposal to lose.

To be fair, the writers do come up with a clever backstory (later elaborated on in "Child's Play"), plausibly explaining how the children came to be in this predicament. And there's a certain charm in seeing a Borg threat turn sideways when "You will be assimilated" turns into something more akin to "Give me my juice box." But the real problem is that there's no threat of a properly manned Borg cube showing up to help out the kiddos, with the writers specifically nixing the idea to turn it into a plot point. (The rest of the Borg decide these kids are not worth their effort to recover, and the little munchkins, who already seem like individuals by the time we meet them, have nowhere to go other than Voyager.) This takes away a potential countdown clock and leaves the episode with an ending that's mostly a foregone conclusion. (Personally, I think it would be more dramatic if the kids were forced to choose between returning to the Borg or adopting a more human way of life, with the fate of the Voyager crew hanging in the balance.)

Nineteen-year-old Ryan Spahn guest stars as the Borg leader, getting the bulk of Borg dialogue while essentially playing an angry teenager. He's joined by twenty-one-year-old Manu Intiraymi, twelve-year-old Marley McClean, and fourteen-year-old twins Kurt and Cody Wetherill.

Most of the kids become recurring guest stars from this point forward. A Borg baby, however, despite being introduced with a lot of whoop-de-do, is never seen again.

Did you know? In a 2000 interview, Brannon Braga said the Borg baby idea was abandoned because the writers felt the Borg adolescents gave them richer material to work with.

"Spirit Folk": D

The characters in Tom Paris's Irish holoprogram begin to believe the Voyager crewmembers are evil spirits.

Air date: February 23, 2000
Written by Bryan Fuller
Directed by David Livingston
TV rating: 3.2

"Something's gone wrong. The people of Fair Haven aren't simple country folk anymore." —Janeway

The holographic characters from "Fair Haven" return in this sequel that sees them grow suspicious of the Voyager crew after witnessing several "supernatural" occurrences.

Unfortunately, the story itself is not just a compilation of worn-out ideas, it's one that doesn't execute any of them very well. As a malfunctioning holodeck episode, it lacks the originality of *DS9's* "Dr. Bashir, I Presume?" or *TNG's* "Emergence." As a holographic village episode, it lacks the heart of *DS9's* "Shadowplay" or *TNG's* "Homeward." And as a study in holographic characters becoming aware of their existence, it lacks the charm, subtlety, and cleverness of *TNG's* "Elementary, Dear Data" and "Ship in a Bottle."

In fact, while "Spirit Folk" still carries an air of Irish charm and shows off the chemistry between Kate Mulgrew and guest star Fintan McKewon, even these positives are simply echoes of the "Fair Haven" prequel which arguably does both better. Quite frankly, it's one of those stories that should have been scrapped before real money was spent bringing it to life.

"Spirit Folk" was, however, nominated for an Emmy for Jay Chattaway's score.

Did you know? In 1985, a twenty-year-old Robert Duncan McNeill guest starred in a segment of *The Twilight Zone* (1985–1989) as a 20th century teenager who, following an illness, finds himself sharing thoughts with a 17th century Puritan girl played by Kerry Noonan. The two characters form a friendship as a result, but the girl's odd behavior leads others in her time to believe she's a witch. Fortunately, the two protagonists are able to use their ingenuity to convince a judge that she's simply gifted with second sight. Afterward, the two teens agree it's best to stop communicating and live their lives separately. The girl, however, leaves one last message for the boy to discover in his own time: their initials carved into a rock.

"Ashes to Ashes": D

A dead crewmate returns to Voyager, pursued by the aliens who revived her.

Air date: March 1, 2000
Teleplay by Robert Doherty
Story by Ronald Wilkerson
Directed by Terry Windell
TV rating: 3.4

"That's how they procreate. They salvage the dead of other races." —Ensign Ballard

Like Season Four's "Unforgettable," the main story here seems like a sequel to an episode from the past that never actually happened with a long-lost character we have never actually met. The first act gives us the "recap," running down the character's final mission with the ship and its unfortunate end. Now, after being brought back to life by aliens, she has returned and wants to reintegrate herself into the ship's crew—but finds it's not as easy to do as she hoped.

If this all sounds like a long and contrived way to set up the episode's drama, which is essentially about someone trained in alien ways trying to become human again, that's because it is. (Why not just bring back the lost woman from "Latent Image" to save a step? Considering that woman and this woman have virtually the same backstory, it's possible that this was the plan but the actress was unavailable.)

Kim Rhodes guest stars as the reanimated Ensign Ballard, playing up the frustration of a person who finds she can but can't go home again, but the bottom line is that it's hard to care about a character we've never met before and will likely never see again, and the viewers' frustration lies in seeing the regulars relegated to supporting parts.

Then there's a short B story, with Seven continuing to look after the Borg children first introduced in "Collective." It's mostly comic filler, with Seven scheduling everything for the kids down to the minute, including "fun." ("Fun will now commence.") But with schools under increased pressure to do the same thing, the storyline actually serves as an interesting allegory.

In the end, however, everything wraps up predictably in both stories, allowing us to forget about it all and move on.

"Ashes to Ashes" was nominated for an Emmy for make-up.

Did you notice? Ensign Ballard's struggle is reminiscent of what Jono goes through in *TNG's* "Suddenly Human," though his story is packaged in a custody dispute. Speaking of which...

"Child's Play": B

When Icheb's parents are discovered, Seven struggles to let him choose between returning to his homeworld and staying on Voyager.

Air date: March 8, 2000
Teleplay by Raf Green
Story by Paul Brown
Directed by Mike Vejar
TV rating: 3.4

"I know what it's like to feel protective towards someone you've helped through a difficult period, but Icheb is an individual now. You have to give him a chance to form his own opinions." —Janeway

For much of this sequel to "Collective," *VOY* sets aside sci-fi plots and hostile aliens to give us a family-oriented custody dispute featuring Seven and one of "Collective's" Borg children. And there's something both frustrating and heartbreaking seeing Seven, who fears losing someone who's become like a son to her, trying to find a reason not to trust his recently discovered parents, who come across as well-meaning and kind.

Manu Intiraymi reprises the boy himself, Icheb, and is a strong enough actor to make the stakes worthwhile, giving us a character-based plot that seems so self-sufficient, no extra layers seem necessary. This, however, makes it all the more jarring—and exciting—when the episode takes a sudden left turn, bringing new meaning to it all and retroactively making sense out of the beginnings of "Collective."

Tracey Ellis and Mark A. Sheppard guest star as Icheb's parents, though Sheppard is only fourteen years older than Intiraymi and the part probably should have gone to someone older with more of a "Dad" vibe. Nonetheless, with scenes set on both the regular stage sets and on location, the family arc plays out effectively, with its twist and turns making the story worthwhile and satisfying.

Did you know? This episode's story was conceived by Paul Brown, a writer and producer for *Quantum Leap* and *The X-Files*.

"Good Shepherd": C

When Janeway learns that some crewmembers have been struggling to contribute, she takes them on an away mission.

Air date: March 15, 2000
Teleplay by Dianna Gitto & Joe Menosky
Story by Dianna Gitto
Directed by Winrich Kolbe
TV rating: 3.8

"The good shepherd went after some lost sheep and ran into a wolf." —Janeway

This character-based shuttle story sees Janeway take three lower decks misfits out for an away mission on the Delta Flyer in an attempt to help them become better officers.

As an episode, it's as vanilla as it gets, amounting to nothing more than paint-by-numbers filler as the Flyer encounters a strange form of life. But it does give Mulgrew an opportunity to work with a new ensemble, and the guest cast doesn't disappoint. Jay Underwood, who previously played an android in Disney's *Not Quite Human* trilogy (1987–1992), plays an introverted officer obsessed with cosmology. Michael Reisz, an anime voice actor, plays a hypochondriac who can't relax. And Zoe McLellan, who would shortly go on to star on CBS's *JAG*, plays a crewmember full of self-doubt who knows she makes a lot of mistakes. ("Shockwave approaching! Contact in four, three, two, one..." [nothing] "...more or less.") Put them all together and you get *VOY's* version of *TNG's* "Lower Decks," but with the captain interacting with them each step of the way.

Does it make for must-see *VOY*? Not in the least. But the dialogue and acting are enough to make it watchable and entertaining throughout.

Did you know? This episode includes one of *Star Trek's* most unique teasers, with the chain of command illustrated through a sequence that literally follows a message from the top to the bottom, bookended by *Citizen Kane*-like shots of the ship (if *Citizen Kane* took place on a ship in space).

"Live Fast and Prosper": B

Con artists aboard an alien ship impersonate Voyager's crew while scamming unsuspecting victims.

Air date: March 15, 2000
Teleplay by Dianna Gitto & Joe Menosky
Story by Dianna Gitto
Directed by Winrich Kolbe
TV rating: 3.1

"I think there's been some sort of misunderstanding." —Janeway

In this fun romp, *VOY* tackles identity theft about five years or so before the issue blew up out of control in real life.

Burger's script itself is somewhat uninspired, content to coast on its unique premise. But director LeVar Burton and the cast give it just the zest it needs to maintain an almost comic nature throughout, and the wardrobe department earns its stripes with some over the top fake Starfleet uniforms, complete with oversized combadges and pips. (I want one of these to wear to conventions just to see who gets it.) Kaitlin Hopkins, who previously appeared as a Vorta on *DS9*, plays a fake Captain Janeway, and although she's joined by a couple of yahoos playing a fake Tuvok and a fake Chakotay, the episode basically belongs to her. Happily, she comes through with a great performance, allowing *VOY* to score on the rare story idea that could fit into any *Star Trek* series.

Still, the writing itself occasionally undermines it all, with an ending sequence, in particular, that can be confusing if the viewer isn't paying very close attention. But "Live Fast" has more than enough good bits to it to overcome any of the bad and is another highlight of Season Six.

Did you know? With identity theft becoming a growing problem in the early 21st century, Robert Maynard Jr. and Richard Todd Davis cofounded LifeLock, a personal fraud protection company, in 2005. By 2014, the company had over three million subscribers.

"Muse": B–

Torres is stranded on a pre-industrial planet where she becomes the inspiration for a playwright.

Air date: March 26, 2000
Written by Joe Menosky
Directed by Mike Vejar
TV rating: 3.3

"It's been a strange couple of weeks. He needs me, or he's the one who's going to die on that stage." —Torres

This planet-based Torres episode features the writer of Ancient Greek-style plays inspired by B'Elanna Torres and Voyager, allowing Joe Menosky to satirize his own occupation and poke fun at the difficulties of writing for *Star Trek* and its characters while simultaneously allowing him the unique opportunity to present the same storyline in two different formats, with Torres's real story mirroring what's happening on the stage before the two stories converge in the last act.

Joseph Will, who has a Bachelor of Arts degree in theatre, guest stars as the playwright, sharing most of his scenes with Roxann Dawson. With a script that's built on their relationship, the chemistry between the two is the pivotal factor. Fortunately, they're quite good together, with Will giving his character a flair for the dramatic while Dawson intentionally underplays him with a deadpan delivery. Together, they give us an episode reminiscent of *TOS*, with two characters in a room talking about their issues, and the drama stemming from there (with dialogue that even includes some not-so-subtle messages to the producers of the show and the producers of television in general). Is it the roller coaster ride fans expect from modern television? Certainly not. But it is *very* Joe Menosky: a bit abstract and out of date, but well written and somewhat rewarding if you give it your patience.

Jo Will returns to play another part in Season Seven's "Workforce."

"Muse" was nominated for an Emmy for costumes.

Did you know? Menosky was still working on this episode's teleplay even as the sets were being prepped for shooting.

"Fury": C

Kes returns to seek revenge on Voyager.

Air date: May 3, 2000
Teleplay by Bryan Fuller & Michael Taylor
Story by Rick Berman & Brannon Braga
Directed by John Bruno
TV rating: 3.4

"You're helping the Vidiians, Kes. Why?" —Janeway

An angry Kes returns to Voyager and travels back in time to Season One to change her fate, with the show bringing the early period back to life through throwback characters, throwback costumes, and throwback hair. (You just have to be willing to overlook the fact that Kes is a little pudgier than she used to be, with Lien coming back on short notice after being out of the acting business.) Like *TNG's* "All Good Things," the end effect is an affectionate look at the past while also seeing just how far the show has come. And to be fair, the high concept is ambitious enough to sustain a certain level of intrigue throughout while being backed by some of the show's more impressive visuals. The problem is that in contrast to *TOS* and *TNG*, there's not really enough *VOY* nostalgia to make it worthwhile, and seeing Kes as a mean, bitter old woman makes it all the worse. (Bringing back Kes is a fine idea, but bringing her back one last time to arbitrarily use her as a villain in need of redemption is not.)

It's a bit of a shame because the episode delivers spectacle in spades. It just lacks any heart or spirit or some kind of meaning to pay it all off, ultimately devolving into a bit of a mess instead.

Did you know? Jennifer Lien was disappointed in her performance in this episode. "There were a lot of poor acting choices on my part in that one," she says. "I was very grateful that they asked me back and that I got to see everyone, but I hadn't been acting for a while, and I wasn't really thinking as creatively as I could have."

"Life Line": B

The Doctor is sent to the Alpha Quadrant to treat the creator of his program.

Air date: May 10, 2000
Teleplay by Robert Doherty, Raf Green & Brannon Braga
Story by John Bruno & Robert Picardo
Directed by Terry Windell
TV rating: 3.7

"I traveled halfway across the galaxy to treat you. The least you could do is show a little gratitude." —The Doctor

While Dwight Schultz and Marina Sirtis return to reprise Barclay and Troi for this offbeat episode, they are both upstaged by regular Robert Picardo and guest star Robert Picardo in this episode that teams up The Doctor with Dr. Lewis Zimmerman, The Doctor's creator.

Yes, it's another *Star Trek* episode with a double role, but unlike *TOS's* "The Enemy Within," *TNG's* "Datalore," or any of the others of this nature (at least up to this point), this one presents the two characters played by the same actor so believably, it's easy to forget about the technical marvel going on and enjoy the story as if Picardo and a twin were expertly bringing it to life.

Shot on some small stage sets representing Jupiter Station, this one is basically a character-based stage play that fleshes out the relationship between the holographic Doctor, who believes he has become something more substantial than his original programming, and his creator, who resents the reminder of the emergency medical holograms he created, as they are considered failures by Starfleet. And from the start, Picardo differentiates the two characters superficially while simultaneously giving them the same stubbornness, helping to give them a ying-yang relationship that's fun to see play out.

Schultz and Sirtis, of course, appeared earlier in the season in "Pathfinder," and they return in a sequel of sorts to it in Season Seven's "Inside Man." This one, however, is a standalone story, with Picardo never reprising Zimmerman again.

"Life Line" was nominated for an Emmy for visual effects.

Did you know? This episode includes a writing credit for Robert Picardo, who helped shape the story idea. Other *Star Trek* actors with writing credits for the franchise include Leonard Nimoy, William Shatner, Brent Spiner, and Simon Pegg, who all helped with scripts for the *Star Trek* movies, and guest star Stanley Adams (Cyrano Jones in "The Trouble With Tribbles") who cowrote *TOS's* "The Mark of Gideon." Walter Koenig, however, remains the only *Star Trek* actor to get a solo writing credit for an installment of the franchise, having conceived and written "The Infinite Vulcan" for *TAS*.

"The Haunting of Deck Twelve": C+

While Voyager goes without power for several hours, Neelix tells the children a ghost story that may or may not be true.

Air date: May 17, 2000
Teleplay by Mike Sussman, Kenneth Biller & Bryan Fuller
Story by Mike Sussman
Directed by David Livingston
TV rating: 3.0

"Gather round. But I'm warning you, this is not a tale for the faint of heart."
—Neelix

Star Trek dives into another ghost story, with Neelix's narration used as a framing device, allowing the writers to present it as less serious than *TNG's* "Sub Rosa" and give it a touch of *Rashomon*. (There's even a point where Neelix gets his technobabble wrong, and one of the Borg kids, like a hardcore *Star Trek* fan, calls him out on it.)

The skeletal story itself, about a nebula life-form integrating itself into the ship, is so vanilla and generically played out, it makes "Spirit Folk" seem like a fresh idea. But with Ethan Phillips's excellent voiceover work and the artistic license that comes naturally to a story presented as a virtual campfire tale rather than a literal reality, the show can get away with style trumping substance in the penultimate episode of the penultimate season. And the bottom line is it's just filler episode that does what it wants to do before clearing the decks for the season finale.

"Haunting" did go on to be nominated for an Emmy Award for visual effects.

Did you notice? As in "Night," Neelix vows once again to install curtains in his quarters. And, as in "Night," he neglects to actually do so.

"Unimatrix Zero": B

Seven is drawn into a virtual reality that some Borg drones visit during their regeneration cycles—a threat to the Borg Collective that Janeway seeks to exploit. (Season finale)

Air date: May 24, 2000
Teleplay by Brannon Braga & Joe Menosky
Story by Mike Sussman
Directed by Allan Kroeker
TV rating: 3.3

"Unimatrix Zero is our sanctuary. When we're here, our thoughts are our own."
—Axum

VOY concludes Season Six by introducing Mike Sussman's idea of Unimatrix Zero, a virtual sanctuary that only exists in the collective dreams of certain rogue Borg, allowing them to associate with each other as individuals and reminiscence about their lives before they were assimilated.

This, of course, doesn't sit well with the Borg Queen (reprised by Susanna Thompson, who took over the role in "Dark Frontier"), who has discovered its existence and is obsessed with putting an end to it, which in turn doesn't sit well with Janeway, who learns of the place through Seven and feels obligated to help preserve it, seeing it as an opportunity to start a Borg civil war. It's a lot of turf for an episode to cover, but that's what season ending cliffhangers are for.

Not surprisingly, the centerpiece of the episode is Seven, with Jeri Ryan getting a rare chance to play both Seven's Borg-side and her human-side, with Unimatrix Zero's nature giving the latter a forum to appear and assert itself, though this leads to some pushback from her Borg-side too. It's well played, and Ryan works especially well with guest star Mark Deakins (formerly a member of the Hirogen in "The Killing Game") with their two characters unsure of whether to reestablish a former relationship or forge a new one. The kicker to it all is that Seven, who is no longer part of the Collective, is the only Borg who can actually remember the sanctuary when she's not there, which simultaneously stymies the Borg Queen's efforts to learn more about the place and stops any renegade Borg from mounting a rebellion, unless Voyager can change the game.

All the same, being all setup with no payoff, "Unimatrix" is somewhat underwhelming as an episode itself, saving most of its bold strokes for the final act. But as a season finale, it checks all the boxes necessary to please most fans.

Did you know? Mike Sussman, born in 1967, was such a *Star Trek* fan growing up, he began writing stories about Kirk and Spock before his tenth birthday.

Season Six Roundup

With the absence of *DS9* and no *TNG* film on the radar screen in the months leading up to the year 2000, *VOY* entered Season Six as the franchise's lone new product.

As such, *VOY* inherited one of *Star Trek's* great talents, Ron Moore, who had previously worked with *VOY's* showrunner Brannon Braga on several *TNG* scripts, including the series finale and the first two feature films, before transferring to *DS9* and staying there until its conclusion. Unfortunately, Moore, upon becoming a co-producer for *VOY*, was unable to find a way to work with Braga and left after just a few episodes.

"When we were partners on *TNG*," Moore later reflected, "I was something of the senior partner because I started before him. But with *VOY*, I was going to work for him, and that was different. I just didn't understand what it would be like to work under someone with a different vision."

With Moore out the door, Kenneth Biller was promoted to co-executive producer, with Biller, Joe Menosky, and newcomers Raf Green and Robin Burger serving as the core of the writing staff while Michael Taylor served as story editor.

The new alchemy led to a daring season, with episodes like "One Small Step," "Pathfinder," "Blink of an Eye," "Virtuoso," and "Unimatrix Zero, Part I" taking risks and paying them off. We even get "Collective," which adds several pint-sized crewmembers to the show, though only one sticks around for the remainder of the series. (Unfortunately, we also get "Fury," which brings back Kes but doesn't know what to do with her.). And yet in some respects, the season plays it safe, with no mid-season two-parter and no giant leaps toward home. But with guest appearances from Dwight Schultz and Marina Sirtis and a connection forged between the Alpha Quadrant and the Delta Quadrant, there's still plenty to like and a feeling that home is closer than ever.

Behind the camera, Robert Picardo took advantage of the chance to direct his second episode of the series, "One Small Step" and even contributed to the writing of "Life Line." Meanwhile, Roxann Dawson made her directorial debut with "Riddles," which would lead to another directing assignment in Season Seven and a recurring spot in the director's chair for *ENT*.

Unfortunately, despite Emmy nominations for costumes, hairstyling, make-up, music, sound editing, and visual effects (which covers just about everything but the catering), the show failed to win in any of the categories, though "Bride of Chaotica!" topped the competition for Best Character Hair Styling at the Hollywood Makeup Artist and Hair Stylist Guild Awards while Jay Chattaway, Dennis McCarthy, and David Bell were once again honored by the American Society of Composers, Authors, and Publishers for *VOY's* music.

With sports teams, of course, they say, "There's always next year." And there would indeed be another season for *VOY*. But everyone understood, thanks to the precedent set by *TNG* and *DS9*, Season Seven would probably be the last.

Season Seven

Production Order
(with air date order in parentheses)

1. "Unimatrix Zero, Part II" (1st)
2. "Imperfection" (2nd)
3. "Drive" (3rd)
4. "Critical Care" (5th)
5. "Repression" (4th)
6. "Inside Man" (6th)
7. "Flesh and Blood" (9th)
8. "Body and Soul" (7th)
9. "Nightingale" (8th)
10. "Shattered" (10th)
11. "Lineage" (11th)
12. "Repentance" (12th)
13. "Prophecy" (13th)
14. "The Void" (14th)
15. "Workforce" (15th)
16. "Workforce, Part II" (16th)
17. "Human Error" (17th)
18. "Q2" (18th)
19. "Author, Author" (19th)
20. "Friendship One" (20th)
21. "Natural Law" (21st)
22. "Homestead" (22nd)
23. "Renaissance Man" (23rd)
24. "Endgame" (24th)

The Seventh Season Cast

Captain Janeway: Kate Mulgrew
Commander Chakotay: Robert Beltran
B'Elanna Torres: Roxann Dawson
Tom Paris: Robert Duncan McNeill
Neelix: Ethan Phillips
The Doctor: Robert Picardo
Tuvok: Tim Russ
Harry Kim: Garrett Wang
Seven of Nine: Jeri Ryan

Notable Guest Stars

Susanna Thompson
Mark Deakins
Susanna Thompson
Manu Intiraymi
Marley S. McClean
Cyia Batten
Larry Drake
Gregory Itzin
Dwight Schultz
Richard Herd
Marina Sirtis
Fritz Sperberg
Megan Gallagher
Ron Glass
Jeff Yagher
Scarlett Pomers
Martha Hackett
Juan Garcia
Jeff Kober
Don Most
John de Lancie
Keegan de Lancie
Neil C. Vipond
Rob LaBelle
Julianne Christie
Alexander Enberg
Vaughn Armstrong
Alice Krige

"Unimatrix Zero, Part II": B

Voyager's crew assists rogue Borg in their fight against the Borg Queen. (Season premiere)

Air date: October 4, 2000
Teleplay by Brannon Braga & Joe Menosky
Story by Mike Sussman, Brannon Braga & Joe Menosky
Directed by Mike Vejar
TV rating: 4.5

"You wanted to destroy Unimatrix Zero. We're just lending you a hand."
—Janeway

What "Part II" lacks in surprise, it makes up for with wise choices. Think of it as a reboot of *TNG's* "Descent, Part II," this time with the kinks worked out. Once again, the Borg Collective is experiencing some internal strife, and once again our friends are caught in the middle. This time, however, Janeway and her crew play a much more active role, Prime Directive be damned.

Susanna Thompson, Mark Deakins, and the other guest stars from "Part I" return to reprise their roles, helping to give the episode essentially three plots. Playing the part of star-crossed lovers, Seven and her old boyfriend (Deakins) reestablish their relationship in Unimatrix Zero, only to discover that outside of this doomed dream world, they live on opposite sides of the galaxy. Giving us the spectacle of some good old-fashioned spaceship fights, Chakotay and some of the renegade Borg battle the Borg Queen's forces. And meanwhile, forming the heart of the episode, Janeway and the Queen herself (Thompson) engage in a battle of wits and wills.

None of these ideas are particularly original, and the episode falls short of the game-changing season openers from *DS9*, unwilling to take the risks its defunct sister show made a living out of. But its various plotlines successfully

202

play to the strengths of the actors involved, as well playing to strengths of the show as a whole, with the writers generously incorporating all the regulars, save for Ethan Phillips, into the action and getting its money's worth out of each.

The Borg return in the series finale, with Janeway and the Queen having a final confrontation.

Did you notice? In the opening of "Alice," Kim and Paris attempt to guess Tuvok's age. (133? 162?) We never get an answer in that episode, but in "Unimatrix" we learn that Tuvok is 113 Earth-years old.

"Imperfection": B

Seven's life is in danger when a crucial Borg implant malfunctions.

Air date: October 11, 2000
Teleplay by Carleton Eastlake & Robert Doherty
Story by Andre Bormanis
Directed by David Livingston
TV rating: 3.6

"I'm sorry for what's happening. You have every right to be angry, but that isn't going to help us solve this problem." —Janeway

This Seven/Icheb episode sees Seven develop a life threatening condition and struggle to accept help while Icheb, initially ignored by the others due to his age, engages in an earnest effort to save her.

The episode itself begins by pushing the other Borg kids out the door, ending their stories. (They never appear again.) And there's also the reappearance of the Delta Flyer, despite its destruction a couple episodes before. (This is explained in the next episode, originally meant to air before "Imperfection.") But the center of the episode itself is an allegory for a kidney transplant. A piece of Borg technology in Seven is failing, and she needs a new one.

Jeri Ryan, of course, is fantastic, taking Seven through the stages of denial, anger, frustration, and ultimately acceptance with a heartbreaking sincerity befitting her character. But it's Manu Intiraymi, as Icheb, who gives another surprisingly strong performance and steals the show, stepping up to assert himself as someone more important to *VOY* than the occasional guest star he was originally conceived to be.

Intiraymi returns for six more episodes in Season Seven, beginning with "Nightingale."

Did you know? As an inside joke, a graphic displaying the name of deceased crewmembers includes several characters from NBC's *The West Wing*. Graphic supervisor Mike Okuda says, "Me, my wife, and graphic artist James Van Over were big *West Wing* fans. We used to joke that the show, with its close-knit family of characters on an idealistic mission, should have been a *Star Trek* spinoff."

"Drive": B–

When Paris postpones a romantic getaway to participate in an interstellar race, Torres begins questioning whether they should continue their relationship.

Air date: October 18, 2000
Written by Michael Taylor
Directed by Winrich Kolbe
TV rating: 3.7

"Tom is a great guy. We've had a lot of fun together, and that seems to be enough for him. But not for me." —Torres

This Paris/Torres episode with a dash of Harry Kim starts off like a lost episode of *Buck Rodgers in the 25th Century*, with Paris, in Buck's role, getting drawn into a galactic race full of alien intrigue, conflict, and drama—and sweet race suits. And as this part of the story moves forward, it sustains its throwback feel, with a reception, a deception, and an apperception that Buck and Wilma might navigate through before somehow finding a way to come out on top.

But Michael Taylor, the writer of *DS9's* "The Visitor" and "In the Pale Moonlight," layers the script with a passive Paris/Torres dispute to give the episode more depth.

Robert Duncan McNeill, reprising his dual roles as ace pilot and Lieutenant One-Liner, is fine as ever, though Taylor misses an opportunity to give his character any kind of growth. (Taylor also messes up his Tom Paris history, with a line incorrectly stating Paris was expelled from Starfleet Academy. Taylor was likely thinking of McNeill's other *Star Trek* character, Nicholas Locarno.) But Roxann Dawson is "Drive's" secret sauce, giving an intentionally restrained performance of a person unsure of how to reconnect with her significant other—and pondering if it's worth the effort.

Meanwhile, former *DS9* guest stars Cyia Batten (Gul Dukat's daughter in "Indiscretion" and "Return to Grace"), Brian George (Dr. Bashir's father in "Doctor Bashir, I Presume"), and Patrick Kilpatrick (a soldier in "The Siege of AR-558" who saves Nog's life) fill out the guest cast, playing the episode's main alien representatives in generic fashion. (Let's just say no one who's watched much *Buck Rodgers* is going to be shocked by who turns out to be a saboteur!)

It might not be the best Paris/Torres episode. ("Course: Oblivion" certainly gives us a better wedding.) But once the main drama gets going, "Drive" covers enough bases to remain engaging throughout.

Did you know? This episode was inspired, in part, by *Death Race 2000*, a 1975 science fiction sports film set in a dystopian future that has since become a cult classic.

"Repression": D+

Tuvok investigates a series of assaults targeting former members of the Maquis.

Air date: October 25, 2000
Teleplay by Mark Haskell Smith
Story by Kenneth Biller
Directed by Winrich Kolbe
TV rating: 3.2

"I can't explain it, Captain, but I can't ignore it either. Someone on board is responsible, and I intend to find out who it is." —Tuvok

Yes, it's another Maquis episode, albeit one coming three or four years after the Maquis-well ran dry.

This time it's a whodunnit Tuvok story polished by an uncredited Brannon Braga, with the Vulcan investigating attacks on former members of the Maquis while the writers liberally borrow from *The Manchurian Candidate*. (No prizes for guessing who the culprit turns out to be!)

Season Three's "Worst Case Scenario" gets away with a similar story because its outside the box approach gives the plot a whimsical charm, imploring us not to take it too seriously. "Repression," on the other hand, wants to be a psychological thriller in the same vein as *TNG's* "Identity Crisis," but lacks the creativity needed to pull it off.

Truth be told, this is one *VOY* episode that probably should never have been made but slipped through the cracks at a time when the writing staff was running out of ideas.

Did you know? This is the last *VOY* episode directed by Winrich Kolbe, director of sixteen episodes of *TNG*, thirteen episodes of *DS9*, and eighteen episodes of *VOY*. He would go on to direct one episode of *ENT* before taking a teaching position at Savannah College of Art and Design. Kolbe passed away in 2012 at age 72.

"Critical Care": B+

After being stolen from Voyager, The Doctor is put to work on a hospital ship where health care is rationed based on social status.

Air date: November 1, 2000
Teleplay by James Kahn
Story by Kenneth Biller & Robert Doherty
Directed by Terry Windell
TV rating: 3.4

"They brought me here to make the hard choices they don't want to make."
—Chellick

This Doctor episode digs into the issues of a bureaucratic health care system ten years before President Obama pushed the issue to the forefront of American politics.

The idea itself is not far removed from *TNG's* "The Masterpiece Society," a story cowritten by "Critical Care's" teleplay writer. In both, the good of society is prioritized over the wants and needs of individuals, turning people into mere cogs in a machine. This one is more heartless, however, with citizens enjoying a higher status able to get medical treatment for nonessential procedures while those with lower status are left to die.

In some ways, such a story is reminiscent of some episodes of *TOS*, with several installments that explore the danger of letting a computer decide who gets what and who lives and who dies. But of all *Star Trek's* chief medical officers, no one is a better fit for this doctor versus an alien-HMO plot than *VOY's* EMH, with the absurdity of the situation throwing The Doctor out of his comfort zone and forcing him to reinvent his approach and learn to game the system. Picardo plays this to perfection, giving his character a smug confidence when he succeeds and a resigned sense of frustration when he suffers a setback. The overall issue, of course, is that the game is rigged, setting him up for failure, and The Doctor knows it. To help flesh this all out, Picardo is joined by a guest cast that includes Larry Drake as Chellick, a bureaucratic health care manager, Dublin James as a dying patient, and Gregory Itzin and Paul Scherrer as doctors for the haves and have-nots respectively.

Meanwhile, in the B story, the Voyager crew attempts to track The Doctor down, chasing the trail of his abductor, Gar, played by John Kassir, the voice of the crypt keeper in HBO's *Tales from the Crypt*. Writer James Kahn keeps this part appropriately short and gives it a comedic edge, which works well to counterbalance the more serious matters in the A story.

Unfortunately, the episode never digs deep into the real problems and solutions associated with real health care systems, content to fashion its own fake system which members of the audience can point to as an allegory for whatever health care system they oppose. And everything doesn't get wrapped up with the finality we've come to expect when *Star Trek* does these sorts of stories. (Kirk would shoot the machine and tell Chellick that he better start looking for a new line of work.) But as a *VOY* medical story, "Critical Care" still stands out as one of the better of the bunch.

Did you know? This episode aired just after the 2000 American presidential debates in which both candidates, Al Gore and George W. Bush, proposed different ways to stop Health Maintenance Organizations (HMOs) from dictating how patients are treated.

"Inside Man": C+

While a hologram of Reginald Barclay interacts with the Voyager crew in the Delta Quadrant, the real Barclay, in the Alpha Quadrant, believes the hologram might have been tampered with.

Air date: November 8, 2000
Written by Robert Doherty
Directed by Allan Kroeker
TV rating: 3.0

"Do you really think it's possible that Leosa stole my hologram?" —Barclay

This Barclay episode brings back all the major players from Season Six's "Pathfinder," including Dwight Schultz and Marina Sirtis, for a small-scale sequel featuring some alien mischief.

Schultz himself gets a double role, as he establishes the titular character, a secret agent hologram who visits Voyager and turns into the life of the party, while also reprising the real Barclay, the awkward dork at Starfleet Headquarters who's trying to figure out what's going on and put a stop to it.

Unfortunately, the caper plot itself is somewhat thin, and the character interactions are simply retreads of what we've seen before, breaking no new ground. And while the episode tries to spice up the visuals with some location shooting on the beach at Leo Carrillo State Park, the setting ultimately proves superfluous.

Nonetheless, Schultz and Sirtis do work well together, and Schultz is especially good as the evil hologram attempting to manipulate the Voyager crew, even if the actor upstages the regulars in the process.

Schultz would return later in the season for "Author, Author." "Inside Man," however, marks Sirtis's last *VOY* appearance.

Did you know? Actor Leo Carrillo (1880–1961), most famous for playing Pancho in *The Cisco Kid*, was one of California's pioneering nature conservationists and served on the California Beach and Parks commission for eighteen years. In 1953, Leo Carrillo State Park, just west of Malibu, was named in his honor. The location has since been used in many film productions, including *Grease* (1978), *The Karate Kid* (1984), *Point Break* (1991), and *Inception* (2010).

"Body and Soul": B

When aliens board the Delta Flyer looking for "photonic insurgents," The Doctor must hide himself in Seven's body.

Air date: November 15, 2000
Teleplay by Eric Morris, Phyllis Strong & Mike Sussman
Story by Michael Taylor
Directed by Robert Duncan McNeill
TV rating: 3.6

"Seven downloaded my program into her cybernetic matrix. An interesting sensation, to say the least." —The Doctor

For the second time in three episodes, The Doctor finds himself a prisoner on a foreign ship. Only this time, he's also in a foreign body.

Like *TOS's* "Turnabout Intruder," the story here is really secondary to the gimmick: Jeri Ryan gets to take over The Doctor's part. This gives the actress her meatiest role of the season, and with the help of both Picardo and a director who's acted beside Robert Picardo for over six seasons, she pulls it off rather well, with a convincing performance Picardo couldn't have done much better.

Meanwhile, Janeway and the Voyager crew have to come to The Doctor's rescue in a B story that also features Tuvok suffering from *pon farr*, the Vulcan condition requiring him to mate. Russ goes for broke with the *pon farr*, but Janeway upstages him with her deadpan delivery of a threat to a hostile alien captain: "We're both reasonable people. I suggest a compromise. Your vessel will escort us through Lokirrim territory. That way you can keep an eye on us, make sure we don't reactivate our holodecks. The other alternative is we destroy your ship."

Both stories play out in generic fashion, with few surprises, but again, that's not really the point here. As a vehicle for Jeri Ryan to step outside her usual box, the episode is a great success, and as a *VOY* episode as a whole, it's quite entertaining, with Ryan and Picardo sharing a touching scene at the end to tie it all up.

Did you know? To assist Ryan, Picardo performed her scenes as The Doctor himself before the cameras began rolling so she could observe his acting choices and mimic what he was doing.

"Nightingale": C

When Harry Kim rescues a crippled alien starship, the grateful crew offers him command.

Air date: November 22, 2000
Teleplay by Andre Bormanis
Story by Robert Lederman & Dave Long
Directed by LeVar Burton
TV rating: 2.8

"I know I can do this, and the Kraylor are giving me a chance to prove it."
—Kim

LeVar Burton ("Timeless") returns to direct another Harry Kim episode, though this one fails to stand out from the crowd.

As a story, "Nightingale" works fine, more or less. Some of the key moments are predictable and forced, but with twists and turns at just the right moments, the plot remains engaging from start to finish. But the concept that Harry Kim is a green ensign who needs to prove himself is an idea that has worn thin by Season Seven. It's as if the writers keep reading a description from the show's original bible and basing all their Harry stories on where the character started, as opposed to accounting for how his experiences have enriched him. (Come to think of it, had "Nightingale" come along in Season Three or Four, it might have been a standout episode, offering Wang a foundation he could build upon for several more years.)

Instead, what we get is just a mixed bag, with Ron Glass giving a wonderful performance as an alien, but the lack of a stellar script making his lone *Star Trek* appearance a wasted opportunity. Meanwhile, Manu Intiraymi reprises Icheb in a B story, used for comedic filler, where the young Borg believes Torres may be attracted to him and doesn't know how to handle the situation.

Nonetheless, "Nightingale," featuring a backdrop of alien intrigue for Kim to navigate through, is a perfectly acceptable hour of television, even if it's only a must-see for Harry Kim completists.

Did you know? Ron Glass is best known for playing Detective Ron Harris in ABC's police sitcom, *Barney Miller* (1975–1982). He also acquired some fame for playing Shepherd Book in Fox's science fiction series *Firefly* (2002) and reprised the role in *Serenity*, a 2005 film based on the series.

"Flesh and Blood": A

Voyager answers a distress call from a Hirogen outpost only to find carnage caused by Voyager's own holographic technology.

Air date: November 29, 2000
Teleplay by Bryan Fuller, Raf Green & Kenneth Biller
Story by Jack Monaco, Bryan Fuller & Raf Green
Directed by Mike Vejar & David Livingston
TV rating: 3.4

"Enhanced memory, comprehensive tactical algorithms, expandable data processing. These holograms have the ability to learn and adapt." —Janeway

This special two-hour sequel to "The Killing Game" brings back the Hirogen for one final story: a chase episode with no expense spared featuring The Doctor and a rogue group of holograms. Like "The Killing Game," it was actually shot as two episodes back-to-back (the first directed by Vejar and the second directed by Livingston), though like "Dark Frontier," a two-hour presentation was planned all along.

It all begins simply enough. The Hirogen, having modified a holodeck to create more dangerous prey, have now become the hunted, and Captain Janeway, knowing it's her ship's technology that created the mess, feels obligated to help end this situation. But from there, everything goes sideways. It turns out that the Hirogen, who aren't used to being prey and who don't know how to take orders from others, are about as helpful as a Ferengi benefactor. Then the holograms abduct The Doctor, and we find out that they're actually rather sympathetic. But hang onto your Klingon khakis, because we're just getting started. As Janeway finds a way to make use of the Hirogens' overambitious pursuit of their enemy, The Doctor begins assisting the holograms, and from there, it's hard to even know who to root for, though it's sure fun to watch everything play out.

The nature of the story, of course, gives many guest stars a chance to appear, with seven of them credited in the opening and an additional five credited at the close. But the episode benefits most from three significant players: Ryan Bollman, a young actor who would go on to carve out a successful television career, plays a Hirogen technician while Cindy Katz, who previously had a bit part in *DS9's* "Second Skin," plays a holographic Cardassian, with both characters getting caught up in moral dilemmas as their superiors lose their focus and judgment. But it's Jeff Yagher who serves as the straw that stirs the raktajino, playing Iden, a holographic Bajoran with strong spiritual beliefs, who is something of an enigma until he reveals his true self in the final act. The writers probably take this too far, with Iden becoming too cartoonish by the end, but Yagher shines in the role nonetheless, making his only *Star Trek* part one of the more memorable guest spots of *VOY's* seven seasons.

212

And yet even with all these oars in the water and an ever-evolving plot that shows off more alien designs than perhaps any *Star Trek* episode since *TAS's* "The Time Trap," the writers still find a way to keep the regulars relevant, with The Doctor and Janeway having to find a way to work through their issues without getting everyone killed in the process. For *VOY*, it's a bold presentation that pays off big, giving the final season a signature piece.

Did you know? The holographic characters in this episode include representatives of the Jem'Hadar and the Breen, the only such appearances of these aliens on *VOY*.

DS9's Jem'Hadar (Photo by Jason Van Horn)

"Shattered": C+

After a temporal anomaly fractures space-time, causing different parts of Voyager to exist in different time periods, Chakotay must find a way to return the ship to a single timeframe.

Air date: January 17, 2001
Teleplay by Michael Taylor
Story by Mike Sussman & Michael Taylor
Directed by Terry Windell
TV rating: 2.8

"On the bridge, it's before Voyager even left the Alpha Quadrant. In Engineering, it's the time when the Kazon took over the ship." —Chakotay

This high concept Chakotay episode, with each section of the ship representing a different time period, gives the writers a playground in which to flex their creative muscles while also allowing for the return of a long lost crewmember. Unfortunately, as a budget saving bottle episode (to help the show recoup losses from "Flesh and Blood"), it lacks the ambition or substance the idea could otherwise merit.

After some initial action and confusion, things quickly boil down to a Chakotay/Janeway mission, with a MacGuffin plot forcing the two to visit each section of the ship to put things right, giving us a tour of different time periods that touch upon Season One's "Caretaker", Season Three's "Basics, Part II" and "Macrocosm," Season Four's "Scorpion, Part II," and Season Five's "Bride of Chaotica!" and "Bliss." (Tim Russ, following his "Amok Time" period in "Body and Soul," continues his recreation of Leonard Nimoy's "greatest hits" with a scene lifted nearly verbatim from *The Wrath of Khan*.) It all will likely mean little to those who haven't watched a lot of the previous episodes of the show, but for fans who have stuck with *VOY* through six seasons-plus, it's not a bad trip down memory lane.

"Shattered" was nominated for an Emmy for costumes.

Did you know? This episode marks the last appearance of Tom Paris's black and white Captain Proton holodeck program.

"Lineage": B+

When Torres becomes pregnant, she must face a private fear rooted in childhood memories.

Air date: January 24, 2001
Written by James Kahn
Directed by Peter Lauritson
TV rating: 2.8

"When the people around you are all one way and you're not, you can't help feeling like there's something wrong with you." —Torres

Like Season Two's "Tattoo" and Season Five's "Gravity," this episode alternates between scenes of the featured character in the present with scenes from the character's childhood, with both parts weaving together to form a narrative.

In this case, that featured player is B'Elanna Torres, and as a character study, the future *Lost* formula works well, with her history and pregnancy making the episode simultaneously about the past, present, and future all at once.

Thanks to a science fiction concept that's rapidly becoming science reality, The Doctor is able to give Torres a chance to look at the future development of her child. But like the best science fiction, the drama isn't about the science itself, but the human reaction to it. She can't help but be tempted to manipulate the development before it even happens.

Along the way, Roxann Dawson gives another great performance, and Jessica Gaona is quite good as well, playing a young Torres. The latter shares most of her scenes with Juan Garcia, who brings some depth to John Torres, a father who is becoming increasingly overwhelmed by the complex husband/fatherhood situation he's fallen into after marrying a Klingon.

The end result, much like "Ex Post Facto," "Tuvix," and many other *Star Trek* episodes, is a story built upon an issue that we will never specifically encounter in our daily lives but can nonetheless identify and sympathize with as if it were a kitchen table topic.

B'Elanna Torres encounters her father once again in "Author, Author."

Did you notice? The big decision John Torres makes at the end of this episode is actually casually mentioned by Lieutenant Torres in Season One's "Eye of the Needle."

"Repentance": B

After Voyager rescues a damaged alien vessel carrying convicts to their executions, Seven and Neelix struggle to accept the aliens' legal system.

Air date: January 31, 2001
Teleplay by Robert Doherty
Story by Mike Sussman & Robert Doherty
Directed by Mike Vejar
TV rating: 2.9

"He was suffering from a neurological defect. He couldn't control his behavior."
—Torres

VOY looks at capital punishment in an episode that displays some surprising depth as it works its way to its conclusions, even if the outcomes are as predictable as the end of a Kirk/Spock chess match.

The nuts and bolts of the episode feature two intersecting plots. In the A story, Seven becomes acquainted with a death row inmate with a bad attitude, though his demeanor begins to shift when he's given proper medical treatment. As a former Borg who did awful things before being saved by Voyager, she sees a lot of herself in him, and she takes an interest in his possible rehabilitation. Meanwhile, in the B story, Neelix befriends a seemingly kind alien who implies he's innocent and claims his people are simply targeted by the authorities because of prejudice.

Jeff Kober, best known as Sergeant Evan "Dodger" Winslow from ABC's *China Beach* (1988–1991), plays the first alien, believably playing a change of heart, while F.J. Rio, best known to *Star Trek* fans for his small role on *DS9* as Enrique Muniz, plays the second, coming across as the perfect buddy. (There's also a guest spot for Tim de Zarn as a warden, allowing him to share the screen with Kate Mulgrew, who knows just how to play Janeway as the captain walks a tricky diplomatic tightrope.)

Neither death row alien, of course, has much of a future, and as the episode moves forward, it illustrates the pointlessness of putting these people to death (whether they repent or not), as their executions are merely a show to please the family and friends of their victims, with their deaths failing to serve a productive purpose. But the beauty is how the show is able to pull this off without manipulating the plot to prove a point or forcing the characters to be overly preachy. It's especially interesting how the legal system in question gives the victims' families the power to choose the fate of those found guilty. This very idea has gained traction on social media, even though it would lead to different sentences for the same crime and open the door for dangerous people to return to society if the victims' families, for whatever reasons, decide it's best.

And yet despite being a solid piece of entertainment, "Repentance" has few real surprises, with savvy viewers likely knowing most of what's going to

216

happen before it actually happens. That is, however, due to the writers making the right choices.

Did you know? In the United States, some states have the death penalty and some don't. But while there will always be political grandstanding, no state without a death penalty has a government eager to enact one. The reason is simple: money. Capital cases, which require two trials (one to decide the verdict and another to decide the punishment), are expensive, requiring more attorneys, more investigators, more time and experts, and a larger jury pool than other trials. And the cost of incarcerating those on death row throughout the lengthy appeals process is significantly more than incarcerating a standard prisoner.

Because of these costs, taxpayers in California alone have spent an average of $308 million for each execution the state performed between 1976 and 2006, its most recent death penalty period. This cost taxpayers $184 million more per year than they spent on all those sentenced to life in prison without the possibility of parole.

Meanwhile, since 1973, over one hundred people in the United States who were found guilty and sentenced to death by the courts were able to prove they were innocent afterward.

"Prophecy": C+

Voyager becomes a battleground for the descendants of a group of Klingon pilgrims, some of whom believe that Torres is carrying their savior.

Air date: February 7, 2001
Teleplay by Mike Sussman & Phyllis Strong
Story by Larry Nemecek, J. Kelley Burke, Raf Green & Kenneth Biller
Directed by Terry Windell
TV rating: 3.0

"I believe the Kuvah'Magh is the unborn child of B'Elanna Torres." —Kohlar

With *Star Trek* author Larry Nemecek teaming up with half the writing staff, *VOY* tries its hand at another Klingon episode, this time with a group of the warrior race arguing over whether Torres is the Klingon equivalent of the Blessed Mary carrying baby Jesus.

As such, "Prophecy" touches on all the Klingon clichés: the petty bickering, the mess hall insults, a fight, and the required variation of "a good day to die." (This time, in a humorous twist, it's Torres telling Paris, "Today would be a very bad day to die.") It all gives it a *TNG* vibe that could have the viewer double-checking the credits to see if Ron Moore's name is in there somewhere. Unfortunately, the number of writers we have in his place only hurts the finished product, leading to an unfocused offering that goes a little wayward at points, leaving the viewer to wonder at times what this one is really about.

Wren T. Brown guest stars as Kohlar, the Klingon commander, summoning his inner Avery Brooks as he champions the idea of a *kuvah'magh,* the savior of his people. (Curiously, Brown appears to wear two different wigs throughout the episode, causing his hair to alternate between scenes.) Meanwhile, Sherman Howard plays his Klingon adversary, T'Greth, who has his doubts. Both actors, having previously guested on *TNG* (in "Manhunt" and "Suddenly Human," respectively), know how to play the game and deliver what's needed. The fact is, however, the story as a whole fails to play to *VOY's* unique strengths and only stands out for being the rare Klingon episode on a show that more often features other aliens.

"Prophecy" went on to be nominated for an Emmy for hairstyling.

Larry Nemecek

Did you know? A version of this story was pitched by journalist/author Larry Nemecek when *VOY* was still in its infancy. "That was from my first *Voyager* pitch session, and they bought it," he recalls. "But that was before the pilot had even aired. So I got paid, but it kept getting bumped on down the road for whatever reason, and I figured, 'They're never going to use this.' Then I visited as they were preparing to shoot the last season, and they asked me if I could locate my notes for that story because they were interested in it but they couldn't find their own notes. So I dug up mine, and then Raf and Ken had to update the story so it would fit in with what was going on by that time, and Mike and Phyllis were then chosen to write the teleplay. So we ended up with half a dozen names on the credits."

"The Void": C–

Voyager becomes trapped in an empty region of space where stranded starships prey on each other to survive.

Air date: February 14, 2001
Teleplay by Raf Green & James Kahn
Story by Raf Green & Kenneth Biller
Directed by Mike Vejar
TV rating: 3.1

"Voyager can't survive here alone. But if we form a temporary alliance with other ships, maybe we can pool our resources and escape." —Janeway

This is essentially a copy of *TAS's* "The Time Trap," though it's unlikely your average *Star Trek* viewer—or the people making *VOY*—were familiar with any of the 1970s animated episodes back in 2001. (Heck, few people are familiar with the series today!)

Like "The Time Trap," we have a number of ships trapped in a pocket of space, and a story that emphasizes the moral dilemma of working together for mutual benefit versus working alone for survival. Unfortunately, to intensify the drama of the choice, the writers create an internal conflict of sorts amongst Voyager's crew itself. This comes across as a bit artificial, with some of the crewmembers too quick to question Janeway's choice to form a coalition, suggesting they become plunderers instead. (Ironically, these sort of ideas, where Voyager becomes trapped amongst hostile aliens and its crew disagrees on the best way forward, were supposed to be a cornerstone of the series as a whole, though this changed somewhat as the show evolved, forcing the writers to create to a new area of space to enable a microcosm of these issues to surface here.)

As an added element, Jonathan Del Arco, best known to *Star Trek* fans as Hugh the Borg in *TNG* and *PIC*, guest stars as an alien from the void who befriends The Doctor in a B story of sorts. But the subplot only clutters up the story and brings up more questions than answers. (How did this species, which requires oxygen, evolve in the void, and how does it survive when there aren't any ships around to hide in?)

Meanwhile, Robin Sachs, an English actor who had previously auditioned for Sisko for *DS9* and The Doctor for *VOY*, and Michael Shamus Wiles, a prolific American character actor who has appeared in countless television shows and movies, don heavy make-up to help round out the guest cast and paint a portrait of alien intrigue.

But really, the story as a whole is done better in "The Time Trap," where Kirk and the Klingons are forced to work together to escape, and as a *VOY* episode, what we get is largely forgettable.

"The Void" would go on to be nominated for an Emmy for make-up.

220

Did you notice? After the series makes a big deal out of Voyager's search for deuterium in "Demon," the writers give Paris a line of dialogue in "The Void" to explain why the hunt for this fuel is no longer an issue: "Why would anyone steal deuterium? You can find it anywhere."

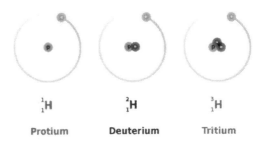

$_1^1H$	$_1^2H$	$_1^3H$
Protium	Deuterium	Tritium

Deuterium Facts:

• A stable isotope of hydrogen
• Discovered in 1931
• Also called hydrogen-2, D, and ^2H
• Not radioactive
• Named for Greek *deuteros*, meaning second
• Found in about 1 in 6400 hydrogen atoms
• Easily found in areas of the Delta Quadrant if you know where to look

"Workforce": A-

Some members of the Voyager crew, with no memory of who they are, begin new jobs on an industrial planet with a labor shortage.

Air date: February 21, 2001
Written by Kenneth Biller & Bryan Fuller
Directed by Allan Kroeker
TV rating: 3.0

"We have a diverse work force." —Alien supervisor

This two-parter, with parallels to "The Killing Game," draws inspiration from *Metropolis* (1927) to paint a dystopian portrait of workers trapped in an industrialized society that depends upon them for manual labor.

The tone is set immediately with an impressive establishing shot of a planet surface before we begin to see the various Voyager crewmembers, including a perky Janeway, settling into their new positions, unaware of their previous lives. Like "The Killing Game" and "Flesh and Blood," no expense is spared in the presentation, with the look of the interiors and exteriors more on par with the *Star Trek* feature films than the television shows of the era, and a bold musical score backing them up, accenting the drama.

About halfway through, the B story finally starts up, with the few crewmembers who have not been captured, including Chakotay, meeting on Voyager to work out what happened and figure out what to do about it, helping to catch us up in the process.

Similar to "The Killing Game," the characters without their memories are still the same characters we've gotten to know over the years. Janeway is still Janeway, Paris is still Paris, Torres is still Torres...they've just been transplanted into a new setting, making new relationships and settling into new lives where people are largely defined by their work. (Tuvok, in a substory, is an exception, as the poor guy is all messed up and must undergo some medical treatments by his abductors to "fix" a memory wipe that didn't quite go right.) There's also a bit of conflict between Kim and The Doctor on the ship which plays well off previous episodes, with The Doctor reprising his role as an Emergency Command Hologram from "Tinker Tenor Doctor Spy" and Ensign Kim, with some command experience of his own, not wanting to be his subordinate.

Meanwhile, former *North and South* star James Read heads up a large guest cast to provide a love interest for Janeway, while others appear in various other roles throughout the episode to create the bustling alien metropolis. (Most of the guest stars are great, but casting Tom Virtue as Janeway's supervisor was probably a mistake, as many fans will remember him as a lieutenant from *VOY's* first two seasons.)

With all these characters, the writers have a lot of moving parts to work with, but they balance all the different subplots quite nicely before leading them

222

all into a big cliffhanger, leaving the conclusion responsible for sorting everything out.

"Workforce" was nominated for an Emmy for visual effects.

Did you know? The actress who plays Umali, the owner of the bar who serves the workers in this episode, first appeared in *Star Trek* as a child in *TOS's* "Miri." She is the brother of Phil Morris ("One Small Step").

Iona Morris, lower left, in "Miri" (Fun fact: the girl behind her and the girl to her immediate left are both William Shatner's daughters.)

"Workforce, Part II": B+

Chakotay leads an effort to rescue his shipmates from an alien planet.

Air date: February 28, 2001
Teleplay by Kenneth Biller & Michael Taylor
Story by Kenneth Biller & Bryan Fuller
Directed by Roxann Dawson
TV rating: 3.2

"My real name is Chakotay. I'm an officer aboard the Federation starship Voyager. Members of my crew were abducted and their memories were altered, and they were put to work here." —Chakotay

Roxanne Dawson oversees a conclusion that relies more on its actors and less on pizzazz than its big budget prequel, giving us a quieter but still satisfying episode.

In this installment, Chakotay must convince Janeway that she's the captain of a starship and her crew needs her to help rescue them, which is like asking someone to take a trip down a rabbit hole. This would be a hard sell in any circumstance, but when someone is happy with the direction of her life, it's especially difficult. Mulgrew plays it perfectly, with Janeway all but rolling her eyes and clearly thinking, "Why is it that when everything is going just fine, this guy has to come out of left field to try to upend everything?"

Meanwhile, Seven, after a Vulcan mind meld with Tuvok, begins an effort of her own to uncover the truth of the situation, with a sympathetic criminal investigator, played by Robert Joy, eventually lending her a hand. These two plots eventually merge, allowing the writers to begin consolidating the characters, while Donny Most plays an evil neuropsychiatrist who serves as the episode's chief antagonist. And as all this is going on, we get a pair of stories on board the ship, as Torres, with Neelix's help, attempts to regain her memories and Ensign Kim and The Doctor try to work while playing hide-and-go-seek with some alien vessels, giving us a few space battles.

Once again, everything is well balanced and well paced, making for another entertaining episode while polishing off another successful two-parter.

"Part II" was nominated for an Emmy for Dennis McCarthy's score.

Did you know? At the beginning of this episode, B'Elanna Torres lies unconscious on a table while The Doctor and Neelix discuss her situation. For the cast and crew, shooting the scene was somewhat surreal, since it meant the director had to lie in the middle of a scene with her eyes closed while the scene progressed around her. Yet this wasn't the first time such a thing had happened. *Star Trek III: The Search for Spock* (1984), directed by Leonard Nimoy, had a nearly identical situation during a scene in which Dr. McCoy talks to an unconscious Spock.

224

"Human Error": B–

When Seven experiments with socialization on the holodeck, her emotions begin to overwhelm her Borg implants.

Air date: March 7, 2001
Teleplay by Brannon Braga & Andre Bormanis
Story by Andre Bormanis & Kenneth Biller
Directed by Allan Kroeker
TV rating: 3.4

"I've been conducting simulations to explore different aspects of my humanity."
—Seven

With shades of *TNG's* "Hollow Pursuits," this Seven episode stands out as one of the more unique offerings of the season, featuring scenes set on the holodeck to give Jeri Ryan a playground in which to stretch her character, beginning with one of *Star Trek's* oddest teasers: 45 seconds of nothing more than Seven playing the piano. And yet from an actor standpoint, it's Robert Beltran who gets the richest material, with the alternate reality giving him an opportunity to create a new Chakotay: a more romantic version who eats meat and courts Seven in a gentlemanly fashion.

Unfortunately, this is all saddled with a vanilla ship-in-peril B story full of technobabble that seems to have come straight out of *TNG*, complete with music that could have been lifted from the sister show's latter seasons. And while it's great to see Seven finally open up, even if it's in a fictitious environment, by the final season fans have a right to expect a more meaningful conclusion than a reset button. Director Allan Kroeker, however, recognizes the episode's strengths and weaknesses and keeps the focus on the former while finding ways to gloss over the latter. The writers, meanwhile, follow up on the fictitious romance with a real one in the series finale.

Did you notice? The holographic version of Neelix in this episode seems as obsessed with curtains as the real Neelix in "Night" and "The Haunting of Deck Twelve."

"Q2": C

After Q's son is banished from the Q Continuum, Q leaves him on Voyager.

Air date: April 11, 2001
Teleplay by Robert Doherty
Story by Kenneth Biller
Directed by LeVar Burton
TV rating: 3.0

"I like you, Aunt Kathy. You've got gumption. But what you don't have is unlimited control of space, matter, and time." —Q's son

Keegan de Lancie, son of John de Lancie (and Marnie Mosiman. a guest star in *TNG's* "Loud as a Whisper"), guest stars alongside his father, playing the titular character in this sequel to Season Two's "The Q and the Grey."

As a story, it's nothing we haven't seen before, playing out nearly identically to *TNG's* "Deja Q," with a Q losing his powers and learning a lesson from humanity. But whereas "Déjà Q" gets away with the concept because of the comic duo of John de Lancie and Brent Spiner, "Q2" feels more like an episode of a teenage sitcom, with an especially tedious early portion that sees "junior" playing around with the Voyager crew. (This week on *Saved by the Bell*, Zach throws a party in engineering and makes Seven of Nine's clothes disappear!)

Once the episode gets past its mischief and settles into the main plot, however, it's an engaging piece held together by LeVar Burton's shrewd directing and Keegan's solid acting, with recurring guest star Manu Intiraymi lending a valuable assist as "Itchy" Icheb. (Writer Robert Doherty generously gives each of the regulars something to do as well, with Mulgrew getting the most substantial supporting part as "Aunt Kathy.")

But while it may ultimately succeed as a de Lancie showpiece, as a Q episode, it lacks the wit and scope we've come to expect and ultimately waters down the species in the process.

John de Lancie doesn't appear on *VOY* again, but he does reprise Q in Season One of *The Lower Decks*.

Did you know? After appearing in a few shows as a teenager, including *The Drew Carey Show*, *Ally McBeal*, and this episode of *VOY*, Keegan de Lancie went to the country of Jordan on a Fulbright scholarship to study Iraqi refugees.

"Author, Author": B

When The Doctor writes a holonovel loosely based on his life, his rights as an author come into question.

Air date: April 18, 2001
Teleplay by Phyllis Strong & Mike Sussman
Story by Brannon Braga
Directed by David Livingston
TV rating: 2.9

"The law says that the creator of an artistic work must be a person. Your EMH doesn't meet that criteria." —Arbitrator

This Doctor episode is basically a rehash of *TNG's* "The Measure of a Man," but succeeds as a fine piece of entertainment in its own right.

The catalyst for it all is the Doc's new satirical holonovel based on his life on *Voyager*, a concept that plays out with shades of the *I Love Lucy* episode, "Lucy Writes a Novel." Filled with audio and visual gags, such as Paris's new name (Marseilles) and new mustache, this portion gives the viewer plenty to smile about.

But the episode's real substance comes when The Doctor's rights as an author become the subject of debate, with the issue, thanks to a new satellite link, turning into a joint Voyager/Alpha Quadrant trial with real stakes, since all the other versions of The Doctor will theoretically be affected by the ruling.

Picardo, who can always be counted on to deliver, knocks the comedy and drama out of the park, essentially carrying the episode (even if he is temporarily upstaged by his own comb-over). But the entire ensemble steps up to assist him, and there's even a B story that gives Wang, Dawson, and Ryan the opportunity to play some poignant moments while their characters Skype with relatives back home.

It all makes for a good "almost home" episode that the show thankfully slips in while it still has a chance.

Did you know? The actor playing Harry Kim's father also appears in *TNG's* "Coming of Age" as the Starfleet officer in charge of Wesley Crusher's Starfleet entrance exam.

"Friendship One": C

Several members of Voyager's crew are captured while attempting to recover a probe.

Air date: April 25, 2001
Written by Michael Taylor & Bryan Fuller
Directed by Mike Vejar
TV rating: 3.0

"If you think murdering one of my crewmen is going to make me more receptive to your demands, you're mistaken." —Janeway

VOY, using the cave set, does an old-fashioned hostage story with a medical crisis thrown in for good measure.

Ken Land, who was a relative newcomer to television at this point in his career, guest stars as the lead heavy, Verin, whose mistrust of the Voyager crew makes him mad, bad, and dangerous to know. This leads to two intertwining stories: one on the planet, where Verin directs his anger at the hostages, and another on the ship, where Janeway, with help from one of the planet's more reasonable inhabitants, attempts to come up with some sort of rescue plan.

This is all bookended with the matter of a fictional 21st century deep space probe, which is indirectly responsible for everything that happens in the episode, giving us a lesson in unintended consequences. But the truth is the episode isn't as profound as it wants to be, never developing into anything more than a simple rescue story.

Did you know? "Friendship One" marks the first appearance of Lieutenant Jo Carey in the regular timeline since his four appearances in Season One.

"Natural Law": C

When Chakotay and Seven crash-land on a planet, they must befriend a tribe of primitive natives to survive.

Air date: May 2, 2001
Teleplay by James Kahn
Story by Kenneth Biller & James Kahn
Directed by Terry Windell
TV rating: 3.0

"They're fascinating, aren't they? I never expected to run into people like these on such a technologically advanced planet." —Chakotay

Location shooting at Griffith Park helps bring to life this Chakotay/Seven "stranded on a planet" episode where the two get to know some nonspeaking locals who use sign language to communicate. The aliens live a simple life free of interference, thanks in part to a protective energy barrier, and this brings forth some interesting questions. Who created the barrier? How does the Voyager crew balance the importance of Chakotay and Seven's lives with the importance of the Prime Directive? And where's Kirok?

Surprisingly for a *Star Trek* episode, all these questions are brushed aside for a story that basically runs in place, with the writers even tossing in a comedic runner featuring Paris getting a ticket and having to take a safety course. Eventually, a twist in the main story—coming a couple acts too late—adds another layer to the plot to bring the A and the B stories together, though there seems so much more to mine within.

All the same, the ground that *is* covered is well handled by the director and the actors, with the xenoanthropological lesson presented with sincerity and patience, and the safety course giving guest star Neil C. Vipond a chance to shine as Paris's stodgy flight instructor.

Still, it's all an odd choice of subject matter for an episode so close to the end of the show's run, seeming more like a rerun from an earlier season.

Did you know? Griffith Park, just down the road from the Paramount studio lot, was the site of the very first scene shot for *TNG*, a holodeck sequence in which Wesley and Commander Riker first meet Data.

"Homestead": B–

Neelix tries to save an imperiled Talaxian settlement.

Air date: May 9, 2001
Written by Raf Green
Directed by LeVar Burton
TV rating: 3.4

"Maybe Neelix could go with us, and we could fight them." —Brax

Voyager bids adieu to Neelix in this simple but heartfelt Talaxian story featuring guest star Julianne Christie as a widowed mom and Ian Meltzer as her son, Brax.

After a roundabout beginning, the episode gets into the substance of a story that has *Star Trek* written all over it: a group of aliens are facing a threat, and our beloved starship crew attempts to assist them. The aliens are Neelix's people, and you might ask how they ended up so far from home. Unfortunately there's no good answer, and the inclusion of these Talaxians, while convenient for the story the writers want to tell, works against the idea that that Voyager is getting closer to the Alpha Quadrant.

What does make the episode special, however, is the poignancy of Neelix finding a new path for himself. It's well written, well directed, and well acted, with Ethan Phillips in particular giving it everything he has. And the bottom line is that a well-executed routine episode with a special ending will trump a poorly executed high concept episode most days of week.

Julianne Christie would go on to play another *Star Trek* alien some months later in "Unexpected," an early episode of *ENT*.

Did you know? Ethan Phillips would go on to make a cameo in *VOY's* finale, but this episode marks the final appearance of Scarlett Pomers as Naomi Wildman.

SCARLETT POMERS as Naomi Wildman

230

"Renaissance Man": B–

The Doctor must become a master of disguise to save Captain Janeway.

Air date: May 16, 2001
Teleplay by Phyllis Strong & Mike Sussman
Story by Andrew Shepard Price & Mark Gaberman
Directed by Mike Vejar
TV rating: 3.8

"Computer, access the holodeck database and locate Commander Chakotay's holographic template. Download the physical parameters into my program."
—The Doctor

Robert Picardo, with help from the ensemble, gets one last Doctor episode in this caper mission that brings back the aliens from "Tinker Tenor Doctor Spy."

The gimmick here is that The Doctor must impersonate members of the crew (as well as an evil alien) *Mission Impossible*-style to trick everyone into helping him accomplish his secret goal, with the audience slowly let in on what's going on as the first few acts unfold. It's a concept that sells itself simultaneously on its mystery and humor, and for the most part it works, with some gems such as when The Doctor, as Torres, gets a smooch from Paris and where Kim figures out the evil alien's true identity.

Meanwhile, Wayne Thomas Yorke, a veteran of over 150 commercials, and Andy Milder, a prolific television guest star, appear in heavy make-up as the conniving aliens behind the curtain, giving some humorous performances of their own as they bumble their way through their plot.

For the Voyager gang, however, it's all just another day at the office, with "Renaissance Man" giving the viewer no clue that it's the penultimate episode of the series. In fact, it's an episode that could have aired anytime, as opposed to "Homestead," which has more in common with the penultimate episodes of *TNG* and *DS9* in terms of providing some closure for a character.

As a filler Doctor comedy piece, however, it succeeds where it needs to.

Did you know? While Ethan Phillips does not appear in this episode, his name, per contractual demands, still appears in the opening credits.

"Endgame": B

Ten years after Voyager's return to the Alpha Quadrant, Admiral Janeway resolves to alter the past. (Series finale)

Air date: May 23, 2001
Teleplay by Kenneth Biller & Robert Doherty
Story by Rick Berman & Kenneth Biller & Brannon Braga
Directed by Allan Kroeker
TV rating: 5.5

"Three days ago, you detected elevated neutrino emissions in a nebula in grid nine eight six. You thought it might be a way home. You were right."
—Admiral Janeway

With elements of "Timeless" and *TNG's* "All Good Things," *VOY's* two-hour finale tries to play against expectations, beginning with a celebration of Voyager's return home (in a hypothetical future) rather than ending with one (in the show's present) before getting into the plot proper: where an elder Janeway journeys back in time to try to get Voyager home faster. It's a concept that doesn't make much sense, with her motivations—the death of two characters and the illness of another—coming across as arbitrary after all the other deaths she's had to deal with over the years, including her *first* first officer (in the pilot).

Nonetheless, the story itself is well presented, with the first half alternating between scenes from the future and scenes from the show's present, with both incorporating elements *VOY* has been developing throughout Season Seven, such as Torres's pregnancy and Seven's experimentation with romance. We even get to catch up with Neelix.

The centerpiece, however, is Janeway herself (times two) with Mulgrew getting a chance to bicker with her older self in a double role. It's well executed by director Allan Kroeker and well acted by *VOY's* leading lady, giving the story its foundation and giving Mulgrew one final chance to wow us with some Janeway magic.

Meanwhile, Alice Krige returns to *Star Trek* to reprise the Borg Queen, a part she originated in *TNG's* second feature film, *First Contact* (1996), and Dwight Schultz and Richard Herd reprise Barclay and Admiral Paris to help flesh out the Alpha Quadrant, as previously established in "Pathfinder," "Inside Man," and "Author, Author."

What's curious about the whole thing is how near it comes to being something other than a series finale, with a teased ending that leaves room for more Delta Quadrant adventures in the future. In fact, this could have been a two-parter in the middle of the season, making for a marvelous story in its own right while still leaving room for the remainder of the series (and a different series finale) to tie up all the issues of the return home that fans would want to see. *VOY* could have even borrowed a proposed idea for *TNG's* Season Six cliffhanger, where Starfleet decommissions the ship and attempts to split the crew up, forcing the officers to deal with a family-like breakup. Instead, what's a good episode on its own tries to resolve the premise of the entire show in just a few seconds at the end, turning what should be a triumphant return home into an afterthought and failing to please just about everyone, from those who have stuck with the show for seven seasons to those tuning in to see just how everything is going to come to a conclusion.

In a way, the show deserves a better sendoff. And yet in a way, the finale fits the nature of the episodic series, encapsulating its strengths and weaknesses in one bite-sized package. It's just too bad that this is it for the *VOY* crew. Outside of Janeway's appearances in *Star Trek: Nemesis* (2002) and *Star Trek: Prodigy* and a recurring role for Seven in *PIC*, these characters are never seen again (as of this writing), leaving the fate of the Voyager family and what a return home means to each of them mostly a mystery.

"Endgame" would go on to win two Emmys, one for Jay Chattaway's score and another for visual effects. It was also nominated for an Emmy for sound editing.

Did you know? Eighteen years after this episode first aired, Marvel released an *Avengers* film with some striking parallels. After giving us a glimpse of a hypothetical future, showing us what's become of the former members of the Avengers team, we see the main characters travel back in time to change their fate. The name of the film? *Avengers: Endgame* (2019).

233

Season Seven Roundup

By the end of Season Six, writer/producer Brannon Braga had been living in the 24th century for ten years and was beginning to feel burned out. "I knew I couldn't do *VOY* anymore," he later said. "I had to do something different." So Rick Berman turned to Kenneth Biller, who had been working his way up the *VOY* ranks for six years, to take over the show. But bringing the series to a satisfying conclusion would turn out to be a daunting task—and one made all the harder by the fact that Berman and Braga began working on a new *Star Trek* series, *ENT*, turning *VOY* into an afterthought.

Biller, nonetheless, soldiered on, crafting a season that delivers a steady stream of good stories within the usual *VOY* box, with "Critical Care," "Body and Soul," "Flesh and Blood," "Repentance," "Workforce," and "Author, Author," providing a solid foundation and "Endgame" finishing things off with an entertaining couple of hours in its own right. And yet all the same, it's clear Biller was content to play it safe, with nothing as ambitious as the gamechangers in Seasons Four and Six and no attempt in "Endgame" to stick the landing. It's something the show could get away with early in its run but something that hurts its legacy overall, with the seven seasons adding up to very little meaning. Mulgrew has told a fitting story about the final shot for the series, which involved just her and four of the crew. "We finished shooting a close-up, and Allan said 'Cut, print, that's a wrap,' and that was it. No celebration. Just people continuing to do their jobs. In fact, I had barely stood up when the crew began dismantling my chair."

There would, of course, be more accolades. Season Seven earned eight more Emmy nominations, winning one for music and one for effects, Jeri Ryan picked up the Saturn Award for Best Supporting Actress, Roxann Dawson and Robert Beltran were honored at the American Latino Media Arts Awards, and Jay Chattaway, Dennis McCarthy, and David Bell were, for the third year in a row, honored by the American Society of Composers, Authors, and Publishers for their scores.

But overall, *VOY* is remembered as a series that never quite meets its potential, lacking a standout episode on par with its predecessors' best and failing to pay off the premise of the series with a grand finale. However, despite these faults, the show does include enough compelling characters, enough poignant moments, and enough memorable episodes to remain popular to this day.

234

About the Author

When J.W. Braun isn't commanding a starship, he's spending time with his wife in Wisconsin. For more information on his books, visit www.jwbraun.com. And please, don't hesitate to review this book! Your feedback is appreciated and is an important part of the author/reader relationship. You can also follow him on Facebook at www.facebook.com/trekkersguides

Printed in Great Britain
by Amazon